The Significance of
Children and Animals

New Directions in the Human-Animal Bond

Alan M. Beck, series editor

The Significance of
Children and Animals

Social Development and
Our Connections to Other Species

Second, Revised Edition

Gene Myers

Purdue University Press
West Lafayette, Indiana

Library of Congress Cataloging-in-Publication Data

Myers, Jr., Olin Eugene
 The significance of children and animals : social development and our connections to other species / Gene Myers. -- 2nd, rev. ed.
    p. cm.
  Rev. ed. of: Children and animals. 1998.
  Includes bibliographical references and index.
  ISBN-13: 978-1-55753-429-3 (alk. paper)
  ISBN-10: 1-55753-429-2
  1. Children and animals. 2. Child development. 3. Child psychology. 4. Human-animal relationships. I. Myers, Gene (O. Gene). Children and animals. II. Title.
  BF723.A45M94 2006
  155.4'18--dc22

                                                    2006016922

Contents

Preface to the Revised Edition

It has been 20 years since I embarked on my scholarly study of children and animals at the University of Chicago's Committee on Human Development, and now over 10 years since the dissertation research reported in this book was completed. Since the Westview Press 1998 edition has been out of print for a few years, there have been steady requests for the book, and a new printing at least was in order. But the invitation from Purdue University Press to publish this paperback edition also offered the chance to update and expand as I saw fit. In choosing to revise this volume, however, I have preserved its character and its flow. Its character is on the one hand ethnographic, and on the other that it advances a careful analysis of child-animal interaction building on concepts from social, cognitive, and language development. My empirical observations are of events involving children and animals that are for the most part common place and familiar; the difference is that I was systematic and theory-building in my intent. I grounded and tested each proposition with data from a classroom where I had extensive knowledge of the setting and its inhabitants. In revising, I have not changed the examples and stories through which the book unfolds, and little further analysis of data has been added. As a grounded-theory ethnography that builds and tests an integrated network of constructs, it is not well-suited to casual browsing.

What I have changed in revising the book, is that I have updated its relationship to the literature. I accessed the increasing stream of research in human-animal studies (or anthrozoology—the status of the field was well summarized in a special issue of *Animals and Society:* vol. 10, number 4, 2002), as well as the kind of basic research in child development upon which the core of the book depends. The result of these updatings is partly contained in the text, but more often in citations and endnotes (I usually found it preferable to preserve the original unity of the book, unless new work called for revision of the argument; nonetheless, much of interest will be found in the new end notes). Given the many fields called upon in my thesis, no doubt there are significant advances I did not tap, but hopefully this revision makes the book current with the most relevant research. In general I have also tried to improve the work's clarity, and to assist the reader through the sometimes complex territories it traverses. The first chapter, largely unchanged, provides a thinly referenced (but hopefully accessible) overview, deferring the scholarly rigor to the succeeding chapters.

I am in a better position now to appreciate and convey the nature and strength of this work than I was when I first wrote it. On the surface it is about a few preschoolers' relations to animals, but I believe it would be a mistake to read it as only that. The book is an attempt to put the study of children's relations to nonhuman animals firmly on the map, in its own right, and not as derivative of some other area of primary interest. I aimed to develop a coherent and articulated theory of children's relations to animals that was based on a reasonably comprehensive picture of the multifaceted phenomenon of child development. I included careful treatment of how several topics, such as the self, concepts of mind and living things, language, morality, and so on shape children's—and by extension older humans'—interactions, relations and concepts of animals. In doing so, the book engages and (necessarily) takes positions on a number of larger contested issues not just in child development, but in the social sciences broadly. These include the role of language and culture in development, the nature of the self, the nature of social development in infancy, the role of the body in self-reflection, the social and societal dynamics of distortion of meaning, pretend, imitation and imagination, moral development, and more, each qualified (sometimes fundamentally) by permutation with "animals." Indeed, a motivating context is set by the discussion in chapter 2 of the omission of animals in our anthropocentric theories of development. In attempting such an ambitious agenda, the book inevitably has weaknesses; hopefully they are balanced by the original contributions.

There certainly are several problems this book does not treat, or treats only in a limited way. It is not directly about personal pets, nor animal therapy, nor animal abuse. It does not catalog the vast writings on or about children and animals. (Each of these things are now done, and done well, by others' works, all cited at the relevant points.) Rather, what is presented is an analysis of how animals can become significant in development, particularly in the development of a sense of self. This theoretical framework has wider relevance for many issues in human-animal interactions (notably, one of its key foundations on the development of self, the work of Daniel Stern, has implications across the life-span). Less obvious, but most foundational, is a debt to the philosophical works of my former advisor Eugene Gendlin; I am with him in attempting to enact a "new empiricism" to show what lies "beyond post-modernism."

Others have found in the book useful and stimulating concepts for original practical applications. It is gratifying to have had a role in shaping the conception of the Hamill Family Play Zoo (HFPZ) at Brookfield Zoo near Chicago. That zoo, and notably its visionary leader, Dr. George Rabb, wished to make the new children's zoo research-based, and brought in a wide variety of child development specialists. Many had influence, as did the zoo staff who constructed the facility with loving care, and who run the programming in the role of special "Play Partners." So I can claim only a tiny credit, but ideas from Children and Animals such as the role of pretend, of embodying the animal, of the importance of individual animals, of the power of hands-on caring, and of respecting and fostering the sense of connection are actualized in the HFPZ. Real animals play only modest roles in this play zoo, which is entirely unlike a traditional petting zoo or adult zoo. The child's creativity and sense of connection are put foremost by the Play Partners. Through the HFPZ (which won the American Zoo and Aquarium Association's 2001 Exhibit Award), these ideas are being disseminated to other such institutions. Other practical applications stemmed from contacts made by makers of toys for infants, film makers, Montessori teachers, *Sesame Street*, animal therapy workers, youth wildlife adventure camps, and various authors. Most exciting recently has been the work of Sarah Bexell, formerly of Zoo Atlanta and a recent Ph.D. at Georgia State University. She found in my book a key germ for an innovative animal curriculum first tried at Zoo Atlanta, and now in China at Chengdu Research Base of Giant Panda Breeding and at the Chengdu Zoo. The curriculum crucially offers "multiple points of contact" with animals. It personalizes animals as individuals, allows sensory contact, validates perceptions of animal feeling and mentality, focuses students on observing animal behavior and understanding its meanings and the animals' needs, connects animals to conservation, and supports moral concern (Bexell, 2006; more extensive research on the outcomes is in the planning stages). What is astounding is the reaction of both adults and children to the curriculum. In a culture known for its open disregard of animals (particularly domestic ones), children and adults exposed to the program have shown an outpouring of emotion and enlightenment upon being provided a framework that validates their hidden feelings of connection and compassion for animals (Bexell, personal communication, 2005). This, perhaps better than any evidence I yet know of, validates the psychological and universalistic thrust of my work.

As questions and ideas about our relation to animals and nature attain greater importance in scholarly communities, other researchers have also been finding the book helpful. To mention a few more prominent examples, psychotherapist Andy Fisher (2002), in an outstanding scholarly treatment of ecopsychology, finds in my book a compatible synthesis of social factors and the body (his work is also strongly influenced by Gendlin). Purdue University psychologist Gail Melson's (2001) review of the child-animal connection follows key ideas from my work in her proposal for a "biocentric" approach to child development. Collaborations with Peter Kahn of the University of Washington and the Mina Institute, whose trajectory parallels mine in integrating child development and environmental morality, have been mutually beneficial, with my work helping shape some of the design of his robotic pet studies (Kahn, 2004, discussed later). Recently I had the pleasure to review (Myers, 2005) an excellent new grounded theory work by University of Colorado at Boulder sociologist Leslie Irvine (2004), which scaffolds partly from my analysis to argue the further position that dogs and cats also have selves in a socially significant sense.

This revision has benefited by interaction with many scholars in anthrozoology whom I knew only via the literature before the first edition. James Serpell, Director of the Center for the Interaction of Animals and Society at the University of Pennsylvania, noticed the book immediately and deserves considerable credit for championing it, for example by including me in special events and by reviewing it in the APA's invitational book review journal, *Contemporary Psychology* (vol. 46(2), April 2001). Valued colleagues in human-animal studies who have helped advance my work in various ways also include Janet and Steven Alger (Siena College and College of St. Rose, respectively), David Anderson of Rockydell Resources, Arnold Arluke of Northeastern University, Marc Bekoff of the University of Colorado in Boulder, Lynette Hart of the University of California Davis, Robert W. Mitchell of Eastern Kentucky University, Anthony Podberscek, of the University of Cambridge, Andrew Rowan of the Humane Society of the United States, Clint Sanders of the University of Connecticut, Ken Shapiro of Society and Animals Forum, and historian Bernard Unti, although there are many more who also deserve mention.

One thing this revision does not do, or only does cursorily, is go past the basic theoretical statement made in the 1998 edition. In the years since the book, I have undertaken a number of research projects that build upon it. One small project looked at whether and how some of the same processes delineated with preschoolers might function between adults and wild animals (Myers and Russell, 2004). Concerning child development, an avenue of inquiry has been how the connection with animals relates to children's concern for animals' environments, and by extension, to wider human ecology. After the family play zoo project, a fantastic research collaboration grew with Dr. Carol Saunders of Brookfield Zoo, and in a series of projects we have explored "caring" as a central motif in children's relation to animals, children's conceptions of animals' needs, and the emotional dimensions of viewing zoo animals. Where relevant, these publications and the directions of my current work are merely noted in endnotes; I did not revise the book to fully incorporate their concerns.

Another outcome, on a different order of magnitude, of the collaboration with Dr. Saunders and others is the coalescing of a problem area we are calling Conservation Psychology. It includes basic research on the psychological dimensions of our relations with the natural world (with anthrozoology in prominence), and operates partly through application-oriented partnerships between researchers and practitioner-organizations (see http://www.conservationpsychology.org/). Compatriots in this growing band, from whose collegiality my work has benefited, include Almut Beringer of the University of Prince Edward Island, Rich Borden of College of the Atlantic, Amara Brook of Santa Clara University, Jim Cantrill of Northern Michigan University, Louise Chawla of Kentucky State University, Susan Clayton of College of Wooster, George Cvetkovich and David Sattler of my university, Western Washington, John Fraser of the Wildlife Conservation Society, Peter Kahn of the University of Washington, Susan Opotow of the University of Massachusetts, Kathryn Owen of the Woodland Park Zoo, Joseph Reser of Charles Darwin University (Australia), Emily Routman of San Francisco Zoo, Wesley Schultz of California State University San Marcos, and many others, some already mentioned.

For the last 11 years I have been fortunate to be part of a vibrant interdisciplinary faculty at Huxley College of the Environment at Western Washington University where my work has been received with interest and support. I am grateful to the contributions of all the above-mentioned colleagues, and others, (including those mentioned in the first edition) to my work presented here. I would like to express appreciation to Tom Bacher, Margaret Hunt, and Becki Corbin of Purdue University Press for their expert assistance and good humor in seeing the book into print. They make a fine team. Yet clearly the book's shortcomings are not attributable to anyone but me.

This book draws from work published in the following sources, whose grant of permission to include copyrighted material is acknowledged here: *Society and Animals* (1996, volume 4, pp. 19–35; and 1999, volume 7, pp. 121–140); *Anthrozoös* (2002, volume 15, pp. 19–36; *International Journal of Sociology and Social Policy* (2003, volume 23, pp. 46–68) and in Robert Mitchell's edited book, *Pretending in Animals and Humans* (copyright Cambridge Univ. Press, 2002, pp. 154–166).

The first edition of *Children and Animals* coincided with the year of my first daughter's birth, which launched my learning about child development and individuality into a yet more intimate depth. She and our second daughter have had no choice but to have a daddy just a little more than normally focused on their lives with animals. I briefly note observations of them at one point, but their contribution to the richness of my life of course far exceeds this, as their multi-faceted development constantly reminds me. Nonetheless, I have found in the experience of watching them grow a confirmation of the deeper themes in my work. I am grateful for their patience as I have missed too many summer days accomplishing this revision. If my work helps ensure their chances for as wonderful an experience of the creatures and ecologies of our earth as I have had, I hope it will have been worth it. Lastly, I am so very thankful to Mardi Solomon for her insights, faith, love, and support.

Bellingham, Washington, 2006

Preface to the First Edition

What transpires between a child and an animal when they interact is at once quite transparent and yet hard to fathom. Many a parent, educator, or interested adult has observed the plain delight, intense interest, and strong feelings animals evoke in young children. This phenomenon alone provokes curiosity. But beneath this sturdy fact, what is going on? What do animals mean in the context of children's blossoming capabilities of language, thought, and understanding of other minds together with broadening social abilities? Do animals provide something developmentally unique? What are the roots of our bonds with and antipathies toward other creatures? These questions initially motivated me to embark on a long study of this rather unexamined topic.

Unexamined—but not entirely; credit must go to a number of astute researchers whose work I review at appropriate places in this volume. Yet I felt a need to understand not just the patchwork of findings but the general patterns found in samples of children by researchers with differing viewpoints. After exploring such possibilities, I settled on a research approach that let me know some children deeply as individuals. What are the various meanings of animals for young children? I hope this book will convey some of the intriguing particularities of different children's approaches.

Sometimes, prolonged involvement with a small part of the world yields insights with broad application. As it turned out, my knowledge of the children in this book led to a new and wider picture. Consider the range of things children do with animals—touching, holding, feeding, imitating, talking to and about them. Hold in mind also all the ways animals differ, and how children do or do not accommodate themselves to the different qualities of animals. Is there any order unique to these arrangements or are they just the playing out of the children's early biases and predilections on fairly neutral others? Or are the children's behaviors just early expressions of their local culture? All these possibilities must be entertained and sorted out. Scrape the surface of everyday phenomena of home, classroom, zoo, pet shop, and the out of doors and a surprising complexity opens out. I believe there is a special pattern in what animals mean to children, and my main thrust in this book is to describe it.

Some readers may find it challenging to accept such a pattern as even a possibility. Animals are one of the most compelling, foreign yet familiar, and available aspects of nature, but there are reasons to look critically at any attempt to understand children's relations with animals. I am aware that the topic is surrounded in popular culture with romanticism—and with skeptical dismissal in reaction to this very sentimentality. And animals are interpreted in many other ways in Western culture. I do not ignore these concerns. In fact, they provide a fascinating intellectual background to my subject.

But this book is certainly more than a study of particular children or a history of children and animals as a topic in Western culture. I have sought to found my interpretations upon solid data and current understandings of child development. And I want to avoid underestimating children's abilities and contributions. Inevitably, however, such an enterprise has limitations. Many of my key findings are based on an intensive study of one group of pre-schoolers. I do not deal with all kinds of animal encounters—the book is not primarily about pets, animal-facilitated therapy, wild animals, zoo animals, or environmental education, although it has much to tell professionals in these areas. I chose to look rather at animals of near-to-human scale, representing a phylogenetic range, and mostly found in the children's familiar settings. I felt these conditions were optimal for the kind of pattern detection I wanted to attempt.

If this book accomplishes nothing else, it should show that children's relationships with animals deserve to be taken seriously. Before starting this project, I spent several years educating children about the natural environment. Stimulated by their responses, I sought to find out why it engaged them so much. To my surprise, I found existing traditions of developmental theory assigned little psychological importance to the natural environment in which we evolved. The reasons for this, pertaining specifically to animals, are part of the story in these chapters. More than a century after Darwin, we have yet to come to terms with our own animality, including the bonds it gives us, virtually ready made, to other species.

Although research on children and animals is young, there are many reasons to advance it. It turns out to be a key arena for studying developmental processes in which the characteristics of interactants might be expected to make a difference (for example, language; nonverbal communication; theory of mind; biological concepts; categories; social understanding; and, above all, the self). Surprisingly, it has not been exploited in such studies to a greater extent. But then, we (perhaps psychologists particularly) have tended to look at animals primarily as lacking in comparison to ourselves so that even such illuminating discrepancies have been largely ignored.

Other reasons to study children's relationships with animals have to do with what is at stake for the children developmentally. Here, the implications reach beyond animals to the ecosystems on which our community of life depends. Many have pleaded for a deeper understanding of the human processes that both tie us to, and alienate us from, our earthly matrix. If this book has one contribution to make in this area, it is toward understanding precisely how a sense of connection to animals, and by extension to a wider subjective ecology, may be a telos, or end, of normal development.

Thanks are owed to many who helped in the long process of creating this volume. Foremost among these are the members of my doctoral dissertation committee at the University of Chicago's Committee on Human Development, where this work began. I want to thank Mihaly Csikszentmihalyi for his guidance and consistent support; one could not wish for a better mentor. Eugene T. Gendlin catalyzed, through his teaching and writings, important intellectual developments in myself and in the framework of what I present here. Daniel G. Freedman was always able to see both the details and the larger whole. All have contributed greatly as mentors, role models, and thinkers to my work.

Other important intellectual influences are John C. Miles and the late David E. Clarke of Huxley College, the late Richard S. Davis of College of the Atlantic, and J. Ronald Engel of the Meadville-Lombard Theological School. Much is owed to current and former faculty, students, and staff of the Committee on Human Development at the University of Chicago—an institution uniquely suited to such an interdisciplinary project. Their influences have been immensely rich, diverse, critical, and constructive. I would especially like to thank Betty Cawelti, Peggy Miller, Rick Shweder, Susan Stodolsky, Bert Cohler, Gil Herdt, Barb Glaessner Novak, Cindy Dell Clark, Daniel Messinger, and the members of the Person-Culture-Body Workshop. The Chicago Bateson Society, Almut Beringer, Rebecca Krantz, Carla Schafer, Dana and Rand Jack, and friends at the College of the Atlantic and Western Washington University all helped me formulate this project. Ken Shapiro also deserves thanks for his support. Portions of chapter 4 appeared as "Child-animal interaction: Nonverbal dimensions" in Society and Animals (1996, vol. 4, no. 1, pp. 19–35), the journal he edits; they are reprinted here with permission. My appreciation goes also to the many child development and human-animal researchers and theorists whose ideas have influenced me.

And there are others without whom this project would have literally been impossible. I owe thanks to the Chicago Community Trust and the Searle Foundation for fellowship support from 1985 to 1989 and to the Spencer Foundation for a Dissertation-Year Fellowship in 1990–1991. Cathy Pusateri and Michelle Baxter of Westview Press guided this project through with stupendous grace, sensitivity, intelligence, and timing; their talents and those of their colleagues are deeply appreciated. Gloria Needlman offered the perfect setting and much enthusiasm for my project. And of course, without the graceful and open acceptance of the children who are featured in this book and the willing cooperation of their parents, little of it would have been possible. If it is worthy of them, it will stand as some sort of a testament to the possibility of a fine human home amid the earth's many other creatures.

Finally, my gratitude is greatest toward those closest to me. Mardi Solomon has supported me intellectually and emotionally throughout. And I wish to thank my parents for their endless generosity, unwavering faith, and love over the years this book has taken to come to fruition.

I

Introduction

The Sense of Connection

One November morning, I sat on the floor of a nursery school classroom with two young boys, watching birds come to the feeder outside. Toby and Scott, each about three and a half, were two of the youngest in the class of twenty-five children whom I was to come to know during this school year. During that time, I shared many events with the children—usually in an avuncular sort of role: I was an adult who was very interested in their activities and thoughts but not inclined to discipline or correct them. Many aspects of life in this classroom were uncovered by my work as what might be called the resident ethnographer, but I focused especially, though not conspicuously, on episodes such as the one about to unfold—ones involving animals.

This nursery school, probably like many in North America, is inhabited by protean animal figures. There are storybook animals of several sorts. Others are animated by pretend—be they stuffed, plastic, or the transformed bodies of the children themselves. Curricular animals enhance preschool-level biology. And there are living animals, outdoors and inside, constituting the locally available slice of the vast diversity of the animal kingdom. One might wonder if the young child's world seems saturated by animal presences.

My task was no less than to understand what this entire mixed menagerie meant to these young children, to find and sort out its core importance, if any there was. Was this too sweeping a goal? Perhaps. In the previous list of kinds of "animals," some seem to spring solely from literary convention or children's television or toys. Animal pretend play is a subset of pretend generally and thus defined by considerations such as social interaction or the acting out of

1

psychosocial issues. In the curriculum, animals are subservient to the child's cognitive development, and teachers know animals are useful in inculcating caring and responsible social behavior. Does such heterogeneity suggest there is no unitary phenomenon here to study? I do not think so. The divisions of our habitual thinking (and in the disciplines) cut across an underlying unity, a more primary level of our encounter with animals.

In his seminal essay "Why Look at Animals?" the sensitive cultural observer John Berger (1980) explained that it has become difficult if not impossible to "centralize" the animal. He meant that we have blurred the animal's distinctness by turning it into a reflection of ourselves—our family roles, our trivial traits. Our metaphors and our zoos reduce the animal to a spectacle and render it passive and marginal to our existence. Encounters are further foreclosed by the removal of animals from our environments, and finally made impossible through the extinction of entire species. More and more, our world is dominated by and—we believe—constructed by our own species.

It should come as no surprise that it seems far-fetched to speak of all the animal presences of early childhood in one breath, since we also marginalize them in our understanding of ourselves and of child development. In this book, I explore these underlying obstacles, but I also offer a response, a different construal. Partly because we do not see animals as fundamentally important to human life, we have dispersed them to the official domains of child psychology—here in conceptual development, a bat that is not a bird; over there in psychoanalysis, the horse that is the father. Encounter is mediated, indirect, because some more important human feature intervenes. But in the actual lives of children, the animal is a whole and compelling presence. We can recover that animal by identifying the biases that have led us to marginalize other creatures and, most important, by going directly to the source—to children and their experience of animals. Thus, not coincidentally, the response this book offers centralizes animals in human development in exactly the way young children themselves centralize the animal other. Here, then, is a key case of how the natural world plays a unique and vital role in human development—a role that could be freshly recognized and cultivated by society in general and by psychology in particular.

That November morning, there were ten to twenty small birds and several pigeons on or near the feeder, which stood near our ground-level double glass doors. I asked Toby and Scott if they could see the birds, and Toby quickly replied, "Yes," adding that one was on the plants. In a tone of great awe, Toby declared he was "amazed." We talked about how many birds there were; the number impressed the boys. Then Toby said in wonder, "You funny birds . . . (pause) you funny birds . . . you funny birds."

Toby continued, "One flew on top [of the feeder]." We were close to a cage containing two diamond doves, recently brought to the class by the teacher, Mrs. Ray. Toby heard the doves, pointed to them, and noted they were making sounds. Meanwhile, Scott left and came back with Scotch tape around his fingertips; he threatened to "cut" us with his fingers thus armored. Mrs. Ray intervened (just as well, since as ethnographer I avoided sanctioning the children lest they hide behaviors from me). But Scott's tape had given Toby an idea. Toby fetched the tape and put some around the tip of his index finger. He came back to the doves and moved this finger along a small area of the wires of the cage. Then he told me, "I cut the cage open." "Why?" I asked. Toby explained, "I'm pretending." "Why?" Toby: "So they can go out there and be with the other birds." Then, with his taped finger, he "cut" a small square in the glass on the door next to the cage. Satisfied, he left to take up another activity.

This sort of episode leads us deep into the significance living animals—even ones with which only simple interaction or merely observation is possible—have for children. In Toby's remark, "You funny birds," there is not primarily a psychosocial projection or an unrealized potential for more rational thought or a partly internalized cultural concept. Instead, there is a young child somehow recognizing and captivated by the nearly ineffable sameness-and-difference of another living animal.

If we were to follow one of those other developmental interpretations, we might find ourselves concluding that whatever sense of awe and connection Toby feels is something that he will, and even should, outgrow with maturity. Perhaps he will. But something of great importance would be lost. Although I observed these children for only a year, the pattern I discerned in their relations to animals may offer its own developmental potential. What is that pattern and what is its potential? What about an animal—and what about a child—causes the child to experience the animal as a vivid and different subjective other? What dynamics of development cause the child's sense of self to arise in relation to the animal, not just to the animal's symbolic cultural meaning or some other factor? What are the wider implications for our understanding of children's relationships and of human development generally? These are the focal questions of this book.

My approach to answering these questions centers on the relational nature of the self as it arises from interactions. Theorists from several schools of research into the child's sense of self agree that the self arises in relationships (patterns of interactions over time); some researchers have even examined animals as "others." But this book is different in taking a comprehensive view of interactive capacities and their implications for self. This will allow us to view the relational self in the context of the child's actual interactions with other species.

The pattern that we find is this: Young children demonstrate finely attuned sensitivities to certain basic and somewhat variable qualities of animals as interactants, even as the children also show certain biases as intersubjective and linguistic young humans. We repeatedly find a small set of core traits of animals (including humans) uniting a whole range of animal-related activities of children. Following the work of developmental psychologist Daniel Stern (1985), I label these traits *agency* (the animal moves on its own and can do things like bite, crawl, look around, and so on), *coherence* (the animal is easily experienced as an organized whole), *affectivity* (the animal shows emotions—or, better, patterns of excitement, relaxation, and many different qualities of feeling), and *continuity* (with repeated experiences an animal becomes a familiar individual). These qualities underlie Toby's responsiveness to the birds. And, crucially, they are qualities that form the child's sense of self and other, beginning at a very early age.

The questions that I raise in this book about the patterns and potentials of the child's relations to animals take on a sharper edge in view of the later part of the example of Toby and the doves. To anticipate a later part of the analysis I present, the birds' capacity for flight—for agency or autonomy—and for subjective well-being mattered to Toby. They mattered enough for him to concoct a fantasy of liberating the doves. In this responsiveness to the doves' condition, we see the early stirring of a moral attitude toward living things. Research into early child development leads us to expect an emerging moral attitude toward other people, which sometimes might generalize to animals. But the pattern I found indicates a somewhat different explanation: The same interactive dynamics underlie early moral attitudes toward both humans and animals. Toby's moral concern could be a generalization from human to animal, but it contains more than that, since the birds' exact animate needs are his focus. These needs of the animal as an agentic subject are closely related to the core traits I referred to previously, traits that apply equally to humans and animals. When these core traits are evident in an interactant, children are likely to feel a morally relevant sense of concern toward the other.

This explanation entails a developmental dynamic with broad implications for our understanding of several different aspects of children; indeed, it goes to the roots of a persistent problem in our psychological theories. This problem is that we see the animal body as simple, reflexive, and entirely different from the complex and autonomous traits of mind that make us human. It is no wonder we marginalize animals in human life and development. The dichotomy of mind and body resides within the person, too, and leads to theoretical quandaries about moral, cognitive, and social development. We are just beginning to learn how our knowledge is grounded in sensuous activity.[1]

Study of the child's relation with the animal adds to this growing understanding because it shows how embodied interaction is at the root of the self, moral feeling, and other mental phenomena. For example, moral feeling toward animals bears the marks of its origins—the child's response to the core properties of animals. Morality is not, as some hold, merely an external social construction children are taught. Nor is it a byproduct of an isolated egocentric self. But culture and language certainly do affect moral development. Children's relations with animals tell us culture and language can foster continuity or discontinuity with embodied experience and feeling. In other areas of development also, this subject sheds new light on some old problems.

Finally, the findings I report here unavoidably resonate with concerns about one context of self and society—the ecological context, of which animals are members. We are more likely to act positively toward something if we perceive it to be indispensable to the well-being of the self. This book raises the strong possibility that our formalized understandings—our theories—of the self and its context have systematically obscured the importance of other species in our development. Greater recognition and cultivation of this developmental potential is an essential challenge for every human group. But it cannot be undertaken without an adequate understanding.

This book is about the obstacles to seeing the importance of animals to ourselves—specifically, to young children—and about the wider problems these obstacles illustrate. And it is about the solutions—solutions that often hinge on finding a new pattern among common but remarkable events. In the rest of this introductory chapter, I will trace the main outlines of these problems and solutions as offered in my book; in the interest of enticing the reader into this territory, I will leave the detailed references to literature and analysis of supporting data to the following chapters. The book as a whole offers an interpretive framework that draws on a wide range of literatures and discourses—small parts of history, anthropology, and philosophy, and larger parts of social and developmental psychology, both general and very specialized. At issue are matters of the body and interaction; language and culture; knowing other "minds" and the self-in-relationship; our evolutionary past and our evaluation of the ties it brings; continuities and discontinuities in development; and, ultimately, the scope of the human sciences.

Although this book tackles an interpretive and theory-building task, the interactions and experiences of the children I observed are a crucial empirical element in the whole project. Most of the examples in the book come from Toby, Scott, and their twenty-three classmates. Since we are already getting to know them, a brief introduction to the children is overdue. About half were girls and half boys. The youngest were three and a half years old at the start of the school year, the oldest just six the following June (this wide range resulted from it being a two-year program; after completion the children entered kindergarten). The children came from a variety of backgrounds, but all spent their days at this midwestern university-affiliated nursery school, in the care of Mrs. Ray and her two assistants, Ms. Wick and Mrs. Tanner. And of course, there are other important personages to mention: Toad, who was frequently fed bugs the children found outside; Snowflake, the class guinea pig (generally to be found in her cage, or being fed on a child's lap); some goldfish; and two diamond doves in a large cage. Outside were urban "wildlife" such as gray squirrels, rock doves (pigeons), house sparrows, and other species that gathered near the bird feeder. In addition, I arranged for separate half-day visits by a wide spectrum of animals: Pogo, a dog accompanied by Mr. Grier; two box turtles brought by a herpetologist, Mr. Lloyd; two ferrets with Ms. Collins; two tarantulas and a spider monkey named Koko belonging to Ms. and Mr. Dean; and two ball pythons raised by Ms. Nol. In the chapters that follow, I frequently include portions of transcripts of videotapes of these visits to explore the children's relations with animals. Other examples come from my field notes, observations, parent journals, and interviews (please see the appendix for more details on the children and my methods). The lessons I learned in this rich setting were fecund for the tasks of constructing and testing ideas and for conveying a sense of the children's varied experiences with animals.

Child and Animal, Self and Other

Living animals are central presences to young children, as shown by several kinds of episodes. Once, after running and playing in a nearby field, the class returned along the sidewalk, when, according to my field notes:

> At the entrance steps into the adjoining building, we pass a quiet dog, apparently waiting for its owner. Several children are interested, and Joe and Toby walk up to the top-step level where it is sitting. Mrs. Ray mentions it's a very nice dog, but that the children need to go on back. Nonetheless, Toby, Joe, Yasmin, Laura, Benson, and Katra wait longer and watch it quietly and intently.

No obvious interaction was happening, but the recently rambunctious children watched the dog silently until they had to go and looked back as they went.

What accounts for such power of animals to hold children's attention? Different examples show children interacting intently with animals, expressing concern about animals' well-being, or finding special symbolic significance in something about an animal. The story about Toby and the doves is illustrative.

All these examples—and we will examine many more—relate to the child's self, which can be conceived of in functional (or goal-oriented) terms, or in terms of the experiences of having and being a self. The self can be seen as the child's system of goals, from self-survival to the continuity of others in relationship to whom the self is defined. In chapter 3, I examine in detail how the child's self functionally incorporates the animal. The data clearly show that the young child's self includes the animal in the sense of caring for it, wanting to continue interacting with it, and finding similarities to it. The problem these data pose for theory is how to understand the development and potential of this kind of self-in-relation to other species.

Animals are evidently vital in the child's sense of the important things in the world and thus should register in the child's *experience* of self. As traditionally defined in social psychology, two experiential senses of self—the subjective and the objective—can be distinguished. We all have the experience of being an acting, knowing, subjective "I." Here, the animal would be experienced as a dynamically interactive and subjective other, through whom the "I" is affirmed in its selfhood. This "I" is traditionally regarded as difficult to study because it is relatively inaccessible to self-reflection. The "me," or objective self, however, has often been studied in the form of a person's explicit self-concepts. Its ontogeny also seems simpler to grasp because its contents are linguistically conveyed in the ways we typify each other and ourselves. Although this self is easier to study, it has a shortcoming from the standpoint of this book. Although many now accept the idea of a socially generated sense of self, theories that stress the linguistic mediation of the self rule out animals as direct members of the community in which the self takes its bearings because they do not speak. Animals might contribute to the self in a secondary manner—as cultural symbols, for example. But this ignores their centrality to the young children. The task posed by my findings is to trace just how animals contribute immediately to the self. We need a way to think about what animals mean to the child's developing subjective self.

An alternative tradition exists that can help us. The pioneering interpersonal psychologist Harry Stack Sullivan, the infancy researcher Daniel Stern, and others argue that the dimensions of the self relate to the structure of relationships—to patterns of interaction over time. The basic contours of the subjective self, the "I," can thus be inferred from a close study of interactions.

In the following, I build especially on Stern's work, extending it in the new direction of interaction between young humans and other species.[2]

Child-Animal Interaction: An Analysis

My claim that animals are directly important in the child's formation of a sense of self is bound to provoke those who hold several traditional notions about children or development. Some, influenced by psychoanalytic traditions, will argue that the child's interactions with the animal are actually projective episodes, in which some intrapsychic conflict is acted out on the animal, with indifference to its distinct being. Others (though this position is weakening) are likely to object that the child's cognitive apparatus is too egocentric to differentiate the animal as a nonanthropomorphic other; instead, the child assimilates the animal to the human pattern. Still others, as noted previously, hold that language and culture are determinative over all else and that the meanings of the animal to the child are explained by such human-generated sources. Obviously, there are truths—or at least Western traditions—behind each objection. But when we carefully unfold interactions between child and animal, none of these objections holds absolutely. Indeed, a more fundamental pattern is evident in ordinary child development. Preverbal, intersubjective, and language abilities all contribute.

Preverbal Aspects

On one occasion, when a small group was with the large snake, Ms. Nol, its presenter, suggested the children were acting afraid of the snake just to get my interested response. This seemed an astute interpretation and fits well with the bias that animals are secondary to the human world in shaping children's experience. But as we will see later in examining this episode, closer analysis showed it was only when the snake pointed its head toward the children that they reacted. And they did this when I was absent, too. Something about the snake's behavior was meaningful to the children. To detect such telling cases requires a close look at interaction.

This book makes a new contribution to the field of human-animal relations because it provides a comprehensive and developmental analysis of such interactions. In chapter 4, the positive and negative aspects of the human-animal bond are reviewed, as are the shortcomings of this concept. To start a new analysis of the differences and similarities of human-human versus human-animal relations, I will begin at the beginning—infancy—and organize an understanding of the structure of child-animal interactions around early emerging and enduring bases of the self.

Many a parent has undoubtedly noticed something recently discovered by researchers: Infants take a special interest in animals. The infant's pattern of responses to animals is not identical to that toward other humans, but not entirely unlike it either. This discovery invites us to ask in more detail about very early social abilities: How might they allow the differentiation of the animal as a special kind of interactant?

When we look into recent infancy research, a very different being emerges to greet us than the isolated and egocentric infant assumed by psychoanalysis or the "blank slate" supposed by empiricist positions. The infant comes prepared to integrate sense experience as a whole and to respond to invariant features of its world—including especially the patterns of its own bodily experience and the actions of other persons. Four particular invariants of self and other underlie the experience of the early "I," or sense of the self as a subject, and the corresponding subjective other. In quite specific kinds of interactions that infants can be observed to undertake, agency, coherence, affectivity, and continuity of self and other are distinct and do not vary across different contexts and actions. From this structure, we can infer the basis of a sense of "I" in relation to the other.

When we look at actual interactions, we can detect precisely how these properties are foremost. Together, they constitute the child's feeling of "core" or "animate" relatedness to the animal, and form the basis for the child's sense of being a human self among an interspecies community of other subjective presences (I mean nothing at all mystical by this term; the meaning is similar to "persons," but I prefer to keep that word's usual meaning). Children announce these experiences, for example, in comments about what was memorable about the animals. About feeding the monkey, Laura explained, "I liked when he scratched my hand," reporting on her direct and tactile experience of the monkey's subjective agency. The importance of animate properties is evident in children's actions and responses. This becomes obvious when we observe that they respond with detailed appropriateness to the differences in various kinds of animals' coherence, affect, and agency. Similarly, continuity is revealed as an important dimension of self-other relatedness with animals by comparing the relations with the guinea pig of children in their first versus their second year in the classroom.

Such sensitive interactive responsiveness by children casts doubt on the idea that children are primarily egocentric and projective or entirely anthropomorphic in their approach to animals. In contrast to the anthropomorphism in what young children are able to report verbally (which has shaped previous major interpretations), their ability to distinguish animals as unique others in interaction is a further growth built on the infant's early skill and perceptiveness. Indeed, animals appear to be optimally discrepant social others by the time of early childhood—offering just the right amount of similarity to and difference from the human pattern (and from other animal patterns) to engage the child. Crucially, animals are social others not as if they were simply behaving inanimates, but rather because they display the hallmarks of being truly subjective others. Such *animacy* is the precondition for another being to serve psychological functions such as those ascribed by object-relations psychoanalysts and others. And, although many activities with animals are framed by cultural practices such as naming and petting, these frames cannot explain the fine features of children's actions. To the contrary, cultural interactive scripts are dependent on the immediate give-and-take of animate relatedness to be possible. Finally, animals are symbolic for the child not in the sense that their meanings are imposed by social or psychic factors (although I do not deny this occurs), but in the sense of confirming the child's own uniquely human self and representing and furthering the living, feeling self in a more vivid form than can other kinds of symbolic carriers of meaning.

Attention, Feelings, and Intentions

Core or animate relatedness is the earliest form of self and other to coalesce from the ongoing experience of emergent self (Stern, 1985). What becomes of agency and so on as first the ability to nonverbally share feelings, and later the use of language, come into full bloom, as happens in early childhood? A comprehensive analysis of interaction must address this problem or risk missing important events and, more crucially, leave it impossible to specify or assess the claim that linguistic constructions are in some sense secondary to animate relatedness. My solution follows the principle that the structure of interactions affects their meanings to participants. If so, then agency, coherence, affect, and continuity will remain important ever after their earliest emergence because they remain as constants in all interactions. We each put this insight into practice intuitively wherever we note meaning in discrepancies between another's (or our own) nonverbal and verbal expressions. The earlier nonverbal modes of person perception remain active. Thus, we might now ask how to characterize the forms of relatedness that emerge later and how to specify how these different domains themselves interact. In chapter 5, I address these problems, building on Stern's (1985) efforts to trace the developing senses of self, on the work of researchers concerned with the child's theory of mind, and on analyses of the pragmatic foundations of language.

The sharing of certain subjective states creates a nonverbal form (or domain) of relatedness that applies between children and animals (as it proto-typically does between humans), but with special qualifications. In general, I found no *confirmed* sharing of affect, attention, or intention such as is possible between caregiver and infant or child and child or, in special conditions, between person and animal. But what I did find strengthens the interpretation that the child differentiates the animal as a special kind of subjective other. The different characteristic vitality affects of different species—the lethargic slowness of the snake, the quick unpredictability of the monkey, the perky playfulness of the dog—were registered by the children; and sometimes I observed a phenomenon like mood contagion, which I consider to be affect attunement.

Although explicitly marked sharing is rare, implicit attention and intentions of animals are conveyed by gaze and action. Some children's most profound experiences occurred when the child was the object of an animal's attention. Significantly, children are biased by their experiences with people to read some gaze and affect cues in certain ways, but they do not necessarily just assimilate encounters with animals to their usual expectations. Animals do not use affect alignment or attunement the way socialization agents such as parents do. As a consequence, animals may be experienced as sharing certain subjective experiences of the child to a greater degree than do adults, and as providing a special interactive realm free of socialization pressures. This was humorously suggested by some children's admiration of animals' freedom from "mommies" and from the requirement to go to school.

Shared attention and intention have interactive developmental bases but also depend on the child's theory of mind, since both concern types of mental state. Four-year-olds attribute mental states to animals in ways consistent with findings of current research. Some children show signs of a further kind of concept not anticipated by a strictly cognitive approach: concepts about other minds that bear a close relation to the interactive qualities of the other, in this case the other animal. For example, children do attribute basic states of mind to animals, but one girl showed she grasped that the monkey did not under-stand her intention to play give-and-take. She scaled back her goal to simply establishing eye contact. The monkey provided the optimal difference for her to experience a sense of relatedness to a divergent other being and to form at least an implicit idea about interactive differences between species.

Animals Through the Lenses of Language

In the course of human development, linguistic communication is continuous from interintentionality (the sharing of intentions between interactants). The recipient must understand that a meaning is intended by an utterance. This capacity first arises in infancy through the conveying of intentions by gestures. Built on such intended communicative actions are the conventional or negotiated meanings of words. Words are thus like "labels" of meanings that may be nonverbal in nature—the "contents" of the "file" labeled by the word. But if this were all there was to the system it would not work, because words do not correspond one to one with meanings. The system must additionally depend on certain assumptions language users routinely make and on their ability to read the social context to discern the precise intended meaning of an utterance. This analysis helps us understand the consequences for the structure of interactions with animals of the fact that young children are linguistic beings.

Younger children in particular talked to animals as if they expected words to work as conventional gestures—that is, as if the animal interprets them as communicative. And in their attempts to understand an animal's actions, the children sometimes "put words in the mouth" of the animal, for instance, providing narration for an animal's exploratory activities. But although language is the implicit model, at least one older child expressed awareness that animals' communication, although like language, must be different in some respects. Animals thus provided a fascinating window on children's conceptions of language.

Children's status as language users has other effects on interactions also, concerning their assumptions that behavior may be "cooperative" and "communicative." The most important result is that children are interested in and concerned about the meanings implicit in core or animate-level interaction and behavior. If they were not language users, children (and people generally) could not wonder and care about animals' experience. The ironic and very underplayed conclusion is that language does not set us apart from animals but engages us with them.

Nonetheless, there is evidence that animals' divergences from human response patterns are not lost on children. Indeed, that the animal is outside the child's linguistic community has important consequences that we can identify. The animal is not part of the impersonal, role-structured, abstractly organized world created by language; again, it offers a special domain of interaction.

Self-Reflection, Pretend, and Continuity

It is certainly interesting to see the fine texture of child-animal interactions, and the material prior to chapter 6 might well stand alone. Yet, my analysis of interactions with animals raises a curious dilemma: If animals are so important to the child's sense of being a subjective self, what about the sense of the "me"—the objective self with traits usually thought to be conveyed only in linguistic interchange? Children's often entertaining episodes at pretending to be animals, I will argue in chapter 6, provide a key to this problem. But, really, the problem is deeper than the formulation I just suggested, for it concerns the relation between the nonverbal domains ("animate" and "intersubjective" I have called them), and the verbal domain and its products—the personal and cultural meanings conveyed by language. It comes as no surprise that an inquiry into human-animal interaction must confront this problem, and, indeed, this study represents a special opportunity to shed light on a host of related issues of broad importance. Some social constructionists would say objective and reflective meanings about the self are just imposed by others' words and by self-talk. But I ask, does preverbal animate relatedness constrain the meanings of culture in some sense? Is there continuity between the experience of preverbal and verbal meanings—and if so, what are its sources and its vulnerabilities? As society struggles to appreciate the significance of cultural diversity, cross-species interactive diversity steps in with an unexpected contribution! Within the constraints of our subject, I will suggest some of these wider implications.

In the tradition of social psychology founded by George Herbert Mead, it is often held that a self-aware sense of self, of the self as an "object," can arise only among the community of language users. This would suggest that animals are relevant to the sense of being a human self only secondarily—for example, as culturally constructed symbols. But if we find—as I do—that this analysis does not square well with what we observe, we might well seek another account. Indeed, there are also independent reasons to question Mead's tradition, having to do with the limits of words by themselves to objectify the self, and with the integrity of the body, which Mead discounted but which is upheld by infancy research. Following the philosopher Karen Hanson (1986), sensitivity to social context, plus imagination—founded on the ability to find pattern, coherence, or invariants in experience—are prerequisites for language to produce self-awareness. But by the same token, other patterns of action besides verbal ones can do so also. And this is exactly what occurs in children's deliberate imitation of, and pretending to be, animals.

The child must self-consciously differentiate the self from the other to typify it in play. Thus many actions in animal-role pretend play reveal the child's concepts of animal other and human self—or rather, in the moment, of animal self and human other! Three such concepts stand out—differences in how humans versus animals orient to the social world, the use of language, and the translation of the human body into the animal's. All of these concepts demonstrated by the form of animal-role pretend play preserve the otherness of the animal, and all confirm my interpretations of the interactively generated meanings of the animal to the child. Children accommodate their bodies in fine detail (as much as possible) to the animals they "become," showing the simultaneous closeness and clarity of the child-animal relationship.

But these results, informative as they are about an area of play that has not received careful study until now, also reveal an important continuity in experience. Self-awareness is not at all divorced from the preverbal realm. This is especially obvious in how the child "embodies" the pretended animal, as shown in this transcription of a videotaped episode:

> Ivy shows what it would be like to be a dog. Mr. Grier, the dog owner: "And what would you use to get [the ball]? . . . Why wouldn't you use your hand?" . . . Ivy: "Because you can't hold—dogs can't hold it up." Ivy holds both arms extended to the floor in front of her, partially lifting her straightened right arm three times.

The fidelity of the words "dogs can't hold it up" in communicating Ivy's meaning pales in comparison to her imitation, which conveyed exactly the sense of the dog's limited motion. A thorough verbal description would have been awkward and even less adequate. As we look at many examples, the familiar core animate categories of agency and coherence (both evident in the example), and affect and continuity stand out as what is salient and represented by the children pretending to be or imitating animals.

Here is a shining instance of a crucial form of continuity between the preverbal and the self-conscious, the embodied and the mindful. Pretending, translating the body into the animal's form, explains how the animal remains a vibrant subjective other—indeed, how it increases in this status once the child can self-reflectively realize the nuanced similarities and differences between self and animal.

Yet, there are many terms for the dichotomy language is presumed to create between these same domains: intentions-in-action versus prior intentions, natural versus nonnatural meanings, and so on. Why is there this exclusive emphasis on language in our self-understanding, in our theories? We need not negate the importance of language, but we can trace another parallel strand in social theory that emphasizes how action and interaction can be immediately meaningful. Other evidence from the psychology of language and gesture and from creative arts sheds further light on the underlying unity of experience—a unity that evidently can be disrupted but also offers important developmental potentials.

Language appears to pose a particular challenge for the developing mind—and often for the adult one, too. It offers the potential for the confusion of word with meaning—the reification of meanings or, in a sense, the forgetting that the word is a "label" for a "file" of meanings. Normally, these labels can be compared across files in metaphor and figurative language. But in some cases, meanings are captured by feeling or thought and made rigid, turning the idea into a thing. I suggest, with the psychologist Patrick de Gramont (1990), that this is one important mechanism underlying the discontinuity of preverbal meaning and verbal grasp. Interestingly, there are special cases—some rare, others common—where reification applies to "human" and "animal" as categories of identity.

The Animal in Moral, Cognitive, and Social Development: Continuities of Concern, Interest, and Community

How can moral, cognitive, and social development further the sense of connection to nonhuman animals? Pretend play and the self-reflective self provide a model by which we can identify similar patterns of continuity and discontinuity in other areas of development. In chapter 7, we examine how cultural meaning and practice necessarily work within the pre-potent core or animate domain—how children's responses to cultural inputs are channeled by their feeling of immediate responsiveness of self and other with the animal. Morality is clearly shaped by cultural inputs, and in the case of our treatment of animals we can point to many moral lessons taught by speech and deed. But these are conflicting lessons and do not explain children's concerned responses to animals' perils. I suggest to the contrary that certain adult cultural practices are called out by children's responsiveness. Some practices protect this responsiveness; others allow it to be subverted by cultivating a sense of distance. None of these practices are arbitrary cultural conventions, I argue, but rather they reflect universal patterns of moral psychology. The roots of morality are fully present at this tender age and are an irreplaceable ingredient of further development. The message is that young children's moral feelings involving animals, equally as those involving humans, must be respected.

Animals intersect with cognitive development in a number of interesting ways. Chapters 4 and 5 include discussions of new work on the child's biological knowledge and theory of mind. But my focus here is on the continuity of intellectual interest in the animal other—the optimally discrepant features (just-right degrees of difference) which make the animal intrinsically engaging to the young child. Again, cultural practices do not just create out of whole cloth (or fail to create) wonder at animals. Rather, such practices encourage or distort a process already functioning in its own way in the child. Cultural styles of objectifying and subjectifying animals are evident in the classroom and matter greatly for the child's potential to grow up with an interest in the life worlds of other species. So also do recognition and cultivation of the particular ways (artistic ones, for example) in which we understand and represent our knowledge of other animals.

Any specific definition of the human self is partly a cultural matter, but given the compelling qualities of animate relatedness, we expect the axis of human-nonhuman is not likely to be neutral in that definition. At least in Western culture, it is a hotly contested question where the boundaries between our species and others lie. This is even true in the nursery school, and young children are active participants in the discussion. And it is in them that identities are being formed. Just as with gender, race, and other categories, children are also learning what it means to be human. Based on what we have learned so far, we know that young children, both in immediate interaction and in self-reflection, experience continuity between human self and animal other. They are by no means oblivious to the differences; these differences are, indeed, what let children locate the human self as one among a community of diverse living others. But to be human can come to mean to emphatically *not* be animal. This is the ordinary reification of "human" and "animal"—the discontinuity I hypothesized earlier. There is evidence of this reification in some individual children's patterns of dis-identification with animals—of averring that they would not "like to be" this or that other creature. Some girls—especially older ones—consistently said "no" when I asked if they would like to be the animals that visited the classroom. What led to this interesting discrepancy? I argue there were factors motivating a reification of human identity. Here, again, culture is not operating on a neutral, formless psyche. The nursery school is replete with boundary disputes, evaluations of the "wild" or the "animal" body, and with rigid distinctions, sometimes motivated out of a need to put at a distance that which is morally disturbing.

Conclusion

The role of the human-animal boundary in the self has far-reaching consequences, since what is experienced as self or as vital to the self determines one's spontaneous "field of care." In this book, I argue that the natural world plays a unique and vital role in human development—that humans have a developmental potential for a sense of connection to the animal world and by extension to a wider "ecology of subjects."[3] This potential is evident in ordinary early childhood development; thus it demands greater theoretical and empirical attention from a wide range of psychologists, social scientists, educators, and others responsible for the growth of young humans.[4]

But if we are to cultivate this potential, we must first understand it. One reason the social sciences dismiss connection to the natural world generally, and animal-human interactions in particular, is the lack of an adequate empirical description and theoretical framework for thinking about them. Indeed, we live in a world dominated by other humans. It is easy to believe that our sense of connection to other humans and their influences on us are real and important. Other people are compellingly present to us, and they influence us through many shared modes of interaction: bodily presence and gesture, as well as language with all its characteristics, such as vocabulary, dialect, and prosody, and its power to constitute or call into existence. These modalities and others allow us to create and confirm intersubjective understandings with others. So powerful indeed do these modes—and our social scientific analyses of them—seem that anything less seems unimportant. This has resulted in a strong bias that the only social factors in development that matter are the human ones, those of which we are most conscious and that we fancy we control most completely!

But as this chapter shows in review and the following chapters tell in detail, children's relations to animals tap processes that lie deep in our own human animality and that bind us not only to each other but also to other species. The preverbal meanings of self-initiated motion, of unitary coherence, of displayed affects, and of sharing a past can transcend species boundaries for us. Children show this clearly, and the substance of their pretend play confirms these as the core of their apprehension of animals. In the intersubjective realm, children again show they distinguish animals as a *different* order of other, even as they use their humanly acquired abilities to read cues of affect, attention, and intentions. In linguistic relatedness, too, children distinguish animals as different. Their language abilities bias them to read meanings into animal behavior, providing a basis for further learning, and making us a species that may be unique in our ability to *include* other species in our sense of who we are. My studies of children's pretend play expand the importance of the animate realm, for they reveal a pattern of continuity between preverbal embodied experience and self-consciousness. This pattern is reflected in other areas of development also, uniting the child-animal relation with other great issues in development and philosophy of mind.

The evidence in this book is essential in correcting the perception that the human world is of sole and paramount importance in child development. Yet, we place human interactive processes foremost in our theories of human development not only because they seem empirically compelling. The underlying reason is that our intellectual forebears handed down to us a peculiar anthropocentrism and dualism in our manners of thinking about what it means to be human, and this has shaped our theories and thereby our attention.

The absence of attention to our connections with other species and the nature of the relationship between the body and our higher mental capacities are two coupled problems. Both stem from the divorce between what are thought of as a simple animal body and a transcendent human mind. Here is the broadest philosophical and historical context for understanding the problems of this book. It reaches into many areas of our culture and psyche: into ideas of social order, into popular conceptions of commonalities between children and animals, into theories of development, and into what we feel ourselves to be. In comparative perspective, it is by no means obvious that our cultural manners of thinking and living out our human animality are the only or the best options. I end this introduction with these anticipations of chapter 2, in which I clarify the import of this book for our common and our formalized understandings of what it means to be and become human. Change in such collective self-conceptions is the greatest possible contribution of this book.

II

Childhood Animality and Development

Child and Animal in Culture and Theory

It seems very natural to associate children and animals in our minds. The reasons are various. Many families with children also have pets; we take children to the zoo; and animals are very common children's toys. Not only do children and animals seem to have an affinity, but more abstractly, they seem similar—perhaps they might both be perceived as unruly or dependent. But despite the ready availability of these associations, we should be cautious about accepting them uncritically. Interestingly, concealed in such everyday beliefs about childhood are roots reaching back into our culture's particular history of philosophical, political, and psychological thought. One prominent example will demonstrate this.

Writing shortly after the turn of the century, Freud (1913/1950) expressed a sentiment that continues to echo in our culture:

> Children show no trace of the arrogance which urges modern adult civilized men to draw a hard-and-fast line between their own nature and that of all other animals. Children have no scruples over allowing animals to rank as their full equals. Uninhibited as they are in the avowal of their bodily needs, they no doubt feel themselves more akin to animals than to their elders, who may well be a puzzle to them. (pp. 126–127)

This passage strikes so many familiar chords that it invites examination as an article of faith. Indeed, words to almost exactly this effect have been repeated by several contemporary authors. Interwoven with the child-animal

19

theme in this passage are mixed feelings about maturity and distrust of bodily instincts, perhaps betraying an anxiety about a fragile social order.

We need to excavate some layers of our cultural history to grasp the nuances of Freud's quote, but it is evident that our response to it may contain several unexamined themes about childhood, maturity, animals, and animality. What roles are played by ideas—Freud's and those of others—that associate children with animals in our culture? Answering that question will take us to the heart of what is at stake in our notions of humanity and animality. Like people in many other cultures, we define humanity in relation to the animal condition and use animals as metaphors in evaluating different human characteristics.

The stakes involve not only children but also our formalized conceptions of ourselves and our development. The implications of these self-conceptions extend to our role in earthly ecosystems. Perhaps, it should not be surprising to find that to understand children's relations with animals we must first examine our inherited ideas about both children and animals; nor should we find it astonishing that this question sends out tendrils to a wide field of concerns about the meaning of human existence. But what may be surprising is that even though we easily associate children and animals, there are deep biases in our thought against granting the nonhuman an important role in human life and development.

Animals and the Symbolic Order

Exactly *which* qualities children and animals share appears to be largely a matter of culture, convention, and figures of speech. Cultures use animals in symbolically ordering human worlds, making comparisons between specific groups of people and certain animals. Child-animal juxtapositions are just a special case of the process[1] which the historian Keith Thomas (1983) described: "The brute creation provided the most readily available point of reference for the continuous process of human self-definition. Neither the same as humans, nor wholly dissimilar, the animals offered an almost inexhaustible fund of symbolic meaning" (p. 40).

A key feature of animal metaphors in human self-definition is their evaluative nature. As Aristotle said, in metaphor a name that usually belongs to one thing is applied to a new subject, and, depending on what sort of comparison one wants to draw, one's metaphor can be favorable to one's subject or not: To adorn, "take your metaphor from something better . . . to disparage, from something worse" (1984, p. 2240). Accordingly, animals may be used in two sorts of evaluative metaphors that contribute to the symbolic definition and division of humanity. On one hand, animals can be used positively as "exemplars" to show that what "we"—the social in-group—"are like" is natural and good. Simple examples would be the use of animals as sporting icons, national symbols, and the like. On the other hand, animals can be used negatively as "bad examples" to illustrate what "we are *not* like," thus making "our" virtues clearer for those who have yet to acquire them. Common cases would be referring to immoral behavior as beastly, epithets such as "swine," and so forth.

Fascinating examples of both patterns are provided by medieval European beliefs. On the positive side, the historian Esther Cohen (1994) discussed the use of animal *exempla* in how a preacher used a tale of storks as an index of piety: They "deserted their nest on top of an excommunicated man's house, returning only when the excommunication was lifted" (p. 62). Popular bestiaries, or books of animals, were full of Biblical and folklore meanings of real and fabulous animals as allegories of virtue and vice.

In a more sweeping sense, animals symbolized negative qualities. Theological writers of the Middle Ages clearly distinguished humans as above animals in the spiritual hierarchy. The human estate lay at as great a distance from animals as possible. Thus, animal antiheroes were common. "Lowly" animals were occasionally hanged along with criminals to emphasize the moral abasement of the latter. Animals were tried in lay courts for certain offenses, especially homicide, according to the historian Hampton Carson (1917). Some animal trials can be traced to the statement by St. Thomas Aquinas that animals are satellites of Satan and "instigate by the powers of hell and [are] proper to be cursed" (Aquinas, quoted by the theologian Reverend Andrew Linzey, 1990, p. 12).

As these examples show, certain groups, at certain times and places or performing certain acts, have been regarded as problematic animal-like humans. In other cases, praise is conveyed by animal metaphor or comparison. These two symbolic evaluative strategies have special expressions in discourses connecting children and animals.

Ideologies of Childhood Animality

Conceptions of human-animal difference are most tenuous and crucial where animals appear most "like" us. Just as our ideas about apes are highly contested today because they are where we now believe "nature" comes closest to "humanity,"[2] so, conversely, are our ideas comparing children to animals loaded with valuational meanings.

We can examine these junctures to discover the underlying meanings and motivations. Animality and affinity with animals are elements in our cultural beliefs or ideologies of childhood, which in turn are connected to political theory and philosophy. This is very evident in the fascination with "wild children," most notably the wild boy of Aveyron, discovered in 1798 and cared for and studied by Jean Marc Gaspard Itard (Malson, 1964/1972/Itard, 1799). Dispute surrounds this and many other reported cases of wild children, but the impression left is that children would naturally be as wild as animals, save for parental socialization.[3] Let us examine three interwoven historical discourses in which animals and children are associated because both are "natural" in comparison with a civilized condition.

The Untamed Child

> "'What is an infant,' asked a Jacobean writer, 'but a brute beast in the shape of a man? And what is a young youth but (as it were) a wild untamed ass-colt unbridled?' . . . Young men, being still unable to control their passions, were only a little better. They were 'like wild asses and wild heifers,' said George Fox; like young colts, thought Gerrard Winstanley."
> Keith Thomas (1983, p. 43)

The sentiments expressed in the above quotation use animals symbolically as "bad examples" in contrast to what is valued. The quality shared by children and animals is original wildness, and culture is valued over such disorderly nature. Children must become "not like" the negatively valued "animal" condition. This theme has a venerable past in our culture, as well as recent expressions.

Although there were ancient expressions of a "bestial" version of human nature, John Calvin and Thomas Hobbes and their followers amplified it greatly. Both employed comparisons of animals to the human "state of nature." For Calvin, the acquisition of religion was necessary, for otherwise "men are in no wise superior to brute beasts, but are in many respects far more miserable. Subject, then, to so many forms of wickedness, they drag out their lives in ceaseless tumult and disquiet" (quoted by the historian Richard Ashcraft, 1972, p. 145).

Hobbes did not insist human nature was wicked, but merely that it was dangerous. Thus, in his famous "state of nature," life was "solitary, poore, nasty, brutish and short" (1651/1965, p. 96). Hobbes's living illustrations were of American Indians, especially evidence, new at the time, of their hostilities. He extended this conception to "our ancestors," universalizing his anthropology (Ashcraft, 1972). Although in Hobbes's *Leviathan*, his political treatise of

1651, the "state of nature" was an analytical construct motivating consent to a sovereign with absolute power, it was interpreted more literally by others.

The precivilized condition was easily generalized to children. Hobbes held that the capacities distinguishing humans from animals had to be learned by instruction and discipline, implying they are not natural to the child. The parallel to acceptance of absolute power in the domain of child raising is socialization-as-taming. The psychologist Eleanor Maccoby (1980) summarized the development this ancient idea had reached around 1700: "Many contemporary writings compared the training of children to the training of horses, hawks, or dogs. And just as there were disagreements about whether horses ought to be broken or gentled, there were disagreements about the most effective approach to training children" (pp. 7–8). So strong was the parallel that some even felt that if animals would only live long enough they too would be capable of social elevation (K. Thomas, 1983, pp. 131–132).

Psychoanalytic thought features turn-of-the-century avatars of the untamed child. Throughout Freud's various formulations, the id was an anachronistic, animalistic part of the psyche. It primarily sought gratification of its strong consummatory, sexual or libidinous, and destructive impulses. The brutish nature of the five-year-old is shown by "the propensity towards cruelty and violence which is a constituent of human nature" (Freud, 1909/1955, p. 270). Just as for Hobbes humans are selfish by nature, for Freud selfishness is never modified at its roots. Consequently, the adult's dreams reveal the child's mind: "Dreaming is a piece of infantile mental life that has been superseded" (Freud, 1900/1965, p. 606). In dreams, animals redundantly represent these atavistic impulses: "Wild beasts are as a rule employed by the dream-work to represent passionate impulses of which the dreamer is afraid. . . . It might be said that the wild beasts are used to represent the libido, a force dreaded by the ego and combated by means of repression" (p. 445).

How does infantile selfishness end up being repressed? The child seeks to gratify its wishes through others but to succeed must conform to their desires. Thus, the "reality principle" gradually supplants the "pleasure principle." Rational thought and "civilized" life are thereby possible, but the pleasures of civilization are dubious. Coexistence of animal-like id wishes with obedience to the dictates of civil conduct means a divided person. But this is the price to be paid to avoid a nasty and brutish emotional life—a sort of Hobbesian politics internalized.

This short summary merely suggests the outlines and persistence of this theme in our culture. Animals have been used symbolically (and without good ethological basis) to represent the innateness of antisocial tendencies in the child. The imposition of a civilized state is necessary, even though the animal within remains unmodified and frustrated. Clearly, this theme is related to many other Western attitudes to children but stems especially from old polarities in political and religious thought. In political thought, there is the tension between social control versus freedom. Christian doctrine also expresses an ambivalence between sin and innocence as humans' original state. Indeed, the positive poles of these dichotomies have also been expressed by animal analogy.

The Child of Nature

The second cultural story contrasts the "natural" with the "civilized" state in a manner diametrically opposite to that just considered. In 1996 at Brookfield Zoo near Chicago, a three-year-old child fell into the gorilla area and, unconscious, was cradled and carried to the enclosure door by Binti, a mother gorilla. The incident garnered interpretations along these lines: Virtuous ape recognizes and helps kindred innocent child (Boccella, 1996). A coincident news item revealed the possible depravity awaiting the youth: With the complicity of adult leaders, a group of adolescents stoned a bear cub to death. Our minds close around such news with familiarity—they tell an old cultural tale.

Here, animality and childhood are conceived of as realms of relative goodness and innocence, whereas civilization is frequently viewed as the corruption of this condition. Thinkers of the Romantic period popularized this view, which, perhaps more than the "wildness" motif, influences contemporary thinking. Animals, like the "noble savage," are apt to be viewed as enviable or even superior beings untroubled by the division that afflicts humanity. Thus, we have the metaphorical animal as exemplar. The "child of nature," according to the cultural historian Peter Thorslev (1972), is like the animal in that both still exist somewhat apart from the fallen world of civilized adults and are thus superior.

A key figure in this strand of thought, Jean-Jacques Rousseau, in his *Emile* (1762/1979), agreed with Hobbes that "all our natural movements relate in the first instance to our preservation and our well-being" (p. 97). But Rousseau also protested that "Hobbes called the wicked man a robust child" (p. 67). Native self-love, for Rousseau, was not bad—his self-loving "savage" was independent, happy, and good in the state of "nature." His savage was not a beastly person but the "savage within": "Rousseau's rediscovery of the Wild Man was the uncovering and rehabilitation of the realm of feeling, which he instinctively felt was essential to an understanding of man and society, and without which social life could not be tolerable or fulfilling," argued the historian Geoffrey Symcox (1972, pp. 233–234).

Indeed, the passion of self-love is the basis of freedom, and showing the way to its preservation was an essential aim of Rousseau's political theory. Before society, there would have been no confrontation with others' wills, and thus no competition with, or need to please, others. But history has placed us in a civil context, and there our selfish tendencies lead us to define and seek what we want through others. This leads to resentment, vanity, self-deceit, inequality, and excesses of pride. Enslaved both by such inner division and striving and by external laws imposed to curtail outright struggle, the civilized adult has lost the natural harmony of savage, animal, or child of nature.

Rousseau took as his task to show how society and person might be rebuilt aright on natural provisions—essentially to harmonize the child of nature with the needs of society as much as possible. To take only one related theme in Rousseau's thought, in his *Discourse on the Origins of Inequality* (1755/1986) he suggested that part of the natural goodness of humans is a capacity for pity—"an innate repugnance to see his kind suffer" (p. 160). He even argued that pity was "so Natural that the Beasts themselves sometimes show evident signs of it" (p. 160). But this simple unreflective pity merely tempers our selfishness and cannot withstand the development of society and vanity. Thus, "reason is subsequently forced to reestablish [pity] on different foundations when, by its successive developments, it has succeeded in smothering Nature" (pp. 132–133).

In this story, although an initial positive commonality (and even sympathy) exists between children and animals, it is ultimately incompatible with civilization. Innocent, natural, and good, the animal-like child easily falls prey to the vanity and corruption of society; only carefully calculated child rearing such as Rousseau outlined in *Emile* can mitigate it. In ordinary socialization, innocence, independence, vitality, and natural acuity of mind are lost, and the person comes to be ruled by the opinions of others and divided between inclination and duty.

For Rousseau, child development and social order required the intervention of a tutor or legislator. But later Romantic idealizations held that the child was inherently good and its inclinations should be unrestrained, according to the historian of psychology Lloyd Borstelmann (1983, p. 24). Thus, stronger versions of the favorable comparison of animals and children echo through much of the culture, for example in the emergence of pet keeping in nineteenth-century America. The historian Katherine Grier (1999) explained that through this period people felt increasing discomfort with the rough pursuit of self-interest that characterized the commercial sphere. In response, the home life of the emerging middle-class family came to be redefined around the virtues of domesticity and geniality. The potential for kindness was extolled by parenting advisors in antebellum America as "natural." As agents of a sea-change in American attitudes toward parenting, they expressed the Rousseauian view that children are innocent, good-hearted beings whose softer feelings should be respected. Kindness to animals, in this perspective, was regarded as a foundation of virtue and an important aspect of character formation.

In this context, Grier (1999) argued, masculine violence stood out as especially problematic. Public and private corporal punishment, wife beating, child abuse, and beating of animals were targets of reformers. If children were naturally good, the special proneness to transgression of boys (later to be men) needed explanation. Childhood cruelty had a "hardening effect," and parents should be vigilant of any sign of boyhood cruelty to animals. Harming an insect could be a step down the slope to domestic violence. Socialization of boys was especially a target of the humane education movement (Unti, 2002). Voluminous literatures provided cautionary tales and exemplars for children. For parents, books gave advice on the importance of instilling self-consciousness of the effects of one's actions, and of dealing gently with young sentiments even when correcting them.

These matters affected not only the family, but the moral progress of society as a whole. For boys especially, pet keeping was thought to be critical for socialization in two ways. A pet in the house provided practice material for children learning to act kindly, and gave mothers the "small world" where they could intervene and instruct at critical moments, such as when a child might be inclined to hurt. Secondly, animals themselves were regarded as exemplars that could teach such virtues as gratitude, fidelity, and enduring love. Middle-class parents were encouraged to keep many different animals for their children (Grier, 1999).

The increase in pet keeping and ideologies supporting it may have created the conditions in 1896 in which the psychologist James Sully could muse: "In a sense a child may be said to belong to the animal community. . . . Has he not, indeed, at first more in common with the dog and cat, the pet rabbit or dormouse, than with that grown-up human community which is apt to be so preoccupied with things beyond his understanding, and in many cases, at least, to wear so unfriendly a mien?" (p. 247). As we will see, some of Sully's peers went further, recasting the middle-class consensus on the importance of animals in child development while advancing a theory with a late-nineteenth-century "evolutionary" and universalistic flavor.

Assumptions of goodness and innocence contributed to the elevation of the moral status of both animals and children. Paralleling the re-evaluation of character traced by Grier, early animal protection organizations attended to the needs of children when child welfare systems were absent or ineffective. In a pivotal episode in 1874, Henry Bergh, founder of the New York City–based American Society for the Prevention of Cruelty to Animals, the first organization of its kind in the United States, obtained the judicial removal of a child from an abusive stepmother, an event reconstructed in detail by historian Bernard Unti (2002). The principles involved in the animal and the child protective movements were somewhat different. The former constrained traditional claims of animals *qua* property, whereas protection of children entailed legal intrusion into the domestic sphere. But both extended social control to protect innocents from individual cruelty. In the years after the 1874 case, Bergh and co-worker Elbridge Gerry founded the New York Society for the Prevention of Cruelty to Children, and similar societies quickly sprang up around the country and in Great Britain. Some of these, especially in smaller communities, served both children and animals. The term "humane" was adopted by many groups to denote their concern with any being that might suffer unjustly (Unti, 2002, pp. 281–296; Singer, 1975).

In recent times, the theme of the child of nature has blended with what Borstelmann (1983) identified as the "child as future redeemer" (p. 30). Today, the corruption from which children may save society is environmental degradation. As in the earlier versions of the theme, society is problematic—only now in the thoroughgoing sense of destroying its own biophysical preconditions. Children themselves did not create this fallen condition and are not held responsible for it; in this they are seen to be like the animals of natural ecosystems. Both animals and children now need protection from environmental pollution and other dangers, and may even stand up to adult despoilers.[4] The animal-child relationship becomes a paradise lost retrospective, as well as a hoped-for ecological Edenic prospective.[5] But at the same time, other agendas continue apace: The child must be ready to survive in the competitive economic world and so on. Too great an attachment to animals might hinder these goals, so interest in animals is seen as a passing stage.

Childhood Animality as a Stage in Evolution Reenacted

The question of stages invokes a key notion of the third discourse. The two themes in modern thought discussed so far link animals and children in the service of ideological evaluations of human qualities and prescriptions for society—especially the need for social control and for the encouragement of freedom. In the third discourse, additional elements lead beyond metaphor to the assertion of a literal child-animal similarity. And actual contact between children and animals is valued—but only at a particular phase of development. Again, an underlying theme is the suitability of the child to a particular society.

The history of ideas about childhood shows scant evidence of interest in children for their own sake until the late nineteenth century. The first careful observational account of a child's development was published in 1787 by the German historian of philosophy Dietrich Tiedemann (1787/1927). But the work of Darwin brought the study of humanity firmly into the domain of natural science. It is thus ironic but expectable that when the scientific study of the child was vigorously undertaken by the American psychologist G. Stanley Hall and his followers at the turn of the century, it came with heavy evolutionary presuppositions. Indeed, in *The Descent of Man and Selection in Relation to Sex* (1871/1874), Darwin tried to reduce the gap between animals and humans by showing that animals had the rudiments of qualities most highly prized in humans—emotions and mental faculties: "The difference in mind between man and the higher animals, great as it is, certainly is one of degree and not of kind" (p. 126). In *The Expression of Emotion in Man and Animals* (1872/1965), he made the complementary case that humans demonstrate many remnants of animality. He showed the adaptive roots of facial expressions and revealed their analogues in other animals.

But although Darwin was cautious in his assertions, others assimilated his ideas to evidence from embryology. They contended that the stages of early fetal growth retrace the steps of evolution, and the similarity of animal and child represents this trend carried on postpartum. Borstelmann (1983) notes, "In the late 1800s, parallels between animals and children, primitive societies and the early history of humans were rampant. 'Ontogeny recapitulates phylogeny' became a slogan of the times" (p. 34). The newfound biological continuity of humans with other species suggested a developmental series common to both animals and young children. The Harvard historian of psychology Sheldon White (1983) notes that no less a psychologist than George John Romanes offered a single ordering of mental activities across phyla and across maturation. The child transcends the animal condition only upon becoming self-conscious at about age three. "What is the nature of the child?" people now asked of comparative anatomy and evolutionary history. According to the evolutionary biologist Stephen J. Gould (1977), "Recapitulation supplied the obvious answer: we understand children only when we recognize that their behavior replays a phyletic past.... Since a human embryo repeats the physical stages of remote ancestors, the child must replay the mental history of more recent forebears" (pp. 135–136).

This perspective underlay and confirmed the conclusions of the Child

Study movement. Led by G. S. Hall and others, turn-of-the-century mothers kept baby diaries; studies based on them concluded that babies go through a quadruped, "prearboreal" stage, as evidenced by a few babies who ambulate on feet and hands. One diarist noted "a curious resemblance between babies and monkeys. . . . Babies sit like monkeys, with the soles of their feet facing each other" (quoted in Gould, 1977, p. 137).

G. S. Hall was a major promoter of recapitulation and suggested, for example, that children's fears of water "originated somewhere since the time when our remote ancestors left the sea, ceased to be amphibious and made the land their home" (1897, p. 169). Hall extended the idea to encompass the entire span of child and adolescent development, considering the later stages to reflect cultural epochs in the development of civilization—the young child as primitive (and vice versa).[6] He held that these stages must be passed in their predetermined sequence. His ideas had other influential exponents, including for a time John Dewey. They were applied in school practice in the United States, and they are reflected in authors of the time such as Sully and Freud.

Consistent with his theory, Hall felt that the demands of schooling were inappropriate before a certain age. Hall and his collaborator at Clark University, C. E. Browne, wrote in 1904 that part of the need for the natural world is a need for association with animals. Thus, not only are children like animals, they need them. M. A. Kaylor (1909), another psychologist at Clark, quotes "Dr. Hall" as having said, "Love of animals is inborn. The child that has had no pets is to be pitied" (p. 206). He then cites a 1902 work by C. F. Hodge, an educational expert, who is even more explicit: "The pet animal is thus for the child, as it was for the race, the key to the door into knowledge and dominion over all animal life. . . . Its fundamental character and value for education are evinced in the passion of children for pets; and as in the race, so in the life of the child, it should be made the most of as a step toward civilization" (p. 206). All of this served to justify Kaylor's own investigations, in which he found children prefer animals suitable to the stage of culture they have thus far recapitulated. By the time children reach age sixteen, the horse—integral to the achievement of human civilization—is most frequently their favorite. Kaylor concluded: "The acquisition of dominion over animals was of fundamental importance to the development of the race. If the child is to epitomize the race's experiences, the pet becomes the cardinal factor at a certain stage in the child's development . . . to deprive a child of association with animals is to deprive him of his phyletic inheritance" (1909, pp. 236–237). What is strikingly evident in this passage is how this theme served the progressive vision of the time while also preserving the Romantic vision of the child as possessing natural goodness, the unfolding—now of an ontogenetic kind—of which must not be obstructed.

Although the strictly recapitulationist stance was discredited in child psychology, it has had lasting consequences.[7] Perhaps one of these is the widespread notion that animals are a good "training ground" for the child's sense of responsibility, morality, and nurturance. Other echoes occur in psychological research. Noting the similarity of methods used to study infants and animals, the Yale psychologist William Kessen (1965) comments,

> The idea of animal-child parallels has been subtly transmuted to remain one of the central postulates of child study. . . . The animal and the child are imperfect adults for the associationist and imperfect in a critically important way. They can be assumed to have fewer, or more simple, units of behavior than does the full man, and their apparent simplicity may permit finding the beginning of the thread that is woven into the inexplicably complicated pattern of adult human behavior. (pp. 113, 116)

Yet it is increasingly clear that child development is not a matter of the simple growing complex nor of a mere unfolding. The child is not like a completed animal or even an incomplete adult. Rather, development is a dynamic process we are just beginning to explore, an intricate dance of biological provision and cultural context. And the culture children encounter is shaped in part by assumptions about human-animal relations.

In all three "stories" or discourses we have seen the interplay of conceptions of nature with conceptions of humanity. The types of natural order are different, but in each one animals index the qualities deemed innate in humans, and the relation of child to animal echoes and evaluates crucial issues of individual and society. Hobbesian "state of nature" conflict is shown in animal imagery—transmuted to childhood animal phobias in Freud; Rousseauian pity is shared by animals, bonding them with children; the inevitable ascendance of industrial humanity over nature is etched over the child's early "animal phase." By consensus, child development implicitly moves from a natural or animalistic state toward one that is distinctively human, regardless of how the initial and final states are evaluated.

Rhetorically, these transformations rationalize the type of person required by associated theories of society. Thus, the themes—or, widely speaking, the metaphors or stories—we have examined are parts of much broader discussions of human existence and development. In dealing with the foundational question of humanity's boundary with the animal realm, however, they constitute a special genre, which might be called "ideologies of childhood animality." Feminists, anthropologists, historians studying mental illness, and others have discerned other patterns of association between animalities and specific categories of persons (see, for example, Haraway, 1989; Urton, 1985; Eaton, 1980; Howells, 1975; Rosen, 1968). Animal-child associations are central to our particular "intentional world," our linguistically generated way of ordering and categorizing our experience. Indeed, as we shall see, our own traditions of child psychology are no exception to the use of animals in the cultural process of human self-definition observed by anthropologists.

Human-Animal Distinctions and Developmental Theories

We have been tracing themes of Western thought that took unsocialized children to be problematic and symbolized key societal anxieties such as authority and freedom with metaphors of childhood animality. Interestingly, these ideas implied that the closeness of child to animal—whether based on wildness, innocence, or ontogeny—is, or must be, outgrown. A primary business of being mature, it seems, is to *not* be an animal. Perhaps, some of this can be written off as mere moves in political theory construction. But in their outlines, such cultural discourses betray a more telling urge. Most of the themes sketched are from the modern period. Yet, if we look back to the earlier discussion of the medieval view of humans and animals, the clues stand out clearly. A rigid and peculiarly Western manner of defining the human-animal boundary is evident. It may underlie both the tenet that the child-animal association must be outgrown and also the pervasive assumption in psychology that animals are of marginal significance in human development. To grasp this manner of constructing the human-animal boundary, some comparisons may help highlight the pattern running through classical, medieval, modern, and—in the guise of developmental theory—contemporary thought.

The Human-Animal Distinction

Human distinctness from other animals does not appear problematic in our contemporary view of life. Biological species, we think, differ in their appearance, habitats, and so on, but especially in their underlying essences encoded in their DNA and produced though organic evolution. Thus, humans are a distinct species within the zoological domain. But just how distinct? Actually, a number of doubts have been raised about our biological classification. The physiologist and writer Jared Diamond asked how the 2.9 percent genetic difference between two kinds of vireos or the 2.2 percent difference between two gibbons makes for different species, whereas only 1.6 percent separates us from chimpanzees, but merits a separate genus (*Homo* versus *Pan*) (1992, p. 23). The linguist George Lakoff (1987) argued that Linnaeus's system of biological classification was inevitably relative to human perceptual and cognitive biases. In biology, the historical rather than factual bases of the classic typological notion of essences underlying species have been revealed. Today, definitions of the species concept abound, many holding that species are fuzzy biological lineages. By such biological or population genetics criteria, we are a unique species, but one with important continuities with other species and with our evolutionary ancestors. Yet, even a century and a half after Darwin we have been inclined to minimize the fuzziness.

The elements of subjectivity in our biological classification of ourselves point to another way in which we understand the idea of "human." Besides denoting our membership as *Homo sapiens* in the zoological kingdom, the term also refers to the "human condition," in contrast to mere animality (see the work of the anthropologist Tim Ingold, 1988a). Other societies also use animals in defining the human, but their human-animal distinctions diverge instructively from our own.

Not all humans everywhere and at all times have believed humans and animals—and gods—are simply distinct. The anthropological and historical literatures are replete with examples of continuity and blurred boundaries. For example, the Barasana people of northwestern Amazonia believe the human status of their souls is precarious. According to a myth about Yeba, the first man, people originally were animal-people. Some were turned unequivocally into animals when they were drunk at a party—they became jungle birds and tapirs and other game animals; some even became garden plants. But in the Barasana "Sōri Masa" myth, humans' souls are taken to the animal spirit house, where they become reincarnated in the bodies of game animals. That such transformations occurred in mythic times is taken as evidence that the same could happen today, according to the anthropologist Thomas Langdon (1975). Consequently, shamans are needed to mediate between these worlds, and special observances surround hunting.

To take a Southeast Asian example, although certain Thai villagers have a separate verbal category for humans, the Cambridge anthropologist S. J. Tambiah (1969) explains why monkeys are not considered food—they are semihuman: "A woman with twelve children ... was too poor to support and feed them. The children therefore had to go into the forest in search of food, and they ate the wild fruits there. In the course of time hair grew on their bodies and they became monkeys" (p. 441). For Koyukans of interior Alaska, reports the anthropologist Richard K. Nelson (1983), present human-animal spiritual continuities derive from a distant past when animals were human and spoke human language before changing into the present forms—humans being created by a raven.

Many Australian Aboriginal cultures hold that such past time is still present in a sense. Inhering in the sensible world is another preexisting, continuing, and generative one known via "the Dreaming." From it, animal spirit entities can take human form. Thus, as reported by the anthropologist M. F. Ashley-Montagu (1937), the Aruntas believe that reproduction is not effected by intercourse but by a child-spirit or *Kuruna* of a particular totem animal entering a woman. For example, a woman might see a kangaroo suddenly disappear and then notice she feels pregnant (pp. 56, 77). The Nuer of Africa illustrate another kind of blurring of the human and animal. *Teknonymy* is the cultural practice of giving a name to an adult that reflects his or her offspring's name. Tellingly, among the Nuer, people are named after their favorite livestock, around which their entire cultural system revolves, according to another English anthropologist, E. E. Evans-Pritchard (1940). The situation cross-culturally is summed up by a comment by the anthropologist Hallowell: "While in all cultures 'persons' comprise one of the major classes of objects to which the self must become oriented, this category of being is by no means limited to human beings" (1960/1975, p. 143).

These other cultures illustrate how the human-animal boundary is intellectually malleable and not necessarily absolute. And they seem comfortable with a degree of "fuzziness." In contrast, we moderns tend to think of humans and animals as categorically distinct. Differences have been overemphasized even in post-Darwinian biological thought. For us, the "human condition" is defined in opposition to the animal condition.

Medieval European thinkers especially were confident in the separate status of humanity. As noted earlier, humans held a special place above animals in the spiritual hierarchy. This idea had roots in the ancient philosophies of Plato and Aristotle. Plato's thought contributed the great dualism of the material world and the sensing body versus the otherworldly realm of ideal forms. If, according to Plato's reasoning in the *Timaeus,* God was "good," this dualism necessitated another principle, that of "plenitude": The entire range of ideally conceivable kinds of things must be represented in nature. From Aristotle, later thinkers took the idea of a single continuum or "scale of nature." The historian of ideas Arthur O. Lovejoy (1936/1961) described the combined result, which was vastly influential up to the late eighteenth century: the idea of creation as a "Great Chain of Being," "composed of an immense, or . . . infinite, number of links ranging in hierarchical order from the meagerest kind of existents, which barely escape nonexistence, through 'every possible' grade up to the *ens perfectissimum*—or . . . the highest possible kind of creature, between which and the Absolute Being the disparity was assumed to be infinite" (p. 59).

In this system, degree of "soul" determined closeness to perfection and thus to God. Just as humans were debased angels, so monkeys were vastly demoted below ourselves. Thus it went, all the way on down to lower forms and even, according to Aquinas, to things deficient in "good" and therefore evil (Lovejoy, 1936/1961, pp. 77–78); as we saw, Aquinas felt animals might well serve the devil.

But within this hierarchical continuity, humans possessed a characteristic distinguishing them from all other living things: an immortal soul. This idea also originated with the Greeks. Plato's dualism hinged on the mind's ability to conceive of the true objects of rational knowledge. These were the "immutable essences of things—of circles and all figures, of all bodies, of all living creatures . . . of the good and the fair and the just" (Lovejoy, 1936/1961, p. 34). A soul with the capacity for knowledge of eternal essences is transcendent.

Aristotle, Plato's pupil, was also struck by the capacity of the mind to discern eternal forms, and through him the idea of a transcendent soul was passed on to Christian thought. Indeed, his long-influential manner of essentialist definition exemplified the mind's presumed ability to perceive unchanging forms. For him, a class of objects was defined by the inhering characteristics that are shared by every member of that class and only by members of that class. Thus, when he came to consider living things in his *De Anima* (*On the Soul*), he discussed the different grades of "soul" evident in the abilities of plants and animals. Although these were not transcendent souls, they were the immaterial organizational principles that explained the living body (the grades or principles of self-nutrition, sensation, and movement) and consciousness and volition. Humans shared these lower grades of soul but were set apart as the only being with a soul capable of reason, which was in turn pivotal to Aristotle's *Politics*.

The idea of human-animal difference thus stemming from the Greeks possessed an immense influence through the Middle Ages; elements of it fit well with the version of creation presented in Genesis. Objects in creation each possessed distinctive inhering characteristics; humans stood in this array of creation, but our unique essence derived from a transcendent spiritual principle. The idea funded conceptions of human life centered on rationality and the idea of an immortal albeit fallen soul.

Of course, to cite only these major landmarks simplifies a complex history that has been examined in great detail elsewhere, but the elements presented are vital to understanding the problem of this book. We must examine one more historical step to link this discussion with the problem of children and animals. A the dawn of the modern era, the philosopher René Descartes radically revised elements of the Christianized Aristotelian view of living things but kept the idea of human specialness. He challenged the idea of an animating principle or soul within the living creature. Partially mechanistic analyses of the body had been invented by the Greek physician Galen (circa A.D. 130–200), the English physician and anatomist William Harvey (1578–1657), and Galileo. But in his *Treatise of Man* Descartes (1632/1972) extended such analyses to explain fully ten bodily functions. These included nutrition, sensation, and movement—the very capacities of Aristotle's three simpler grades of soul. Descartes argued that these functions

> follow naturally in this machine entirely from the disposition of the organs—no more nor less than do the movements of a clock or other automaton, from the arrangement of its counterweights and wheels. Wherefore it is not necessary, on their account, to conceive of any vegetative or sensitive soul or any other principle of movement and life than its blood and its spirits, agitated by the heat of the fire which burns continually in its heart and which is of no other nature than all those fires that occur in inanimate bodies. (p. 113)

In effect, his argument convincingly eliminated the role of the old formal-causal concepts of the vegetative and animal souls, replacing them with what he supposed were the movements of fluids, of filaments in the nerves, and of other material cause-effect processes.

But Descartes stopped short of assigning rational thought a mechanistic origin. His own experience with doubt and volition and his ability to conceive of ideas such as "perfection" and geometrical proofs (all recounted in his *Discourse on Method*, 1637/1971) convinced him of the unquestionable reality of the rational soul. He believed this soul interacted with the body (at the pineal gland) but stood in contrast to its simple material-mechanistic nature. The fact that animals lack language "is evidence that brutes not only have a smaller degree of reason than men, but are wholly lacking in it" (Descartes, 1637/1971, p. 42). Descartes notoriously concluded it was defensible to study such mechanistic beings by vivisection.

The general effects of Descartes's skepticism, however, were corrosive on humans' exceptional status in creation and helped launch empiricists such as Locke, Hume, and Bacon. John Locke, for example, agreed with Descartes's physics and physiology but rejected the idea of a soul possessed of innate ideas. *All* knowledge comes from experience, he insisted. Demonstrating another vein of skepticism, Hobbes reasoned that men's equality (he ignored women, since his concern was with political rights, which at that time were usually exclusively allowed only to men) derived not from rationality or divine status but from their ability to kill each other, which critics complained made men more barbarous than beasts (Ashcraft, 1972, pp. 150–151).

The dividing line between humans and animals fell more in doubt and contention.[8] In response to the breakdown of the old order, people tried to strengthen the traditional distinctions where they seemed most problematic, for example, I suggest, in the themes of childhood animality. If humans were no longer automatically assured of special status and the basis it provided for social order or salvation, civilized status might still be *acquired,* and animals were apt analogies for those humans who had yet to acquire it. If hope was to be preserved, that similarity to animals had to be outgrown. Even the Darwinian view of humanity was co-opted into this pattern by those positing a cultural evolution through which the child ontogenetically progressed. But any attribution to animals of consciousness, reason, and other traits thought to make humans unique was contested: Animals have only the mechanistic, instinctual body. Thus, Western culture clung tenaciously to a clear distinction between humans and animals and at the same time conceded more and more continuity, partly by the device of a childhood animality that was to be transcended. This pattern has carried over, as we shall see, to the domain of theories of human development.

Animals and Human Development

Psychology, like other social sciences, grew out of the philosophical traditions discussed above, and bears their marks. The Darwinian revolution and the focus on biological bases of behavior notwithstanding, psychology, when it seeks to define its subject as the mental life of humankind, often defines humanity by what makes us unique among species. Consequently, when our human sciences look at our relations with animals, humans and animals are unavoidably split by such basic assumptions. These premises invisibly marginalize relations with animals, even when these relations are addressed. This applies to the traditional and still-dominant perspectives on child development—and thus on children and animals.

"Human development" is conceived of in a number of ways. Some theories focus on changes that vary across contexts, emphasizing environmental mechanisms. Other times, development means maturation, especially in the case of changes that appear to be fairly invariant across different environments and thus are driven by genetics or some robust mental structure. In reality, development is multidimensional and includes both of these kinds of change. Whatever the mechanism of change, however, development often implies directionality and progress in some trait that is of special interest. Many theorists have conceptualized development in terms of some goal or end point—some valued vision of maturity toward which development does or may proceed.

Which end points, or—the Greek term which is often used—*teloi,* are thus enshrined in our theories of development? They are the features of humans that Western philosophy has chosen as most unique and thus putatively essential to humans—rationality, self-consciousness, and related notions. Such features were classically seen as transcendent of the animal body. Thus, psychologists formalized old philosophical doctrines when they answered the question, "What distinguishes the mature person?" with one of these capacities. At the same time, they also participated in a culturally specific form of using animals in defining the human being—a form that assumes a value-laden difference. The result is a certain sort of anthropocentrism in our formalized psychological ideas about ourselves.

Of course, to view growing up as the realization of categorical human differences that allow creative and responsible autonomy is not in itself misguided. Examples we will examine shortly include development conceived of as psychological adjustment to social reality, as the attainment of rationality, and as the exclusively linguistic mediation of the self-in-society. Despite the fact that these concepts have led to many important insights about ourselves, for the purpose of understanding children's relations with animals all produce a systematic circular denial of the importance of such relations:

1. Development is the realization of some valued human capacity;

2. What is valued in humans is what makes us unique;

3. Thus the mature human has actualized its difference from other species.

In this manner, any central importance of animals in human life is dismissed by one's very assumptions. While children may be seen to have some commonality with the animal (perhaps including some form of affinity to it), such connection is secondary or spurious in light of an especially human capacity that develops with maturity. Animals can mean nothing fundamental to human development within such frameworks. If the matter arises at all, it is as an interesting application or illustration. As we might expect given the origins of these endpoints of development, not only relations with animals, but also the body are marginalized in modern theories of development. Let us now explore how this is played out in three traditional *teloi* in developmental theory: psychological adjustment to society, rationality, and the self-in-society.

Psychological Adjustment to Society. The metaphoric closeness of the child, the animal, and the body—all conceived as asocial or antisocial at root—is very strong in the psychoanalytic tradition. As we saw, in Freud's conception, the id evokes a strong child-animal parallel; it is infantile and instinctual, animalistic and selfish, even destructive. The psychoanalytic tradition posed the end of development as the optimal psychological adjustment of this selfish core to the demands of society. This is inevitably a compromise, and a difficult one. The necessity of accepting realistic partial fulfillment of id wishes gradually gives rise to the ego. The ego is essentially oriented toward the human world, and it must channel instinctual urges away from awareness and direct expression. Thus, in general outlines, psychoanalytic theory assumes a biologically based commonality with animals, but this is normally expected to be transcended with development.

This attitude about animals has characterized psychoanalytic thought since its inception. One of Freud's prime cases of how animals represent repressed material was Little Hans (1909/1955), a young boy who expressed his fear of his father in a phobia of horses. The horse was merely Han's vehicle for Oedipal anxiety; the real content was the family drama. In dreams and jokes, animal material also revealed the id—and a lapse of ego functions. Freud, like many others of the time, interpreted severe mental illness as regression to earlier animalistic phases.

Perhaps inspired by Freud's ideas, animals play roles in other branches of psychodynamic thought also. Freud's collaborator Ferenczi (1916) saw animals as symbols of the "totemic" self. Carl Jung saw hostile animal images as the projection of the "shadow" side of the self (1971, p. 147). Menninger (1951) interpreted his patients' bestial fantasies or acting-out as repressed childhood sexual or hostile urges. Animal phobias may betray psychodynamic or sexual anxieties (McLinton and Meir, 1978), though fears of animals may be of a more ordinary sort (Bowd, 1983, 1984; see Heerwagen & Orians, 2002, for an evolutionary/ecological view of children's fears, including of animals). Others have said animals represent security or authority figures, the latter in the case of dinosaur play (Woods, 1965; Schowalter, 1979). Because of their symbolic meanings, some clinicians beginning in the 1950s felt animals—usually in fantasy—were useful in the working-through of conflictual issues (Heiman, 1956, 1965; Bettelheim, 1976; Kupferman, 1977; Sherick, 1981; Van de Castle, 1983; Levinson and Sanders, 1986). In a more positive vein, real or stuffed animals may serve as "transitional objects" in the young child's creation of a stable world of symbols (Wolfe, 1977; Soares, 1985; Harris, 1993; Triebenbacher, 1998). Recently, projective therapy techniques calling for identification with real or inner animals have emerged (Houston, 1982; Gallegos, 1991). The mythologist Heinrich Zimmer (1960) anticipated this trend: "The interior animal asks to be accepted, permitted to live with us, as [a] somewhat queer, often puzzling companion" (p. 129).

These examples, while encompassing considerable theoretical diversity, reflect the attention and importance given to animality by the psychoanalysts. But as noted earlier, these are largely negative animal metaphors; animal images relate to a temporary phase of immaturity, antisocial urges, psychic stress, or ill health. And ultimately, if they are important at all, animals are merely symbolic, inner, or projective. In therapy, they are but a means toward a mature social—that is to say, human—ego in a mono-species adult world. Of fundamental concern are the distinctively human psychic-symbolic process and mental health. The child's early similarity and connection to animals is based on an inferior form of functioning, one that is outmoded with social adjustment and maturity. Notably, psychoanalysis also holds that mind and body coexist uneasily. Our animal nature is assumed, but the animal body is asocial and the ego must artfully exert control. Occasionally, the mind or ego fails and some forbidden content disconcertingly breaks free from repression, but normally the mind governs over the animal body.

Omitted so far from the discussion of schools of psychotherapy is the huge boom in animal-facilitated therapy of many sorts, stemming from the work of the child therapist Boris Levinson (1969; 1972). And, one should add, the work of his dog co-therapist! Levinson, and those who have followed him, granted relations with individual animals psychotherapeutic worth in their own right. Although it is far too extensive to review here (and because authoritative volumes are available, e.g., Fine, 2000), it is fair to say that much of this newer literature does give animals a real role in human development. But sometimes such animals are valued only instrumentally. A similar subtle bias is evident in research on animals' role in fostering developmental goals such as empathy, social skills, cognition, and other concerns (see Poresky, 1996, for a nonetheless admirable example and list of similar studies). While no doubt such research strengthens our understanding of the importance of animals in human development, the key variable of interest, the child-animal relationship itself, needs to be the object of understanding.

Maturity as Rationality. Not surprisingly, given the history of Western thought about human nature, rationality is considered a marker of humanity and maturity. It connotes consistency, detachment, objectivity and dispassion. Freud said the ego obeyed the reality principle, but this is only one expression of the idea. Rationality has meant instrumental or practical reason—the ability to coordinate means to reach a predetermined end. Rationality also may mean discursive or critical reason—dialogue to clarify knowledge and purposes, as well as means. In Karl Marx's vaunted comparison of the architect and the bee, both construct elaborate buildings (practical reason), but only the human does so from a deliberate plan (discursive reason). In the guise of scientific thought, criticism of knowledge was wedded to instrumental ingenuity. The result inspired a distinctively modern vision of development.

Jean Piaget, the great child psychologist, conceptualized the mental development of the child as approaching a posited endpoint, "hypothetical-deductive reasoning" (Inhelder and Piaget, 1958). Through activity in the physical world, the child's logic became increasingly complex and created more adequate conceptual patterns or "schemata." For Piaget, activity and cognition were the origin and cause of development, including of language. On the one hand, this does not necessarily imply a drastic split from animals: Neither instrumental thought nor possibly innate sources of it are necessarily restricted to humans. Piaget looked at knowledge from an organismic standpoint. But on the other hand, no particular closeness with animals is implied either. Piaget's standard for rationality is high—some of the young child's thought is animistic and anthropomorphic and therefore inferior.

Piaget called attention to the infant's impressive bodily or "sensori-motor" intelligence but showed that later the young child's thinking is quite deficient in understanding physical causality and the actions of living things. The child "animistically" projects intentionality onto inert events (see Piaget, 1929/1975). Such errors are corrected by a gradual process of decentering.

I do not deny the importance of insights generated by research into cognition, but theories in this tradition have tended to regard thinking about animals mostly as just instances of some more basic thought process, and not of interest in its own right. Again, the importance of animals in human development is assumed away at the outset. One exception is a new focus on the child's "biological knowledge," which we will discuss in chapter 4. But at this point, it is worth briefly noting fundamental problems with the elevation of rationality as the end of development.

The prizing of rationality as the point of development seems hardly contestable. Our science has flourished with the realization of its potential. Perhaps more important, the objective quality of moral judgments of fairness and justice depends crucially on discursive rationality. Yet, an exclusive focus on rationality has been vigorously criticized for the distortions it can encourage in our thinking, especially when rationality is conceived in a way that disjoins it from the human animal body. Philosophers going back at least to John Dewey emphasized the unity of cognition with emotional and bodily aspects of activity. But the epistemology of science holds that such subjective processes are not observable. Even though the scientist could observe them in herself or himself, felt bodily processes (not proprioceptive sense, but ironically including aspects of creative thought) cannot appear in the world of constructs through which the cognitive scientist observes other beings. But in both animals and humans of all ages, the body and the mind are inextricably intertwined. We do experience in our bodies our interactions with the world; and this complex sensing must fund "higher" cognitive activity (Gendlin, 1962).

Thus, the experienced bodily complexity of lived interactions shows up neither in our science nor in the conception of thought we derive from our own scientific or other activity. It is therefore omitted from our account of child development. Without asking about the possible value of the child's naive sense of psychic "participation" in nature and felt closeness to animals, it is assumed the child must develop away from this incorrect apprehension.

Language and the Human Self-in-Society. A third unique attainment of the growing person is membership in human community and culture—unquestionably of great value and deserving of status as a telos, or end of development. Cultural systems are supraindividual since they are reproduced in successive generations of persons. Thus, symbolic media must somehow impose their patterns on individuals, and language is thought to be the principle medium. Membership in the human community is thus a matter of coming to share linguistic meanings, and many cultural anthropologists assume no development is needed, just mere acquisition. Yet, even very domesticated nonhuman animals cannot participate in language as proficiently as even the least socialized humans.

Thus, this theory assumes a drastic gulf between humans and nonhumans. It allows that cultures may appropriate nature for symbolic purposes, but it holds, as the English structuralist anthropologist Mary Douglas (1975) bluntly stated, "In the last most inclusive set of categories, nature represents the outsider" (p. 289). Indeed, thus far in this chapter, we have been viewing the construction of animality and humanity as a culturally malleable affair, in which nature has no voice. But we can invert this perspective, stepping into the shoes of other cultures, as hinted in Tim Ingold's remark: "If humans everywhere and at all times have engaged in the activity of world-making, perhaps the difference between Western and other cultures is that the worldview of the former incorporates the idea of man as maker . . . whereas those of the latter incorporate a denial of human authorship" (1988a, pp. 11–12). Only a few anthropologists have followed up by taking other cultures' insights seriously.

The perspective enshrining the human self-in-society as the defining unique quality of humans is founded upon a basic—and important—distinction between the human and the nonhuman animal. Language is important not only because it allows the transmission of knowledge and meanings but because it allows self-reflective thought. Descartes and his latter-day followers set the criteria of rationality very high: "Thought" means reflective self-aware-ness. Hegel voiced the idealist version of this widespread consensus: "What distinguishes man from the beasts is the faculty of Thought manifested and first laid down in . . . human Language" (quoted by the philosopher Richard Routley, 1981, p. 412, n. 2).

The same bias is clearly repeated in George Herbert Mead's (1934/1962) influential theory of social interaction: "Man's behavior is such in his social group that he is able to become an object to himself, a fact which constitutes him a more advanced product of evolutionary development than are the lower animals" (p. 37, n. 1). Mead explicitly replaced the Aristotelian and Cartesian markers of human difference—"soul" or "mind"—with a secularized (and operationalized for research) version: language behavior. The "verbal gesture" enables self-reflectiveness, the only means by which the person integrates the various perspectives of others. Thus, selfhood is only attained in the context of a society of other language users, in which animals are not participants.

Examples from sociological and anthropological studies illustrate the consequences when animals do step onto the social stage: the animal is too hastily subsumed by the mesh of human meaning and social interaction. In an otherwise path-breaking book, the ethnographer of childhood William Corsaro (1985) sampled episodes of children's animal pretend play—but only to the extent human social roles were enacted. The anthropologist Billie Jean Isbell (1985) described how, in an Andean community, a sequence of animal metaphors were applied to the individual's identity across age-statuses and "moved" the person through the life cycle. Sociologist Clinton Sanders (1990, 1993b) theorized that the human-imposed frame determined the moves and meanings when dog owners interacted with others. The anthropologist James Fernandez (1986) watched older children attain human "mastery" roles over younger children's subservient animal roles in pretend play in a northern Spanish village, commenting, "They fully become subjects, that is, themselves, by becoming masters of animals" (p. 35). It is as if he saw the children reca-pitulate the "linguistic" human origin story told by cultural anthropologists. The child acquires knowledge of the meanings of the animal through words; any role of the real animal is secondary and subject to interpretation, usually as structured by adult discourse. Such cases reduce animals' significance to symbolic meanings. Linguistic interaction is presumed to dominate over modes in which the animal is a more equal participant, and other humans are presupposed to be the significant environment of the person. The diversity in cultural meanings of animals attests to the constructive power of language and other cultural forces, but again—since what is essentially human sets us apart—we find the circularity by which animals possess no fundamental importance to us.[9]

But doubts have been raised about this separation. Not unexpectedly, they involve a re-examination of the role of the body as well. The sociolinguist Harvey Sarles (1977) has criticized the use of language as a species boundary marker in social theory. Although language is described via numerous abstractions (grammar, meaning, sound, lexicon, structure), it is typified as *not* being other things—emotion, paralanguage, analogue; "and whatever language is, animals don't have it!" (p. 62).[10] As Sarles indicates, this perspective can also be criticized for splitting aspects of the person, as if meaning exists on a separate plane from action. Similarly, Jackson criticized the intellectualist bias of much social theory and argued that cultural analysis should not "reduce embodied experience to a mere sign" (1988, p. 328). G. H. Mead can serve as an illustration. His theory eliminated the body as a source of the sense of self, because, curiously, "We cannot get an experience of our whole body" (1934/1962, p. 136). As the philosopher Karen Hanson (1986) observes, Mead's "denial of . . . the body's reflexivity verges on a denial of the body's integrity" (p. 72).

But evidence of infants' amodal perception reported by Stern (1985), and our familiar proprioceptive sense of our body's position and motion suggest a more central role of the body in meaning and the sense of self. The outlines of this insight were traced by the phenomenological philosopher Maurice Merleau-Ponty (1945/1962), who objected to "linguocentrism" such as that criticized here. He rejected the isolation of the inner subject who must construct the world from externally transmitted meanings, and held that our actual experience is one of discovering ourselves already in the world. Others are known to us more immediately than through speech only. He rejected the solipsism of an opaque non-meaningful outer world of others who can be known only as they tell about themselves, a position that also overestimates the role of speech in how we know other humans. The possibilities opened by Merleau-Ponty simultaneously break down not only the isolation of person from person, but that of mind from modes of embodied experience, and also that of person from animal.

We find again, as in the other approaches discussed here, the familiar circularity and the parallel theme we have been tracing alongside children and animals—the separation of animal body from "higher" human faculties. It is time to amplify this parallel.

The Self-Organizing Human Animal Body

At this point, our line of thinking has linked the seemingly simple topic of children and animals to cultural history, to major theories of development, and to philosophies of mind. A fuller exploration of these topics demands book-length treatment, but this survey is sufficient to illuminate the broader significance of this book. In particular, two negative consequences are evident from our review of the history of developmental theories and how they treat our relations with animals.

First, such theories disjoin humans and animals. When our social scientists have looked at our relations with animals, they have unavoidably done so through the lenses of their theories, and these, embedded in Western philosophical traditions, define human nature and virtue in ways that hinge on what makes us unique. Humans and animals are split by the very assumptions of the theories, invisibly marginalizing relations with animals. A divergent trend is set between children and animals as "unique" human qualities are actualized in maturity. Thus, when children's (or adults') interest in animals comes up, the animals end up being incidental, of secondary importance to theory, or worse still, a regressive focus in development. The older assumptions discussed here still typify much of the empirical work on children—or humans generally—and animals. But research on human-animal interaction is fertile ground for new discoveries because animals present variations on the characteristics of a social interactant. To be open to these discoveries, we have to grant that unique phenomena may be present, and we have to be willing to assume, at least provisionally, that the animal contributes to the interactions in equal measure as the person or child. But despite the efforts along these lines by researchers such as Shapiro (1989), Sanders and Arluke (1993; 1996), and Alger and Alger (1997), relations with animals are not regarded as central psychological/developmental problems.

The second negative consequence is much broader—it is the implied dichotomy in the person's functioning. The theories posit, on the one hand, a simple and mechanistic body with either primitive instinctual order or no inherent pattern at all; and on the other, a conceptual order imposed by an impersonal logic of the mind, society, or culture. Since the body is simple and unreflective, mental or cultural structures necessarily derive from some interposed percept, concept, or schema, placed there psychodynamically, by the ascendancy of rational thought, or by linguistic symbolism.

The underlying theory requires there to be no inherent relation between embodied knowledge and what we think as cultural beings. The body becomes socialized but offers no order of its own that can help determine the outcome. We build up our world from the objects of perception and cognition, such that animal or human can be known only as an object. The subjective self, including the experience of embodiment, falls out of the legitimate subject matter of psychology. Theories embracing this epistemology must conclude that a sense of connection or intersubjectivity is epiphenomenal or secondary.

As we can see from repeated previous encounters, there is a link between the perceived lack of value in relations with other species and the problem of the relationship between the body and our cognitive, ego, or linguistic capacities. Both arise from the assumed divorce in our theories of a simple animal body from a transcendent intellect, today most often identified with language—the most structural, mindful, and independent form of behavior. This divorce is questionable from the standpoint of our evolution. The bodies of many mammals (and other taxa) are not asocial; they imply many social moves in long relationships. And in our case, language evolved in already very social bodies, which inhabited, moreover, an interspecies context. The divorce is also subject to a developmental critique. Evidence of how interaction and language are united in the developing human animal body would address this dual quandary. Research of many sorts is now examining the coupling of body and language in precise detail (discussed in chapter 6). Indeed, in our explorations of child-animal interaction we will find just such evidence.

Our culture has labored under the impression that we are an isolated species, alone in lofty (or anxious) detachment from this-worldly bonds. In the old account, the child's understanding of animals comes from egocentric projection, anthropomorphic reasoning, or cultural meanings. But if children and animals interact directly on a bodily level, then the meanings children make about animals derive from the experience of interaction. Simply put, animals may be directly meaningful to us. Perhaps, our language is even a factor that unites us with other creatures.

But not if our language (or other cognitive order) first divides our very person. This book also addresses this schism. If children's meanings about animals demonstrate a fine sensitivity to the differences animals present as interactants, this would be no inferior grade of ability to be overcome by imposed verbal order. Instead, this would show that children's embodied understanding is capable of being carried forward in more than a single or projected human pattern (although we may find the familiar—psychodynamic, culturally learned, and so forth—patterns also). We may even further see how these interactive meanings work within and after language—that is, if children's meanings about animals do not just stop at those imposed by language, this would be evidence for how the human animal body is self-organizing in a way that includes and surpasses simple linguistic orderings.[11] By the later chapters of this book, I hope to have explained and demonstrated how this is indeed the case.

Of course, abstract conceptual thought and language are marvelous human achievements, but we may have been mistaken in assuming they are what make us *most* human. Rather, children's relations with animals show that what is most human is something deeper and older in us—indeed, something that connects us with other animals. Language and mind can make us yet *more* human only if that older connection is not lost.

Conclusion

Cultures—perhaps universally—define the human in comparison to nonhuman animals. But Western culture may be exceptional in positing categorical human/nonhuman *contrasts.* Being human means *not* being an animal! This view has permeated our thinking about social categories, including the category of childhood. Ironically, even psychology has affirmed that as children grow, they become less like animals. This kind of self-conception fosters alienation from other living things, and it also exacerbates our ongoing confusion about how "mind" and "body" relate.

Now that I have introduced the full depth of the problems motivating this book, I will focus on children's interactions with animals. This primary subject—intrinsically interesting in itself and relatively uncharted—will lead us to insights and suggestions of broader importance by the end. I begin by showing that children do indeed incorporate a fine-grained appreciation of animals in their sense of self. Contained therein are clues to the sources of this self in direct interaction. What are the bases of such interaction, and what are its full implications? Not only will I show how animals are an inevitably and uniquely important part of the world in which children take their bearings as persons, but I will also show how interactive "bodily" knowledge intricately reflects interaction. It forms an essential basis for adjustment, thought, and language, but more importantly it influences and surpasses the paths these more "human" abilities take with development.

III

An Ecology of Subjects

Animals and the Child's Self

A young boy ventures out onto the Florida beach "monster hunting"—spending his days watching the intertidal life, waiting for the shadow of a passing giant stingray below the dock, and listening for the messages of the wildlife around him. This could have been many a child. But the story comes from *Naturalist,* the autobiography of Edward O. Wilson (1994), one of the century's premier students of biology and originator of the term *biophilia* for the possibly innate human tendency to take an interest in living things. Wilson's career demonstrates the developmental potential for engagement with other species. Early on, he narrowed his focus to one group of insects, the ants, and become the world authority on them; but later he also applied biological insights to humans; made key contributions to ecology; and, turning interest in life into concern for it, is a leader in the fight to save biological diversity.

Of course, Wilson's life story shows the many circumstances that came together to produce such an exceptional biologist. But it also hints that the roots, the earliest beginnings, of the lifelong love affair with the world of other creatures may be the heritage of every child. Indeed, it is especially appropriate to introduce this chapter with Wilson because he has also promoted the study of biophilia—the idea that we humans are genetically inclined to take an interest in living things. Perhaps, he is right. Yet, even if we have biologically programmed learning rules for biophilia, we need to account for this potential in the context of our full human capacities. Especially, biophilia may mean interest in the *subjective* side of other creatures; we may be the species that locates itself in an ecology of subjects.[1]

47

If our past thinking about animals and children has been biased by our ambivalent evaluations of the "animal" and the body, or if the topic has simply languished from a lack of interest, that does not prevent us from looking at it freshly. We are somewhat freer today to acknowledge our biological continuity with other organisms and certainly aware it would be wise to respect our interdependence. To be sure, not every aspect of our relations with nature can be revealed through children's time with animals, but it is an area calling for new visions. The neglect of animals in child research does not fit kids' behavior.

Indeed, we can look at the child's relations to animals as a subject in its own right and search for structure in what we find. My year in the nursery school produced a wealth of episodes, stories, observations, and recorded interactions that showed striking patterns. And several of these, we shall see, reinforce the idea that animals are important to the child's sense of self.

Understanding how important animals are in the child's sense of self is the main purpose in this chapter. First, I will present a range of episodes from my transcripts and field notes. Next, we will see in greater detail how they add up to a case for the child's self-in-relation to an ecology of subjective other beings. To anticipate, several patterns of activity relate directly to animals: interest in them as shown by attention, a desire to interact with them, and caring about their needs. Animals are also potently symbolic to children in a special sense—a sense that reveals the power of certain core properties of living beings. I will show how these all contribute to the self, which can be considered both a complex system of goals, and a special integration of experience. But a good place to begin is with the most simple kind of interaction of child and animal—times when virtually nothing appears to take place.

Children sometimes merely watch animals with rapt engagement, as when the children I was observing, themselves observed a dog in silence. *Something about animals is able to truly hold young children's attention*—a commodity of notoriously short span. Some children showed this inclination especially strongly; Solly was one such boy. Late in the school year, Mr. Lloyd brought two turtles to the class. During discussion, they were placed on a table in front of the class.

> Solly works his way close to the table and looks at eye level at the baby turtle, making a smiling, curious face. He reaches to touch the turtle, but is prevented by Mr. Lloyd—"We're answering questions now." Solly removes his hand but sits up closer, puts his hand on the table, and looks at the turtles again, still with a closed-lipped smile, eyebrows up. This close attention continues another minute. He is not oblivious to the discussion, about whether baby turtles survive in the wild (which most don't), as his lips become a frown. Fully two minutes after he started watching, Solly

> looks away briefly and then finally touches the little turtle with one finger.
> It moves toward his edge of the table, causing others to exclaim. Solly looks
> up at Mr. Lloyd, smiling in open-mouthed wonder. Mr. Lloyd moves the
> little turtle back. It crawls again. Solly and others reach to touch it.

Solly's focus lasted nearly two and a half minutes, despite an ongoing class conversation in the background and the fact that the turtles had been in the class an
hour and forty minutes already. The others were attentive enough to register the
little turtle's approach to the edge of the table. That young children have a great
interest in animals is of course not an original discovery; the psychologist and
educator Susan Isaacs showed it systematically in 1930 (Isaacs, 1930).

Examples of pure attention to an animal were not uncommon in my
observations, but even more frequent was direct interaction between a child
and an animal. Interaction structures and sustains attention. It also presents
many new dimensions, which we will explore in depth. The children had opportunities to interact with the larger turtle on the floor in groups of four, with
the supervision of Mr. Lloyd. In one small group comprised of the younger
children Dimitri, Mindy, Toby, and Rosa, interaction was lively and continuous.
Here is my transcription of less than a minute of it:

> Mindy gets the turtle in her hands and turns it around; the turtle faces
> her; she moves out of its way. Dimitri and Toby reach for it; so does Rosa.
> Toby talks to himself; otherwise the children are only intent on interacting.
> Toby looks closely, touching it several times, saying, "That feels so funny."
> The turtle faces Mindy and she moves back again suddenly: "Oooo!" Rosa
> moves back also, both girls in sitting positions. Toby: "Yikes. He looks
> mad, he looks mad." Mr. Lloyd: "Does he look mad?" Toby: "Yeah. Yikes.
> He's going to . . . he almost went over here"—Toby gestures to the floor
> between his legs. Dimitri now has his hands on the turtle; Mindy moves
> forward again, and actually picks it up, but then sets it down. Dimitri moves
> aside from the turtle as Toby and Mindy move closer. It crawls toward the
> bookshelf, all children around it. Toby: "Just let him go—just let him go
> where he wants." Dimitri: "Go this way"... Dimitri turns the turtle, looks
> at Mr. Lloyd, and smiles. Mindy and Rosa come around to be in front of
> the turtle. Toby touches the turtle: "I just touched, I got to feel one of his
> claws." Dimitri touches it also: "Me too." Toby: "Hey, do ya wanta feel his
> shell?" Toby touches turtle and pulls his hand away quickly.

Even without describing the finer motions of the children, this is clearly intense
interaction! Yet it was almost all nonverbal, save for some interpretation of what
the turtle was doing or might do. The children were engaged in anticipating and
responding to its actions. The point here is simply that animals are compelling
as interactants. The children ignored the next group, each other, and much of
what the adults said to them.

Another important theme emerged in the young children's time with the turtle. We just heard Toby ask the others to "let him go where he wants." This became the repeated and defining desire of the boys. But eventually, the turtle went too far away and they decided to bring it back, indicating a tension between wanting the turtle to be free but also wanting the interaction to continue. The evident concern over the turtle's autonomy is only one instance of a whole class of examples we will explore in this chapter. They involve the expression of *concern for the animal's well-being*, and they are central in understanding the significance of animals to children.

In a related case, the spider monkey that visited the class was very active. Although it was not dangerous, its owners held onto its tail, preventing it from moving freely or getting too close to the children. Drew, Solly, and others wanted them to stop this:

> Drew, interrupting, says to Ms. Dean: "Let go!" Solly: "When will you let go?" As Ms. Dean pulls the monkey back by its tail, Katra exclaims, "Aaaa!"

Later Drew directly challenged the monkey's keepers about the way they were holding its tail:

> The monkey strains briefly to get crumbs on the floor. Drew: "Why don't you let go of his tail?" Ms. Dean: "He's got my hand. I'd let go in a second if he'd let go of my hand." Actually, her hand is tight around the monkey's tail but its prehensile tip is visibly relaxed in her hand. Drew points to this, gesturing with one hand on the other: "He's let go'd of your hand. . . . He let go of your hand.". . . Ms. Dean holds her hand behind her leg, out of Drew's sight.

These examples of children expressing concern for an animal's autonomy hint at one of the core features of animate beings that are most obvious and important in children's perception. The ability of an animal to move on its own, to have authorship of its actions—in short to show agency—is not only perceptually compelling. For children (and the rest of us except solipsists), it also conveys subjectivity—a sense of the animal as possessing its own interior life and goals. In response, children are inclined to respect these goals, in effect caring about the animal's own well-being. We will observe the same pattern in relation to other core animate properties.

There are more complexities to the child's concern for an animal's well-being. Ivy complained about the confinement of the baby snake:

> Ivy: "I don't think you should keep it in that cup, know why?" Ms. Nol, the snake keeper: "Well, I just brought it down in there, so it protects it from getting hurt." Ivy: "But know why? But know why?" Ms. Nol:

"Why?" Ivy, indicating the size of the snake with her hands: "It could get bigger and it might squeeze"—she hugs her knees up tight to her chest, as if extremely cramped.

In passing, we may note Ivy's use of imitation, an important theme to come. But her complaint was not about restricted agency or about direct harm, as shown by her ignoring Ms. Nol's justification. Rather, it was that the baby snake could not grow. Ivy's concern extended to the snake's development. The animal can represent the child's own issues, paradigmatically in this case the inwardly experienced imperative of maturation shared by all young organisms. Animals—*just because they are living things*—may "symbolize" such issues. I put "symbolize" in quotes here to indicate a special and powerful sense of the term, one not to be reduced to cultural construction.

I have just highlighted central aspects of children's experience of animals, using examples akin to those many parents may have observed. But such observations—showing that animals command children's attention, that interactions with animals are compelling, that children readily care about animals' well-being, and that animals symbolize important issues for the child—although perhaps familiar, do not alone provide a theory or framework for understanding animals' importance to children. We must ask, is there an underlying thread of significance?

I suggest that the thread is the child's sense of self. The self is a uniting concept. It embraces activity, thought, and feeling; world and identity in it. And as many psychologists have argued, the self develops from patterns of interactions with others over time—that is, from relationships. Let us expand this to include animals among the "others" of the self. We feel a sense of relation to other species that seem to have "someone in there"; and we can explain something of who we are in reference to them. Animals provide clarifying points of comparison for the child and for our attempt to understand the self in general. And because animals interact differently with us from the way humans do, they can give us theoretical insight into the self in relation to other humans, too.

How does the idea of the "self" make sense of child's response to animals? First, we can view the self as a system of goals. These goals produce patterns of observable behavior. But the self is nothing if not also a subjective experience. This second sense of self we cannot observe directly. At the end of this chapter, I confront that problem and suggest a solution.

The Self as a Pattern of Goals

The self is a psychological "unit" with a high level of integration. For simplicity, we can think of it as an organized system of goals. This description agrees with the ordinary meaning of self, as in "self-interest." Continuity of the self is our primary goal. The bottom line is the survival of the organism, but the self is more than the organism, and its goals are not limited to bodily survival. Many different forces shape the self's various goals, among them genetic dispositions, social approval, and specific values promoted by society as well as those reflectively chosen. But since the "self" arises from relationships, continuity of the self also entails the maintenance of relationships. Thus, having a self predicts interest in significant others.

We can further infer that maintenance of relationships implies the exercise of the faculties that gave rise to them. Such exercise increases the person's skill, expanding his or her ability for furthering relationships. Thus, increase in interactive skills is evidence that a relationship (or kind of relationship) contributes to the self. From such an upward spiraling of ability and challenge, which the psychologist Mihaly Csikszentmihalyi (1990) terms "complexification," more elaborate relationships become necessary to maintain the self. Indeed, the very process of increasing skill may itself become a derivative goal. In a final logical step, maintenance of relationships requires continuity of the others to whom the self is related; thus, their well-being may become a goal of the self as well.

An advantage of this goal-oriented theoretical approach to the self is that it allows inferences—from observed patterns of behavior—about aspects of the self that do not appear in conscious self-reports as well as those that do. Persistent attempts, for example to maintain engagement of another, may suggest one of the self's goals. The meaning of an event to the self is found in its consequences, as shown partly in behavior: we respond to events in ways that reveal their significance for our goals. If someone dies or is otherwise lost, our reaction to that reveals that person's importance in our self's constellation of goals. Thus, a specific system of self can be inferred from behavior expressing the person's goals. Such behaviors include action toward the basic ends of the self such as survival; socially derived, or deliberately chosen goals; directed attention; persistent and varied attempts toward a target; preferences or values; and strong or revealing responses to certain events, especially those involving significant others. What goals of the young child's sense of self do patterns of such behaviors involving animals reveal? We will now examine three central goals.

Interacting with Animals

Most of the young children I observed wanted to interact with animals. At the minimum, interacting meant sustained attention. Such "interest"—literally, "holding between"—means engagement. In a step still more engaged, children gave strong reactions or excited comments in response to actions by animals. For example, the monkey grabbed the children's shoes. Being the recipient of its action was indeed exciting! Solly said, "He bited my shoe!" and Drew exclaimed, "He was pulling on my shoe!" When the turtle scratched Mindy, she retorted, "Aaaaaa! You scratched me!"

The children had a strong preference for interacting with animals.[2] We have already seen one case: the young children with the turtle were not dissuaded from interacting even by the interference of adults—a clear instance of how the child actively shapes his or her own experience and socialization. More direct evidence comes from data I gathered in one-on-one sessions: I asked each child to choose one of several activities (I randomly varied the order in which these were presented). The choices were to draw with crayons; play with dolls; play with animal puppets; play with trucks; or feed the classroom guinea pig, Snowflake. Of the twenty-four children, nearly two-thirds chose feeding the guinea pig as their first choice of the five options—a striking result, since by that time, midyear, all of the children had had plenty of chances to feed the guinea pig.

"But what about children's spontaneous choices?" one might wonder. In the course of everyday activity, how important are animals? In the spring, I used rigorous focal-individual/time sampling methods to observe several children systematically and found that of thirty-eight animal-related episodes, twenty-three involved live animals, eight involved pretend, and in the remainder animals were the subject of talk or books. Of the children's total time, almost a tenth was spent in animal-oriented activity. Although this is not a huge figure, it is still substantial and comparable with time spent in other play activity settings that adults consider developmentally significant. Interacting with animals is a preferred activity and (among other things) expresses a goal of the self, that of maintaining the sense of self by engaging in relationships with important others. In these cases, the others are animals.

Expanding Relationship Skills

Over time, relationships with animals became more important to these young children. Interactions with the resident guinea pig show this increasing importance of the animal. I could determine this because Snowflake was familiar to returning students but not to those attending for their first year. During two months at the start of the school year, 39 percent of the instances I recorded of children involved with the guinea pig were of children new to the class (n=12), and 61 percent were of children returning for their second year (n=13). The individuals doing this accounted for 85 percent of the returning children but only 58 percent of the new ones. In other words, proportionally more of the children with the previous year's history of interacting with Snowflake chose to interact with her, and they accounted for more of the interactions. By May and early June, there was a more equal distribution: Fifty-eight percent involved "new" children, whereas 42 percent were ones who had been there the previous year also.[3] The children's interest in interacting with Snowflake appeared to increase with experience.

Were the children getting better at interacting, too? Was a process of complexification at work? Most of the children's interactions with animals were not characterized by high degrees of "meshing," the term used by the ethologist Robert Hinde (1976) for the precise coordination between the two participants' actions. The most intricate interactions were with the guinea pig; it was also the animal most accustomed to the children. The children could successfully feed it and hold it on their laps; they observed it in the classroom and helped with various needs like changing the newspaper in its cage. I did detect some improvement over the span of ages in the class, although I did not quantify it. The younger children tended to have less knowledge and less skill at holding and feeding the guinea pig.

Regardless of age, however, differences between individuals showed that experience in interacting goes with and maybe causes increasing skills. Four children in the group who seemed especially adept at observing and interacting with animals spanned a one-and-one-half-year age range: Ivy (five years, eight months in the spring), Joe (5 years, 4 months), Solly (4 years, 11 months), and Toby (4 years, 3 months). In addition to their interactions with the guinea pig, these children had multiple animal-related experiences outside school, which may help explain their abilities. Ivy had fish at home, had been to the zoo four times in the past year, and had kept Snowflake in her home over spring break. Joe made frequent visits to the zoo. He had exposure to dogs in relatives' homes, his parents read to him about animals often, and he once had hermit crabs and a goldfish. Solly had fish and a toad and was still very attached to the family dog, which had died in the fall. His mother reported he was always looking for insects and liked to watch birds; she herself had long kept animals. Toby had spent time on his grandfather's farm, where there were cows; at home he had an ant farm. We have already seen examples of each of these children being involved with animals; these instances will multiply.

Similar examples in the classroom are harder to come by for other children, such as Mindy. Her mother reported only three exposures to dogs or cats in the current school year and no pets in the home. Mindy said she preferred to talk about guinea pigs rather than pet or feed the one in the class. Actually, she did have frequent interactions (six) with Snowflake at the beginning of the year, the most of any of the new children. But these were often brief and awkward—enough so that Mindy evoked intervention from others:

> Mindy shakes the cracker box with the guinea pig in it. The other children tell her that'll hurt it or it'll die. . . . Later she lifts it up and down in the box, too quickly for my comfort. I try to get her to not do this. Then she fumbles the box and it hits the floor, hard. Kevin helps her empty the guinea pig from the box onto her lap.

Most children were awkward with Snowflake occasionally, but Mindy seemed consistently so. During observation periods especially focused on Mindy, I saw few incidents where she was involved with live animals; the most involved interaction I observed her in was squashing bugs near the classroom door.

Another child toward Mindy's end of the spectrum was Dimitri. In the fall, five times he took action apparently just to make an animal react, more frequently than any other child. For instance, he chased pigeons and teased the guinea pig, once dropping a toy helicopter in the cage, and then hitting the top of the cage, prompting Chris to admonish, "Don't do that." Dimitri's interactions with Snowflake were chaotic. He attentively fed the guinea pig, but like Mindy tried to control it physically:

> Dimitri wants to hold the guinea pig. Mrs. Ray helps him ask Rosa for it and puts it on his lap as he sits, legs extended, on the floor. He feeds it greens for a long time, sometimes straining to see its mouth. He tries to feed it a pellet of food. It doesn't take it. The guinea pig drops to the floor between Dimitri's legs; he holds it there and says, "I got you."

Actions such as these were performed by most children at one time or another, but this pattern of control was typical of Dimitri. Data from Dimitri also do not entirely support the idea that experience and skill spiral upwards. He had extensive animal experience: year-long relationships with two cats, a neighbor's dog, and several visits per year to a pig farm and the zoo. During the year, one of his mother's cats was sick, but got well, thanks to a "doctor who fixes cats and dogs," whom Dimitri admired very much. But toward the end of the year, Dimitri was noticeably more adept at holding and feeding the guinea pig. Of course, not only individual differences in background but also instruction, development, and life events increase interactive skills and self-in-relationship.

The Animal's Needs

A child may incorporate the animal's well-being in his or her own sense of self, since this serves the child's goal of continuity in relationship. Altruism and caring are possibilities for humans on several theoretical grounds, and a sense of self-in-relationship is one of them. Examples of children's strong reactions to events and stories about animals, and actions they take as a consequence, reveal that meeting the animal's needs may become a goal in the self's underlying goal structure, related to empathy.[4]

Drew's desire to see the monkey move freely and Ivy's concern for the baby snake's growth share a common denominator: concern for the animal's freedom. In another example, the ferrets were put in harnesses, but they could wiggle out, and they chewed at their leashes. This attracted the children's attention:

> Billy looks and points: "Look what he's doing. . . ." Solly turns to Drew: "They're trying to get out of that." Drew had been straining to look. At this point he starts chomping his teeth together.

Concern for free movement was expressed with less energetic animals, too. Toby asked that the snake be let go: "Why don't you let it just crawl around?" Ms. Nol did not reply but set the snake on the floor. Later, just before his small group time, Toby asked again, "Why don't you let him crawl around?" As we saw earlier, this was a strong theme for Toby. With the monkey in its cage to go home,

> Mindy and Rosa are on the floor looking in. Toby arrives: "Look [he's] trying to get out of his cage. He's trying to get out of his cage. Yikes.". . . Ms. Dean: "Do you think he's happy in his cage right now?" Toby: "No, see he's trying to get out." Mr. Dean: "You think he wants to get out?" Toby: "Cause look-it, he's sticking his claws out."

When the monkey's movement was constrained, the previously implicit and unspoken meaning of the monkey's action—its expression of the monkey's agency—was revealed. Sometimes, children actually intervened with each other or with animals:

> Abeo pushes at the turtle's head again. Chen: "Don't push him, don't push [his head] inside"; he removes Abeo's hand.

In the introduction, we saw Toby "free" the caged birds—a fantasized intervention. These children clearly are concerned for animals' agency and autonomy—key aspects of their well-being.

Another concern, for the animal's health, was revealed in children's caring response when an animal was harmed—distressed, injured, or killed. Even merely reported mild injuries were troubling to the children. The dog owner, Mr. Grier, told the class a story about one time when Pogo, as a puppy, came to the grade school class he taught:

> Mr. Grier: "And the kids really enjoyed me bringing him in, and he got used to them and they got used to him, and you know, they could still

even do their work and he would be walking around and he might sit with them and they would pet him.

Well, let me tell you what happened one day. One day, the class was all kind of seated down, and I was talking to them. And I'm talking and I started walking backward a little bit, and I guess I didn't look where I was going and I didn't know that Pogo was right behind me and as I was walking backward I stepped on him. And he let out a squeal, you know." The children's faces are quiet, attentive; Yasmin nods. Mr. Grier: "Like a yelp . . ." Someone makes a high faint squeal. Mr. Grier: "When you hurt, it wasn't just like a bark. It was really, he was in a lot of pain." One or two children are making squeals now. Reuben: "It was like this, go . . ." He makes a closed-mouthed forceful and pained squeal. Mr. Grier: "Uh huh, something like that." Other pained squeals continue.

The children's sympathetic response to a violation of the animal's integrity and the pain it caused is familiar to anyone who knows young children. The incident was reported by two of the children to their parents. Joe told his mother about it:

Joe: And the bad story when they were leaving our class, um was when . . . ah . . . uhh . . .

Joe's Mother: Did something happen?

Joe: Uh huh, um, um.

Mother: Did something happen with the turtles?

Joe: No, with um the dog.

Mother: Oh, what happened with the dog?

Joe: When he was a little puppy, his owner was a teacher, and he brang him to school, and he was dr—, and he was going to draw on the blackboard with a piece of chalk, and he didn't know that Pogo was right there, so he stepped on him by accident. But then everybody looked, but from then on all the kids were saying um "Don't walk around when Pogo's right there."

The incident was referred to later by Joe as the "bad story." Dawn brought up the story as soon as her father asked her about the dog's visit:

Dawn's Father: And what about the dog?

Dawn: A . . . ahm . . . when he was little um the . . . in the um . . . in thaaaa, ah, when he was little and he came to school with Mr. Grier when he was a teacher, and he laid on the kids' laps and it, it didn't even bother them. But and um as Mr. Grier was walking back, he stepped on it.

Father: He accidentally stepped on the pup?

Dawn: But he didn't get hurt.

It was fairly unusual for any event involving the animals that visited the class to be reported to parents, and these examples stand out.

The children's responses were more striking when the harm occurred to a living animal in the class. When an animal the children knew first hand was harmed to the point of death, even more intense emotions—and another aspect of the child's incorporation of the animal's needs—were revealed. Drew was very interested in the turtles' feeding behavior during their visit. He revealed why:

> Drew said to Mr. Lloyd: "My turtle died." Mrs. Ray to Drew: "Was your turtle that big?" Drew: "No . . ." Mrs. Ray: "That was sad." Drew: "And it wasn't eating its food."

In fact, Drew's turtle had been a fifth-birthday gift, and after a brief life of six weeks it had died, just ten days earlier. He had been careful in caring for it and was "very upset and sad to discover it had died one night," according to his mother. Drew discussed this further in his small group with Mr. Lloyd. He wanted to know what Mr. Lloyd was feeding his turtle and if it would "eat other stuff." The death of Drew's turtle was talked about among the other children, and Dawn reported it to her father.

The entire class suffered the loss of another animal, coincidentally on the same day that the turtles visited. The classroom's pair of doves had finally succeeded in hatching one of a series of eggs. The offspring was only a couple of weeks old when it was found motionless that morning on the floor of the cage. Ever since the egg had been laid, and especially after it hatched, the baby dove was an object of great attention. Mrs. Ray discussed its death extensively, including the cause—perhaps it caught cold or the mother did not have enough "crop milk." The children talked about this loss, and Dimitri brought it up with his mother. And in yet a further coincidence, another dead animal appeared on the same quite death-ridden day—a gray-cheeked thrush whose "sad eyes" impressed Mindy. All these dead animals were mentioned to Mr. Lloyd minutes after his arrival:

> Drew: "You know what?" Mr. Lloyd: "Hmm?" Drew: "I have a turtle except it died." Mr. Lloyd: "Why did it die?" Drew: "It wasn't eating its food, turtle food." . . . Abeo: "We found a dead bird outside." Mr. Lloyd: "You did, what did you do . . ." Drew (interrupting): "Brunged it inside . . ." Mr. Lloyd (interrupting): "Did you just leave it there?" Drew: "And our baby bird died inside here, today."

The death of a close animal is recognized to be a traumatic event, as the study of people bereaved of their pets has shown (see the work of the human-companion animal researcher Lorann Stallones, 1994, and also Stewart, 1999).

It carries dual aspects. On the one hand, it constitutes a breach in a relationship within which the self had taken its bearings and thus threatens continuity of self. On the other hand, through relationship the goals of the other—goals like continuity and well-being—may have come to matter for the *other's* sake. Death can seem an ultimate violation of those goals.

American parents tend to feel responsible for how their children's development turns out. Theory reinforces this with the idea that we construct every experience for the young. In some of the preceding examples, adults attempted to moderate the impact of harm or loss. But the impact had occurred; the adult's intervention was just a response. Even when the event was anticipated, its impact was felt despite adults' attempts to construct the problem in a more positive light. Of course, this is not to deny children's need for help in dealing with painful feelings! But it appears that events within children's own relationships with animals can determine children's responses. The effectiveness of adult construal is limited. Indeed, the meaning of such events is "overdetermined" by children's own forms of self and relating. Events such as we have examined here—ones concerning an animal's agency, affect, coherence, and/or continuity—are fundamentally important to children themselves. We are beginning to see how the separation of person and animal assumed by traditional theories presents a limited view of our potential.

Symbols of the Animate Self

In the preceding chapter, we looked at animals as cultural symbols. Such symbols have come to be regarded by cultural psychologists such as Richard Shweder (1984) as an "arbitrary code." In this view, little except other cultural meanings determines what an animal (or any other entity) symbolizes. But the meanings of animals to the children I observed related to specific psychological and developmental issues, such as loss and bereavement, coping with physical harm, or concern for a baby animal's need for room to grow. Indeed, for this latter concept, the developmental psychologist Karl Rosengren and colleagues (1991) showed an early developmental basis. By age three, most children understand that growth over time is a property of animate things. In fact, so salient is this conception that they over-generalize it to inanimate objects. By age five, children's performance does not differ significantly from adults'. Growth is a conceptually pre-potent feature of living things. For us, however, what is at issue is not just children's conceptual grasp but the psychological significance of such meanings.

Children evince a fine appreciation of the meanings implicit in the features of living or animate things. These features resonate with the child's own self. Turtles, for example, had a particular symbolic meaning related to coherence. During the first session of the class as a whole with the turtle, the following exchange occurred:

> Mr. Lloyd: "How do you think it feels, what does it feel like to be a turtle?" Solly: "Safe . . . *Safe.*" Mr. Lloyd: "You think it feels safe, why?" Solly: "Because you have a shell."

Solly stated it first, but this theme was repeated many times. The children identified readily with the younger turtle, but they also expressed the desire to be invulnerable by identifying with the turtle's ability to "be safe" in its shell. Here is another example, from a younger child:

> Billy: "When a shark comes . . . when a shark comes to get the turtle, it—he pulls . . ." Sam tries to join in. Mr. Lloyd: "Let's let Billy talk." Billy: "He just puts his whole body in his shell, and he just puts it right in." As he says this, Billy pulls his arms in tightly toward his sides. Billy: "And then he, and when it's all gone, when the shark is all gone, when the shark is all gone, he just puts his body back out." Billy extends his arms back out again.

For Billy, the turtle symbolizes not only safety and coherence but also the whole affective experience of surviving an imagined life-threatening situation. Notably, Billy's symbolization took the embodied form first of a tightly closed-off protective posture and then of an expansive, mobile, and agentic one—conveying affective qualities that would be hard to represent verbally. Imitation and incorporating the animal's well-being were united in this symbolic activity.

One time, I asked two boys if they would want to be the guinea pig. Their response showed both empathy and their interpretations of confinement:

> Mr. Myers: "Would you like to be like the guinea pig?" Drew: "No. In a cage? Would you?" Mr. Myers: "I don't know." Solly: "And crawl in things!"

Drew disliked the idea of a cage, but the agentic potentials of being a small animal appealed to Solly. Agency is a key value for children's own sense of self, and animals' autonomy symbolizes it.

The death of an animal is significant because it symbolizes issues of loss-in-relationship. A day after the baby dove's death, Dimitri explicitly brought up his own father's death in a talk with Mrs. Ray. For him, the bird symbolized the basic issue of continuity of self and other. *The qualities animals potently symbolize for young children are not just arbitrary.* They include agency or autonomy, coherence or wholeness, feeling, and continuity. These qualities will become quite familiar to us and are central in the child's own experience of self. Animals represent them because they display them with immediate compelling vitality—a fact with broad implications for our understanding of symbolism.

To summarize, the functional sense of self posits the goal of self-maintenance; when translated into relationships this means interest and engagement in, and increasing abilities for, interaction. It also means caring about the others who help constitute the self for their own sakes, and experiencing one's own vital issues through the other's experience. Following the German philosopher Martin Heidegger (1962), we can describe the essence of human being with the term *Dasein* (German for "being-there"), which "itself is to be made visible as *care*" (pp. 83–84). The self emerges in the context of relationship and shows itself by links of caring. In this section, we have seen such links. They attest to our developmental potential for a sense of connection to other animals. *The young child's self takes form in the available interspecies community, constituting itself among an ecology of subjects.* But we have yet to understand in detail the exact interactive sources and full implications of these relationships.

The Self as a Pattern of Experiences

Before moving on, I want step back to our discussion of theories of the self to address the problem of the subjective self. The early American psychologist William James (1890) provided an enduring analysis that designates two meanings to the "self" as it is experienced by each of us. Experientially, he said, the self refers to the sense of a "me," or self-concept that one can describe in objective terms. On the other hand, it also refers to an ongoing experience of a *subjective* "I," meaning our feelings of continuity, agency, wholeness, and awareness. The "I" and the "me" have their origins in interaction with others and help elucidate the interactive sources of the goals of the self as a functional unity, as I described previously. But these two meanings also pose a dilemma for studying the self and its development.

James said the "me" is "the sum total of all a person can call his" (1892/1961, p. 44). In other words, it was the person's material possessions, social positions, and distinct mental qualities including consciousness, thoughts, and psychical mechanisms. These are all "objective" properties, and so James called this the "objective" self. This is what many psychologists mean by the "self-concept," and it can include *knowledge* of one's subjective self, or "I," but *not* the "I" itself. Many researchers have focused on what a person thinks of himself or herself, which is assumed to have a strong influence on the person's conscious choices, social relations, and so on. Such ideas about ourselves are typically communicated in words, and have traditionally been studied via language.

An example is a child's narrative about the self, which expresses self-attributed categories such as gender. The process of language socialization is crucial to this kind of development. In the school years, children make comparisons with others, leading to the perception of group and individual differences, including psychological traits. Such aspects of the self are clearly influential in a child's experience and are shaped by his or her particular speech community.

But there are limitations to an exclusive focus on the objective self. The American psychologist Jerome Kagan (1990) criticizes the nearly exclusive contemporary focus on the self-concept. It overvalues consciousness, he argues, reflecting our conviction that our conscious intentions are important. This bias, translated into methods that ask the person to report on the contents of his or her mind, constrains the material available for study and thus stunts our theories of the self. Many biological and psychological processes lie outside of awareness, inaccessible. Objective measures of mood and feeling tone "usually have very little relation to self-reports" (Kagan, 1990, p. 364). Adults can report their thoughts, but most cannot explain how they (even successfully) solve certain problems. Particularly telling is the fact that people's self-reports rarely contain inconsistencies, although inconsistency across situations and time, and contradictory ideas are typical of much of our lives. There is also the difficulty—especially acute for young children—of forming grammatically comprehensible linguistic responses to self-concept questionnaires or interviews. For all these reasons, Kagan predicts that the meaning of "self" in future studies "will emphasize a family of processes rather than a unitary one" (Kagan, 1990, p. 365). Interaction with varying interactants, such as animals, is one place to look for such multiple processes!

James's concept of the "I," or subjective self, is the personal moment to moment experience of individuality and is underlain by processes such as those Kagan seeks. James discerned four features: (1) an awareness of one's agency over life events, (2) an awareness of the uniqueness of one's life experience, (3) an awareness of one's personal continuity, and (4) an awareness of one's own awareness. These four kinds of experience, which make us aware of the "I," all have profound consequences. Agency leads to the belief in the autonomy of the self and the sense one actively structures one's experience. Distinctness produces the sense of individuality—that "other [people's] experiences, no matter how much I may know about them, never bear this vivid, this peculiar brand" (James, quoted by the social psychologists William Damon and Daniel

Hart, 1988, p. 6). The experience of continuity lends stability to the self; it and the sense of distinctness are especially important to identity and self-concept. Self-consciousness allows one to reflectively define what one's identity means. But the "I" *is* just that aspect of ourselves that can never be pinned down—the dynamic present sense of self. Whereas the "me" is the self-as-known, the "I" is the "self-as-knower." It is not static in the way an objectively labeled trait of the self can seem, and it enters into the person's every action and interpretation as the backgrounded acting, knowing self. This is especially evident from the fluidity of agency and reflectiveness.

Wonderful and recognizably true as this description is to us, the fluid-ity and privateness of these experiences of self inclined many philosophers as well as James and his followers to despair of ever "capturing its essence in a scientifically objectifiable manner" (Damon & Hart, 1988, p. 4). Still, the self is not just a fiction; people do report experiences that endow the self with a compelling reality. Since it is not open to consensual validation, however, it can only be studied indirectly. But the alternate research focus on the self concept collapses the "I" into the "me." Some researchers ameliorate this reduction by studying, as did George Herbert Mead, the "me"'s concepts *about* the "I"—that is, what the person believes about his or her agency, uniqueness, continuity, and self-awareness. But this still is not equivalent to "self" in the full sense, and it has a further disadvantage in our case. Young children do have basic concepts of others' minds, and of their own, as entities possessing beliefs and desires. But more advanced concepts of psychological traits are some years away. Thus, mea-sures of children's *knowledge* of the self's subjective qualities will misconstrue and underestimate the self's actual nature, extent and detail. We *have* subjective selves long before we can tell much about them. If we want to understand how animals come to have such important places in the child's self as we have seen they in fact have, we need another way of asking about it.

Fortunately, there is an alternative approach. It depends on a degree of inference, but within a theoretical structure this is customary in studying subjective experience. Recently, Daniel Stern (1985) has modified James's set of characteristics of the "core" subjective self to comprise agency, coherence, affect, and continuity. Basic experiences of self are attained in infancy through interacting with others—others whose actions allow the infant to make critical contrasts about who (self or other) is the source of agency, continuity, and so on, at the moment. Crucially, Stern bases his ideas on the new body of empirical studies of early and probably innate talents of the infant. Stern explains James's fourth feature of the subjective self, self-awareness, as an acquisition based two further kinds of interactions—intersubjective, and verbal—that define two more senses of self and other. But preceding the core, intersubjective and verbal selves (and also continuing with them) are experiences of self coming into being. This not-yet-gelled feeling of self Stern calls the "emergent self." Stern thus describes four interactively defined domains of relatedness and self: emergent, core, intersubjective and verbal. The first is least amenable to study, but is active whenever the other senses of self are coming into being or changing in the midst of new experiences with different interactants. While experiences of emergent self probably recur at every stage, we will be most concerned to demonstrate empirically how animals shape the three latter crystallized forms of self in young children.

Adopting the general strategy suggested by Stern's solution, we can make some inferences about the subjective "I" by studying the structure of interactions and relationships within which it arises. This is a similar strategy to that of Harry Stack Sullivan (1953), who wrote that the structure of a relationship is a clue to its significance to the participants. In studying children's interactions with animals, we can employ this strategy in a productive way since the characteristics of the interactants vary in interesting and regular ways.

We have already seen that children's incorporation of animals in their range of interests and concerns foreshadows the importance of the core subjective features of agency, coherence, affect, and continuity. A close study of child-animal interactions will teach us exactly how animals attain such importance in the child' sense of core self and other. That is the task of the next chapter.

IV

The Immediate Other

Animate Relating

One day, Dawn's father brought her baby brother to visit the preschool. Dawn begged her father to let her show Peter, who was barely able to walk, around the classroom. Finally, he acquiesced. First, they "walked" (Dawn lugging Peter along) to the guinea pig's cage and stood before it. Next, they stopped to watch the other children making Halloween "witches' brew." Then Dawn awkwardly carried Peter to the glass doors and they looked out at the birds on the bird feeder as he rested his hands on the glass. The next stop was the pair of doves, to which they returned shortly after a visit to another activity table. Dawn was nearly five, and this was the beginning of her second year in the class. As she introduced Peter to her familiar setting, it was clear that the animals were important members of her classroom community. Perhaps Dawn felt that her infant brother would be interested in animals, too.

Why do young children take such an interest in animals? Perhaps it is simply because animals are a novel stimulus—especially for urban children who have little contact with animals. Can the "novelty hypothesis" adequately explain children's interest in animals? It is of course possible that animals are no different from other phenomena that are equally novel. The idea of novelty applies to occurrences in which a person loses interest once he or she is habituated to the stimulus. It might account for Peter's interest, but Dawn had the ability to be very absorbed even with familiar animals like Snowflake. What accounts for the spiraling engagement, as if "novelty" continued indefinitely, seen in people who spend their lives working with animals? "Novelty" fails as

65

an explanation, for it is too general: It tells us nothing about the particular structure and challenge provided by continued interaction with animals.

In fact, research now backs up what may have been Dawn's intuition that infants take a special interest in animals. As we will see, insights from infant studies provide important pieces in the complicated puzzle of why animals matter to us. In brief, from a very early age infants have the ability to construct a coherent experience of self and other from "invariant" properties of interactions (properties of self or other that are the same across varied specific interactions). Because animals are like other humans—but not identical to them—in their properties as interactants, they provide unique opportunities for the development of the self. I have made a case for them being important to the self, and I have introduced the basics already—agency, coherence, affect, and continuity; in this chapter we will explore these basics more fully as I show how the animal emerges for the infant and young child as a truly *subjective* other whose immediate presence is compelling.

An objection could be raised to the idea that the differences animals present as interactants matter and contribute a different dimension to the developing self. Indeed, we might expect several objections based on the traditional ways child-animal interaction has been interpreted. Is not the child merely being anthropomorphic when he or she experiences an animal as possessing an inner, subjective life? Is not the child's feeling toward the animal rather based on egocentric projection or culturally constituted linguistic meanings? Is the child cognitively "fooled" by certain properties, and would thus respond the same to a sophisticated robot? Why should we think the child's feelings are based on a genuine sense of self-in-relation, with all that implies about the dynamic adjustment to the other?

Today, it is rather easy to suppose that human mental and cultural constructions so override the natural world that the latter cannot have any inherent significance for us. The assessment of animals' importance to children is only one case in point. But the sense of subjective immediacy that arises in infancy and childhood is not secondary; we will see that it both precedes and continues after the child learns cultural frames. After analyzing the dimensions of this sense and learning its basis in early development, we find one fact stands out: Children's interactions with animals *vary* systematically depending on the animal. And these variations provide a response to some of the objections mentioned above. But we must start with a close examination of actual interactions. Indeed, until we have a clear account of the structure of human-animal relationships, we may be bound to look at them as distorted human-human relationships.

The Animate Other

One morning, the teacher instigated a game of "circus" with small slugs in the play yard. The children held sticks as the attached slugs dropped slowly along their strands of slime. My first impression was that the children treated the slugs as essentially objects, manipulating them mechanically. I do not mean they "objectified" the slugs in the sense of disrespecting their subjectivity—for it seemed there was no question of such an inner aspect of the slugs at all. In another case, which like the other examples in this chapter was transcribed from my videotapes or field notes, the children turned the turtle in its tracks to make it change direction:

> All kids seem to have their hands on the turtle; then Chen has hold of it.
> Drew: "Turn him around." Other kids sit back; Chen turns the turtle.

The animal seems essentially passive, inanimate and without its own agency. These examples involve slow, relatively non-motile, "passive" animals. But the children also moved the guinea pig around physically, manipulated it, and ignored its own activity, such as the time Mindy shook it in the box, or a time Drew and Solly played with it, trying to control its motions. Is it possible for children to see animals as if they were not alive?

Consider an alternative interpretation. We can reverse the "parsing" of such events, focusing not on the child but on the animal as shaper of the child's responses.[1] In this light, in interacting with even such a passive animal as a slug, the child *had to* adjust the height and position of her hands in ways that were responsive to the animal's movement and slime trail. When the children lifted the turtle, its ability to bite *caused* the children to avoid putting their hands near its head. This language may seem stretched, but in context it makes sense. Part of the fascination of the slugs was that they were not fully predictable, and seemed to start dropping out of their own volition. And when the children did treat an animal as inanimate and unable to initiate or respond, they were often stopped in their tracks by some action of the animal or, in the case of Drew and Solly, by the guinea pig's squeal alerting an adult!

Is this kind of reinterpretation just conceptual sleight of hand, making much of the animal's supposed agency where at first glance it seems to play a minimal role? At the root of this problem is the child's concept of animates versus inanimates. Jean Piaget studied "childhood animism" by asking young children about inanimate objects such as the moon, clouds, and wind—"Why do they move?" The children told him it is because they intend to move (1929/ 1975, chap. 7, esp. 215ff.). This is "animism." They confused animate and inanimate causality. We now know that for a number of reasons, including linguistic cueing, this pioneering researcher underestimated children's true conceptual abilities. Fortunately, recent work shows even infants have a clearer animate-inanimate distinction than Piaget concluded.

Infants and Animals

Some of the earliest evidence that children put animals in a special category stemmed from James Watson's "conditioning" of a fear response in an infant. In 1920, Watson, a booster of behaviorism, and his graduate student Rosalie Rayner paired an unpleasant loud noise (the unconditioned stimulus) with the sight of a live rat and showed that eleven-month-old "Little Albert" quickly learned a fear reaction to the rat. In behaviorist theory, it should not matter at all what the conditioned stimulus is—instead of a rat, it could have been a rock. But in 1934, the psychologist Elsie Bregman tried replicating the infamous experiment, only she paired a loud noise not with a live rat but with wooden blocks and pieces of cloth. After numerous attempts with fifteen infants, she found no evidence of long-lasting conditioning. We can take this as a clue that an animal is not the same kind of stimulus as just any other thing.[2]

Others have found more direct signs that infants are prepared to notice animates. Three-week-olds give different responses to the sight of inanimate versus animate objects according to the psychologists and infancy researchers T. Barry Brazelton, Edward Tronick, and Mary Main (1974). The psychologist Lonnie Sherrod (1981) showed that six-month-olds clearly distinguish animate from inanimate—although in these and other studies the only animates presented were people. Another psychologist, Gail Ross (1980), found a distinct category for animal stimuli by twelve months. In another study reported three years later, the psychologists Roberta Golinkoff and Marcia Halperin (1983) found similar affective reactions to most animal stimuli as opposed to non-animal stimuli in one eight-month-old boy. Although only one living animal was used (other animates were merely drawings), they also concluded he possessed a preverbal category for animal. The psychologists Kenneth Roberts and Martin Cuff (1989) determined that at age nine months infants have the ability to discriminate basic categories including "bird," and at fifteen months, they have the superordinate category "animal." Notably, animal words and sounds are among the first in the infant's vocabulary (see also the work of the psychologist and researcher of language development Eve Clark, 1979).

The strongest evidence about infants' mental category for animals comes from research employing living animals. The psychologists Aline Kidd and Robert Kidd (1987a) studied 250 infants of ages six, twelve, eighteen, twenty-four, and thirty months and found an increase across this range in proximity-seeking and contact-promoting behaviors directed to the family pet as compared with a novel battery-operated toy dog. From twelve months on, babies smiled, vocalized, and maintained interactions longer with the pet. And finally, the work of the Canadian psychologists Marcelle Ricard and Louise Alland (1993) stands out for presenting a living animal with which the infant was not already familiar. They found differentiated patterns of response to a rabbit versus a strange person or a mechanical toy between ages nine and ten months. The rabbit evoked an intermediate mixture of responses. The infants tried to get closer, as they did with the toy but not with the stranger; they made fewer communicative smiles toward the rabbit than toward the stranger but more than toward the toy; and they did an equal amount of looking at the rabbit as at the stranger. With both the rabbit and the person, the infants looked back at their mothers less than when encountering the toy. The authors concluded, "The spontaneous familiarization behaviors they resort to when confronted with an unfamiliar yet not frightening animal suggest that they do not confound this class of objects with people or with inanimate toys" (p. 14).

These rather little-known infancy studies contain a big lesson: Very young children do differentiate between humans and animals, and, moreover, children's concepts of nonhuman others may be based on and exhibited in *interactions* with them. And both of these conclusions have implications for the self. Instead of looking only at what the child can say about self and other (which would reveal James's notion of the objective self, or the "me," which is usually what is studied), we can come closer to the elusive sense of the "I" by looking at how actual interactions are structured, as we noted in chapter 3. Young infants respond to basic features of other animates. As children mature, they become able to handle more complicated kinds of interactions; later we will explore the consequences of children's more complex abilities, for example, language. But the basic or core features of animates do not just vanish as the child gets older; they continue to structure the interaction, providing a basis for a sense of core or animate self and other that persists across development. Looking at children's interactions with animals, the features that stand out are the main constituents that Daniel Stern (1985), blazing the trail beyond where William James left off, showed are necessary for the first coherent sense of the core self or "I."[3]

Agency

Agency is a cardinal feature of animals as young children encounter them. The animal can initiate action. For example, the animal's ability to bite was of concern to the children I observed, and it came up with every animal. Early on, fears that the snake was poisonous were raised and discussed among the children:

> Joe: "Is it a rattlesnake?" Chris: "No." Ivy: "What kind of snake is it?"
> Laura: "If it was a rattlesnake it would bite."

Even the snake owner's reassurances did not settle the matter, and the snake's potential to bite remained salient in the children's interactions. During one small group session, the snake's presenter suggested that my presence might be cueing the children to act out fearful responses, since they had been calm before I arrived. I reviewed the videotape and, sure enough, there were some fearful gestures when I was present. But this explanation ignored the snake's movements. While the children were calmly attentive, the snake's head was toward its keeper. When I was present, the snake happened to be positioned with its head outward, and each child pulled back precisely when its head was pointed at him on her. Indeed, *before* I arrived, the three exceptions to the calm attentiveness each occurred at the moments the snake's head was pointed at a child.

In other cases, the children verbally expressed concerns with biting. While feeding the ferrets, Dawn observed, "He's biting the bottle." The ferret presenter later cautioned the children repeatedly not to put their hands near its mouth, but this became relevant to Billy only once the animal was free on the floor. Then he asked, "Does it scrape and bite—bit people?" The monkey was very interactive and liked to bite at feet, which pleased Solly: "He bited my shoe." Katra, however, was not amused. I asked her, "Are you afraid of him, Katra?" She shook her head. Mr. Dean added, "A little bit?" Katra nodded twice. Further questioning revealed biting as her reason. Indeed, as Toby observed, "Everything we give him he bites."

The monkey initiated interactions in other ways besides biting. Its activity was regularly punctuated with attempts to grab the children's feet, which were extended toward it on the floor. It would first look away and then slide its body, arms extended, toward a child's foot. Mostly, this resulted in the children's quickly withdrawing their feet, but sometimes they permitted the contact. Once, the monkey crouched down by Ms. Dean and then hopped first toward Yasmin and then across the semicircle to Chen and Drew. Chen retreated, exclaiming, "Hey!" The monkey touched Drew's shoe. Drew leaned back laughing, touched his shoe, and said, "He was pulling on my shoe."

Biting was not only something initiated by animals; it was also a potential response to action by the child. Anticipating bites, the children registered agency not only from overt action but also from the omission of possible action. When the dog visited, Billy asked if he bit cats; he was told the dog chased cats. Sitting next to the dog a little while later, Billy reached for its face and then sat up. He proclaimed: "I touched his tongue. . . . He *let* me touch his tongue." Mr. Grier responded, "Really?" Billy: "He didn't even bite me."[4]

Recent research supports the importance of agentic action to young children. It pervades their causal thinking about animates, as shown by many researchers since Piaget; see, for example, the work of the psychologists D. Dean Richards and Robert Siegler (1986), who looked at the features children attribute to living things. The developmental psychologists Susan Gelman, John Coley, and Gail Gottfried (1994) reported experiments in which young children were asked to judge whether videotaped unfamiliar objects and animals moving across a surface were moved by an external cause (a person moved it), an internal cause (something inside it moved it), or an immanent cause (it moved by itself). Some children saw all the target objects being carried by a human hand; others saw them all move without any apparent human help. Surprisingly, Gelman and colleagues found that four-year-olds "consistently deny any external cause to explain the biological events, even when a human bodily carries an animal. Rather, biological events [i.e., the moved or moving animal] are viewed as resulting from immanent cause. Children regularly appeal to intrinsic factors even without knowing the internal mechanism" (p. 349).

It could be objected that children attribute agency to animals because of cultural conditioning—for instance, the pervasive personification of animals. Some of the examples given do indeed occur within cultural scripts elaborated around petting/being petted, holding/being held, and feeding/being fed. Often, all three of these co-occurred with the guinea pig, and the children themselves transmitted this cultural practice within the nursery school. But although such interactions occurred in a cultural frame, the detailed moves are not deducible from it. Instead, such activities, as well as touching/being touched, biting/being bitten, pursuit/escape, seeking/hiding, and throwing/fetching are examples of "complementary" interactions (defined by the ethologist Robert Hinde, 1976, as when the action of one organism elicits a different but linked action by the other). Most interactions observed between children and animals were of this contingent form.[5] Partaking in extended bouts of linked moves is a social activity based on fine-grained responsiveness.

In a complementary interaction, either the child or the animal may be the initiating party. One example is "chase." Most often, the children pursued the animals, but the activity can occur the other way around:

> The turtle starts walking toward Billy. He gets up and goes behind Ivy, then moves to one side as the turtle approaches Ivy, who moves away backward. Ivy: "Oh oh, he's coming at me." . . . Billy continues avoiding it.

Being the recipient of the animal's own agency is a significant experience, as being touched by the monkey was for Solly and Drew. Mindy said she wanted to squeeze the snake. After having her hands on the snake for a while and evidently squeezing it, Mindy proclaimed five times, "I squeezed her." Then, the snake's reaction registered. Mindy interjected, "I feel the muscle, I felt the muscle." Children easily recognize and respond to the agentic qualities of animals, just as we would expect from the preparedness for such interaction that they have exhibited since infancy. The interactions which this move-by-move responsiveness makes possible are the constituents, rather than the effects, of what may become routinized behaviors including learned cultural scripts.

Coherence

The second key feature of animals is their coherence. Young children perceive animals as paragons of coherence. First, children receive a basic impression of wholeness from the animal's body. Young children are very concretely oriented in their approach to animals.[6] Petting an animal is culturally framed, but it also provides a tactile, concrete sense of the animal. It is a highly sought-after activity, and the children asked repeatedly for turns to touch the animals that were brought to class. When they were not allowed to do so, they tried on the sly. The children commented on the surface textures they felt when petting the animal, such as its softness.

Some petting or observation focused on a part of the animal. The children remarked on animals' teeth, claws, paws, and so on. Benson touched the turtle's hind foot and remarked, "I touched his claws and he didn't scratch me." Pogo's bushy tail was another such part; it drew the attention of a group of the younger children for its sweeping motion: Drew pointed to it, saying, "Look [what] it's doing; it's sweeping the floor." Solly suggested the dog's name should be "Sweeper." Then, Mindy moved close to Toby and the dog's tail; Dimitri and Rosa also approached, and all put their hands under the dog's wagging tail.

The body parts the children remarked on in this way stand out from the whole animal, which possesses an unmarked primary unity revealed by the child's readiness to hold an animal. The small size of the resident animals in the classroom, which the children often petted, enabled them to touch the entire animal—giving a very concrete sense of its coherence. This sense is reflected in a comment Dimitri made while feeding Snowflake: while holding the animal between his legs, he told her several times, "I got you." Dimitri had created a space for the small, calm, furry guinea pig that matched its whole, complete, warm and vibrating body. The child's readiness to hold an animal often thus reflected its specific shape and character. On the other hand, one animal literally held the children:

> Yasmin: "I want to do, could you do that to me?" . . . Ms. Nol puts the big snake around Yasmin; she is calm and laughs. Ms. Nol: "It's got ya. It's just holding on tight." Yasmin, fairly calmly: "It's just squeezing me." Ms. Nol: "It's got its tail under your arm, just holding on—it probably thinks you're a tree." Yasmin: "Maybe." Ms. Nol: "A good solid branch to hold onto so he won't fall—she, she." Yasmin: "It touches. Please don't touch." She keeps her hands away from the snake: "Make it unravel by itself." Ms. Nol lifts it off.

The large, mobile snake embraced the children as it constantly extended and changed its position, tracing, as it were, not only its own, but also the child's basic experience of being a coherent unity.

Naming is a cultural practice that works within the reality of organismic coherence. One of the first questions children asked about a new animal was "What's its name?" Although they also wanted to know the kind of animal, species identification was not sufficient. It did not mark the animal's primary individuality. Sometimes, I invited the children to make up names for the animals. Here are some distinctive names they gave the ferrets:

> Laura: "What's his name?" Mr. Myers: "What do you think would be a good name for a ferret?" Laura: "Ferr-at." Dawn: "Ferrie." Solly: "Duster." Dimitri: "Duster." Angela: "Buster." Chris: "Nibbles." Sam: "Drinker." Ms. Collins: "Drinker?" Sam: "Yeah, because he drinks a lot [from the bottle]" Chen: "Drinker." He repeats this many times. Adrienne: "Furry." Ivy: "Furry, 'cause it's, it's furry." In the back, Adrienne and Dawn are saying "Ferrie" over and over.

Once they learned the ferrets' names were really Ben and Bojangles, they used those names frequently in talking about the animals. Naming is a cultural practice that merely underscores the animal's particularity and individuality—the child's overwhelming sense of uniqueness between subjective self and other.[7]

The animal does not talk to the child. Later, we will explore all the implications of this, but here we can gain insight into animate coherence by contrast with the verbal relatedness. Since it does not talk, the animal is unable to place the child in the "double bind" described by the family systems pioneers Gregory Bateson, Don Jackson, Jay Haley, and John Weakland (1956)—that is, the animal cannot persistently present contradictory messages through verbal versus nonverbal channels of communication, as do significant human others who essentially tell the child two things at once. For this reason, animals may not foster fragmented self-perception in the child but rather reinforce self-coherence.

Affectivity

Affect also consistently enters the child's experience of animals. How? One possible route, much studied in human affect, is facial displays of discrete emotions like "happy," "sad," "angry," and so on. These are powerful human emotion carriers and may be universally recognizable. Nonetheless, they are likely to be a weak route in our interactions with animals, since animals' facial musculatures are relatively less intricate than humans', their facial structures are so different, and most of us lack the species-specific ethological knowledge needed to guess well. This is not to say that people do not frequently make wrong guesses—anthropomorphic attribution based on facial emotion display is not infrequent. Certainly without knowledge of a species' patterns of expression, errors are likely.[8] But in fact, facial expression may not be the main way people get information about animals' emotional states.

Another dimension of affect besides categorical emotions is called vitality affect. Vitality affects are patterns of arousal over time and are displayed by both humans and animals through qualities of motion and prosodic qualities of voice. Words that describe some of these subjective affective patterns include "surging," "rushing," "drawn-out," "dragging," and "fleeting." Such qualities are perceived across differing sense modes and situations and can be evoked by internal feelings or the actions of others. Stern (1985, p. 56) likens the expressiveness of vitality affects to that of music, of dance, or of the way puppeteers utilize a vocabulary of arousal patterns that could be designated by such terms as "lethargic," "jaunty," "forceful," and so forth. All convey feeling despite a lack of facial information.

For humans, perception of vitality affect has roots in early infancy and is critical in human emotional communication. Within a certain range, these affects are also communicable across species. The writer Elizabeth Marshall Thomas (1993, pp. xvi–xvii) described how her dogs rapidly and accurately read her moods from her behavior, even at a distance. Masson and McCarthy (1995) catalogued a multitude of examples of animal emotion, many of which hinge on vitality affect. Granted, the "vocabulary" may not be identical across species—excitement for a sloth must have a different rhythm, for example. Other species' affects may have no analogue in humans at all, and, conversely, humans may be capable of feelings that no other animals have. Little research has been done on these clearly difficult questions. Nonetheless, we—children included—perceive that animals experience changes in arousal and affect quality.[9]

The children I watched responded to affect intensity and the qualities of arousal of the animals. The kinds of responses varied but usually included an unlabeled but enacted recognition of the animal's affectivity. In a simple example, when the children were invited to throw the ball for the dog, the animal's excited and expectant affect was conveyed to the children by its quick pacing and turning; the alertness of its face; and its nondirected, nonthreatening barking. The children's response showed recognition of the mood—they were very excited. For all, this mood waxed and waned with each episode of ball throwing and fetching. The children's excitement did not just come from wanting to throw the ball, which could be interpreted as the governing cultural frame of the interaction. That a deeper level of vitality affect was operating was shown by the variety of overt responses showing a similar experienced affect. Two girls scrambled around and clung to each other, as if afraid. But they were smiling and verbally denied they were really scared. Their arousal contours followed the dog's excitement, illustrating how vitality affects can be expressed or experienced in a variety of concrete actions.

The ferrets provided a contrasting affect. They were initially too active to be let free and had to be kept in hand, where the children took turns feeding them with a bottle. From being held and fed a cloying oil-vitamin mixture, the ferrets became extremely passive, an affect reinforced by the way they relaxed when the presenter held them by their neck skin, a standard way to carry them. Reflecting this predominant vitality affect, the session ended up being the least arousing of all the animal visits.

Vitality affects associated with activities the children experience in their own lives provide another avenue to the animal's affective side. Feeding the toad provided an analogy to familiar mealtimes. The children never tired of watching the toad eat. The teacher would place it on a sheet of paper along with whatever bugs the children had gathered from outside. Toad searched the paper, then stalked and finally snapped up the bugs it found. The vitality affects of these episodes were shared by the children: eager anticipation in avidly collecting bugs to feed it; building tension shown by the children's crowding around the paper to watch; and satisfaction upon completion.

Continuity

The three aspects of animals discussed above can give the child the feeling of being the *same* self in relation to the *same* other if there is continuity over time. Young children remember previous episodes of interaction with animals and generalize about them, transforming interactions into a relationship. The case is strongest when interactions with the animal are repeated many times and attain a degree of regularity in the actions of each participant, as in the children's relationships to Snowflake. A concrete history existed on both sides: The guinea pig had long been in this environment, where it felt, saw, heard, and smelled the humans' activities; and since some children were in the class for a second year, a culture of guinea pig knowledge was passed on not only by the teacher but also by the children. This history included such things as the enacted knowledge for the children of having the guinea pig sit on a towel on their lap and holding food for it—and the enacted knowledge for the guinea pig of being placed on a child's lap and chewing the food and not the child's fingers. Where a relationship has a history like this, interactions can become predictable. For example, over repeated feeding episodes hesitant children who withdrew the food learned that the guinea pig was persistent; fidgety children learned the guinea pig would leave if they tossed it too much on their laps. In both cases, the children—often with encouragement—increased their success in feeding the guinea pig.

In the preceding chapter, I noted that the children returning to the class for a second year showed a greater sense of relatedness to the guinea pig, as indicated by the greater proportion of interactions with it and the percentages of children partaking in such interactions at the start of the year. Data on interaction with the diamond doves provides a comparison. The doves were new in the class at the beginning of the year. Among the instances of children being involved with the doves, however, the attentions of the two groups of children were more equal: 53 percent involved returning children, and 47 percent involved new children. Furthermore, these represented more equal proportions of the two groups: 62 percent and 75 percent, respectively of the returning and new children. Thus, the difference in the guinea pig data may not be due to the older age of the returning children but, indeed, to the role of continuity of self-with-other.

In a developed relationship, differences between children in interactive style become evident. Ivy frequently "babied" the guinea pig, cuddling it closely or rocking it proudly. Dimitri, by contrast, regularly attempted to scare the guinea pig, by banging on its cage or dropping in toys; he told me he did not like the animal. On the other hand, Mindy, one of the new children, accounted for a third of the guinea pig episodes from that group, and like Dimitri she sometimes provoked it. But she also told stories about a guinea pig she had known in a city in which she had previously lived and how someone who had been afraid of it learned not to be. Both a sense of grappling with the scary agency of the animal and of growing continuity were reflected in her tales.

Out of these basic invariants of experience, a core animate domain of self and other takes on compelling reality. This is the reality of comings and goings, touching, observing, and responding to each other's overt actions and affects; and from all this, apprehending a basic sense of the other's inner experience.

The Infant's Social Self

We began by noting that even infants differentiate animals from other kinds of living and nonliving things on interactive bases such as the ones just discussed. At this point, a short theoretical digression will underscore the significance of these findings by showing the continuity between experiences of infant and young child.

According to the associationist tradition, which was very strong through much of the twentieth century, infants are born unable to perceive the world in a coherent fashion. The stereotype was that the infant's world was, in William James's words, "blooming, buzzing confusion." Even Piaget believed that much learning had to precede the ability to represent external reality (1936/1963). Today, a revolution in infancy research is showing that infants are prepared to notice many invariant features of experience. So far-reaching is the new work on infant perception that the infancy researcher Bennett Bententhal (1993) has commented, "No longer can we assume that basic concepts about number, people, causality and so forth must await the development of concrete operational thinking . . . or even preoperational thinking" (p. 175).

The invariants infants notice are patterns of "sensations, perceptions, actions, cognitions, internal states of motivation and states of consciousness" that are *analogous across sense modes* and so are experienced in terms of "intensities, shapes, temporal patterns, vitality affects, categorical affects and hedonic tones" (Stern, 1985, p. 67). It has long been known, for example, that *intensity* of stimulation is analogous across sensory systems (e.g., loud sound, bright light, and intense jostling share something); we now know this is true for infants and in all preverbal modes of perception. For infants as early as the age of one week, features experienced in one sensory channel—the bumpy texture of an unfamiliar pacifier in the mouth—can be represented and recognized in another—at first sight the infant can distinguish the bumpy from a smooth pacifier visually. According to the older Piagetian perspective, such an act was not expected so early, since it would require development of different touching and seeing sensori-motor schemas *and* of coordinating schemas between them.

Stern (1985) suggests that "infants do not attend to what [sensory] domain their experience is occurring in" (p. 67) and that data from the different senses are fused in "highly flexible and omnidimensional" mental representations that have a global quality. This is perhaps clearer in contrast to language, which alone allows us to abstract visual, auditory, and tactile sensations from the amodal representations of concrete situations that the infant's body and brain automatically create. Language also lets us label objects in a way that can make them seem independent of experience. As we will discuss more fully in the next two chapters, none of that is possible without the generalized reality created by language.

All of the foregoing has special relevance for the self, because certain invariants of interaction give the infant the data that reveal where self ends and other begins. Before the age of about three months, no organized, globally represented self has coalesced. During this time, Stern (1985) suggests, the infant may have experiences of "emergent self" when a new pattern of stimuli comes together as a sense of "I." But after three months of age, the infant now responds as a social being to others, as is so well recognizable in its "social smiles." We can identify the invariants in agency, coherence, affect, and continuity as critical ingredients in this core or animate self.

The infant experiences authorship of her on his own action through at least three routes: "(1) the sense of volition that precedes a motor act, (2) proprioceptive feedback that does or does not occur during the act, and (3) predictability of consequences that follow the act" (Stern, 1985, p. 76). Evidence of these includes volitional motor plans such as hand-to-mouth, gazing, and sucking skills and, later, at four months, shaping the hand to fit an object being reached for. As is clear from studies already cited and from studies on animate versus inanimate motion, infants notice the agentic quality of others too (see the work of the infancy researchers and developmental psychologists Elizabeth Spelke, Ann Phillips, and Amanda Woodward, 1995). Variation in the mother's role in helping the infant self-regulate "permits the infant to triangulate and identify what invariants belong to whom" (Stern, 1985, p. 106). In other words, the infant's sense of agency arises as the infant uses its native abilities to discern the common origin and quality of many varied daily acts initiated by the self versus those initiated by others.

The infant also experiences self-coherence, or "unity of locus." The infant visually orients to the source of sounds and is thus in a position to see that others' behaviors are specific to them and different from the infant's own. Coherence of motion, temporal structure, intensity structure, and form add more information. Especially important is the demonstration that four-month-old infants detect cross-modal synchrony. For example, when viewing two films simultaneously, they watch the one to which the sound track they hear corresponds (Spelke, 1979). This finding supports the contention that the infant can coordinate all sensory inputs emanating from another person into a coherent whole.

Affectivity and the emotions are higher-order self-invariants based on experience with a range of feelings. The discrete emotions (joy, anger, surprise, disgust, and so on) give unique invariant organizations of feedback from stereotyped facial displays, patterns of internal arousal, and specific qualities of feeling. Patterns of arousal over time may be perceived with or without a co-occurring categorical affect and are experienced as vitality affects.

Continuity, or self-history, is based on memory of the other invariants. Infants are well known to register perceptual events in memory and to have motor memories, or what the developmental psychologist Jerome Bruner (1969) called "memories without words." Episodic memory, or "memory for real-life experiences occurring in real time" (Stern, 1985, p. 94), enables integration of the other invariants, from specific to more general episode classes. The infant generalizes several similar memories of interactive episodes to create her or his first integrated sense of self and other. In the core sense of self that these invariants make possible, "The emphasis is on the palpable experiential realities of substance, action, sensation, affect and time. Sense of self is not a cognitive construct. It is an experiential integration" (Stern, 1985, p. 71).

Let me hasten to clarify what early infancy realities mean for the young child's relation to animals. First, they provide a plausible explanation for how the infants we met earlier distinguish animals from objects and people. Animals are core others for the infant. This is to say, they are apprehended as first of all *subjective* others who display their own invariant patterns of agency, coherence, affect, and history. Because of this, they can also affirm the infant's self-invariants. The child receives roughly this experience from the animal: "I (the child) actively reach and touch; you affirm I did so by rubbing against me (or leaving, striking back, and so on). Your lively action, breathing, warmth, and gaze make you vividly here. We fill a present together."[10] I will have more to say about this shortly.

Second, and crucially, each form of self persists—once present, it continues to function even as later forms of self become operative. I have touched on emergent and animate (core) forms of self. As more abilities come "on-line," a preverbal intersubjective self gels from the awareness that subjective events can be shared. According to Stern (1985), this happens at around seven to nine months of age. This self is virtually unavoidable, because the caregiver often matches the infant's vitality affect *in a different modality,* for example, cooing in response to the infant's calm hand motions. This *communicates that* the infant's *inner state* has been detected and shared. But note, with this achievement core or animate relating does not cease! As we all know, it is possible to nonverbally deceive others about our true feelings, and to an even greater extent, feelings can be at odds with what is spoken. The verbal self arises around twelve to eighteen months, when symbolic play and representation first occur. Like the earlier abilities, these new ones *create* a new domain of interaction. The verbal self-and-other domain vastly increases our potential for self-consciousness, but the other organizations of self persist with and after it.

The reason that the different forms of self persist is that the specific aspects of concrete interaction characterizing each domain continue to be present throughout life. Senses of self, as used here, are not developmental stages of the sort we are accustomed to thinking of, like Piaget's stages of logical operations, which overtake, subsume, and transform the preceding one. Rather, domains of relatedness emerge and then coexist: "The subjective experience of social interactions seems to occur in all domains of relatedness simultaneously" (Stern, 1985, p. 31). Thus, this framework allows us to look at enduring senses of self-and-other in development beyond infancy.

Third, and most important, since experiences that are relevant to the self entail correlative actions by other persons, every sense of self necessarily emerges interdependently with the "other." The infant is social from the beginning, and the same "other" becomes more complex in the infant's perception as the infant's abilities blossom. Each new domain of relatedness depends on developing cognitive and other abilities, but each is realized through the use of these abilities in interactions. Since animals as interactants have different capacities for interaction from those of other humans, the child's interactively derived sense of self with the animal differs from that derived with another person.

From these three theoretical reference points—the subjectivity of animate self-and-other, the endurance of senses of self, and the interactive interdependence of self-and-other—we can see how the animate, intersubjective, and verbal domains together constitute the child's relations with animals. Succeeding chapters will flesh out the picture. But before we move on, we can answer the question of how the differences of different animals register in the domain of core or animate subjective relatedness.

Optimally Different Animals

At the start of this chapter, we considered the idea that animals are interesting because of their novelty. The problem with this idea was that it failed to account for situations in which a balance between environmental novelty and the person's capacities leads to development. Optimal arousal theorists and others, such as Csikszentmihalyi (1990), note that a challenge that just exceeds the person's present skills offers an optimally discrepant environment for development. And this is just what animals offer as interactants: new information—incongruities, interruptions of expectation, challenges—in the context of familiar otherness. Animate otherness underlies children's connection with animals; but within this otherness many challenges are available. Cognitive researchers suggest that the young child's explicit concept of "animal" is of a mammal-like creature. But on the animate or core level all animals offer *gradient variations* on the themes of agency, coherence, affect, and continuity—and thus opportunities for differentiated experience and thought.[11]

Qualities of animals' agency vary across taxonomic groups and across other factors such as domestication, training, and individual history.[12] Toward one extreme are highly responsive animals such as well-trained dogs. At the other are invertebrates—informatively, for example, insects. Arthropods' agency and affectivity are radically different and seem especially unpredictable to us mammals.[13] The children were shown how to let a tarantula walk on their hands and how to make it twitch slightly by puffing on it. But some children blew too hard, causing the spider to make a dramatic jump, which elicited even more exaggerated responses in the children! Occasionally, a fly would get into the classroom. In one exciting instance, Toby noticed a fly and stood up, exclaiming, "Fly! Fly." Chris, Ivy, Katra, Dawn, and others also saw it and joined in, calling, "Fly!" Katra pointed to it and Chris put his hands out to clap them over it, but in vain.

There is a huge variety of animals, each dictating a particular response to its whole form. The range of animals in this book clearly shows this. The very act of touching or holding another creature calls for sensori-motor accommodation to the size, shape, textures, temperature, and other qualities of the animal. Animals vary greatly in size relative to the person, and this can have great impact. Immediate contact conveys the unique, concrete coherences of animals to the child.

Interestingly, different species convey characteristic vitality affects. The monkey's unpredictable and stealthy way of approaching the children's feet created an atmosphere of suspense and liveliness. The characteristic vitality affect of an animal may be vivid enough that it overrides even strong societal biases about the species. For example, these four-year-olds knew enough stories to make them afraid of snakes. But in actual interaction with the living snake, many were remarkably calm. Had the snake's movement not been lethargic and smooth, even the reassuring presenter would have had difficulty keeping the children calm, as evidenced when the snake did make a sudden move or point its head toward the children. Contrary to stereotyped images, the children kept more distance from the monkey than the snake. Conspicuous differences in the vitality affects of the tarantulas, the ferrets, and the dog were also registered by the children.

Variation in self-other continuity is implied by all these differences in animal interactants—compared to humans and compared across animals. An important dimension of interactions is the meshing or synchrony of moves by each partner. Meshing is never perfect, thus contributing to the distinctness of animate self-and-other. To the extent higher degrees of meshing happen, for example, with the guinea pig, continuity would gain clarity and depth, heightening the resolution of the animal's discrepancies from human patterns.

These observations can be generalized and are central to understanding how the children are not egocentric or anthropomorphic in their approach to animals. *As interactants*, animals present both important continuities and important discontinuities from the human pattern. Indeed, we saw that even young infants discriminate animals from humans. Carey (1985) found that four-year-olds put humans in a separate category from animals, and she concluded that they do not develop a domain of biological concepts that is independent of human social behavior schemas until middle childhood (see also the work of the psychologists Frank Keil, 1990; and Graziella R. Rusca & Francesco T. Tonucci, 1992). But more recent work suggests that the domain of biological knowledge (such as how living things are classified) has origins independent of psychological knowledge (Coley, 1995; Hirschfeld & Gelman, 1994; see Coley et al., 2002 for an overview of the current state of knowledge). Enlightening work on this question by psychologists and anthropologists Norbert Ross, Douglas Medin, John Coley and Scott Atran (2003) compared urban American majority culture children (similar to the populations used in most previous studies, including Carey's) with rural children of the same culture, and with rural Native American children. Their results showed that only the urban children tended to import a human model into thinking about animals' behaviors, as opposed to even the youngest rural majority culture children, who reasoned in biological terms. All ages of the Native American group used biological and ecological concepts in thinking about animal behavior. Both culture and experience play a role in development of thinking about animals.

These studies, and other recent ones comparing children's interaction with robotic dogs versus real or stuffed toy dogs[14] help make the case that animals offer unique contours of interaction.

Children generate and draw on knowledge both of biology and of other minds in interacting. Children's interactions demonstrate they have implicit knowledge of the classificatory and behavioral differences of animals. No child interacted with Snowflake exactly as she or he would with another human—not even Ivy, whose tendency was to baby her. Children cannot be simply anthropomorphizing when they adjust interactive moves to fit the animal. Indeed, interaction is what produces new explicit concepts and distinctions.[15] For example, many names the children proposed for the animals—such as "Sweeper," "Drinker," "Duster," and "Nibbles"—bore close relationships to the actions of the animals.

Because animals, like other humans, are animate others to the child, relatedness grows in similar ways. But the animal is a discrepant other. By preschool age children are adept at detecting and responding to these differences. The discrepancy is often optimal: the animal is neither human nor categorically separate but offers gradient differences (or differences in degree). This triggers differentiation of basic interactive abilities. The children I observed did not treat animals as humans; nor did they treat all animals identically.[16] When we look at interactions, we see a refinement of the infant's discrimination of animals as a unique class, not just assimilation to a human pattern. This will become clearer as we add other interactive abilities to our analysis. And pretend play, as a window on the child's nonverbal concepts, will confirm it.

The Animal as a Subjective Other

The animal is a subjective other to the child; thus it can serve important psychological functions. Many interpretations of animals' significance agree on this but assume that these functions must be projective and egocentric. Before looking at some illuminating episodes, let us review some of those interpretations. In chapter 2, we already encountered the psychoanalytic interpretation of animals, illustrated by Freud's case study of Little Hans. Following the child psychologist D.W. Winnicott (1971/1989), personality theorists have supposed the child projects his or her creative powers through the animal-as-transitional-object (see the work of Cecelia Soares, 1985, on pets in the family system; Triebenbacher, 1998). The psychiatrist Karl Menninger (1951) argued that almost any action or attitude toward animals revealed unconscious motives—usually sexual or hostile repressed childhood urges. Animals may be security or authority figures. Because of these projective meanings, many clinicians believe animals are useful in the working through of intrapsychic conflict.[17] Even psychotherapy techniques specifically calling for identification with "inner" animals have emerged (Houston, 1982; Gallegos, 1991).

The idea of a psychologically potent human-animal bond has been the focus of much research also, as reviewed by the human–companion animal researchers Beth Ellen Barba (1995) and Gail Melson (2001). The idea is derived from the psychiatrist John Bowlby's (1969) theory of mother-infant attachment.[18] It is a compelling idea, partly because it is easy to see pets in the framework of human-human relationships, especially those between parent and child.[19] The parallels include the need for continual care; the need for protection from dangerous ingestibles, things, and situations; the need for having problems explained to the doctor; and the performance of behaviors at the owner's will, such as petting and touching, as enumerated by the psychologists and pioneers of pet-person relations Alan Beck and Aaron Katcher (1996). Both pets' and children's range of movement is restricted, their sexuality controlled, their excrement tolerated, and their dependence accepted. Pet keeping occurs in many cultures (Erikson, 2000; Bodson, 2000), which the animal behaviorist James Serpell (1986) and others hold is because an innate nurturant response to infantile features makes us react positively to animals with large eyes, round faces, and other "cute" looks (see also Lawrence, 1989).

The idea of a bond, projective and anthropomorphic though it may be, highlights how the subjective meanings of an animal may be positive, neutral, or negative. Positively, animals provide enduring interactions and good feelings. Contributions here have been copious about the use of pets in therapeutic settings of every kind. The psychotherapist Boris Levinson (1969, 1972) was a founder of the movement that now includes the use of dogs, cats, birds, horses, and dolphins, among others, in such settings as psychotherapy, residential programs, geriatric care, jails, and rehabilitation. Animal-assisted therapy has been used to augment treatment of medical conditions as well as psychological problems including loneliness, depression, ADHD, under-stimulation, adaptation to illness, enhancing self-esteem and social skills, and autism spectrum disorders for patients at many points in the life span. (See Aubrey Fine's handbook (2000) for a thorough overview of animal-assisted therapy.)[20] Pets also contribute to normal social development and family integration in a number of ways, the classic statement of this being psychologist Boris Levinson's book *Pets and Human Development* (1972).[21] Recently sociologist Arnold Arluke (2003) has helped delineate the early development of individuals at the extreme positive end of the pole of the human-animal bond in his study of "supernurturers," or children with an extraordinary degree of active everyday concern for animals.

Arluke's astute qualitative research unearthed important roles of parents, a sense of reciprocity with the animals the children helped, and the child identifying as an "animal person" and assuming responsibility (Arluke, 2003).

The negative pole of the bond is shown in tragic cases of children, severely victimized by abuse or war, who torture animals and may later show sociopathology, according to the psychologists Frank Ascione (1993; see also Ascione et al., 2000) and Alan Felthous and Stephen Kellert (1987). In recent years a more differentiated analysis of several causes of cruelty to animals has emerged, particularly in the works of Arluke (2006) and Ascione (2005).[22] Yi Fu Tuan (1984) suggested that a less extreme urge to dominate often co-occurs with making the other an "object" of one's affection. Unfortunately, history abounds with examples of human cruelty, including toward pets. Institutionalized gratuitous provocation and cruelty to animals is found today in rodeos, and in every historical period and across cultures.[23]

We can take from this evidence the indispensable insight that animals are psychologically potent to us. But the challenge, as posed by two consistent contributors to the study of animals across the human life span, Aline Kidd and Robert Kidd (1987b), is to determine how the human-animal bond *diverges* from the human-human bond and from two other models: animal-animal and human-object. Interestingly, research on the mother-infant bond focuses on dynamic interactive and affective processes. We can use the same approach to understand how the animal is a *different kind of subject* for the child.

My focus on actual interactions with animals showed increasingly finely tuned actions. The child's basic abilities as a social being are not just set in one (human-human) pattern but are capable of differentiation. The child is not merely projecting onto the animal. Such a view would miss the most concrete and basic relationship of the child to the animal. For example, a child cannot long mistake a living animal as a transitional object, since the animal's independent agency would conflict with the child's projected sense of authorship of the object. Core connection to the animal suggests an alternative frame of interpretation of animals' psychological importance.

Specific Subjective Qualities

Then what subjective dimensions of the animate other are evident in children's actions? First is a nearly ineffable sense of "aliveness" that children can experience with others of any animate species. Vitality affects are continuously present in the other's action and in the self's inner experience; animals unavoidably convey them in the qualities of their movement. Stern (1985) argues that for the infant vitality affects are a more primary way of experiencing others than seeing each behavior as discrete. In a stream of interaction with the animal, its subjective presence is continuously available and (my second point) thus *confirms the child's own self.*[24]

For example, the animal's agency confirms the child's, as seen when children I observed provoked an animal to react. The children delighted in chasing common urban outdoor animals, such as squirrels and pigeons. After such episodes, some children reported, "I made it fly" or "I scared it." These children focused on their own agency, but agency here means something achieved only with an animate other. In flying away, the action of the pigeon confirms the child's own agency in a way that an inanimate thing cannot. Even a child such as Solly who was usually very mild toward animals was capable of using an animal this way:

> As Ms. Collins retrieves the ferret, Solly moves his right arm up and down, roughly in karate-chop fashion, aimed just behind the ferret's tail. Solly: "Can't get away from the snapper, snap, snap," bringing his hand down on the "snap"s.

Mindy seemed unusually obsessed with pest animals, mentioning how there were mice and ants in her home, and at other times wanting to squash bugs. She also liked to tease the guinea pig—which is not a pest:

> On another attempt to poke the guinea pig, Mindy pulls her hand out fast, making a noise on the cage, and the guinea pig jumps. I point this out, which leads her to drag her hand on the cage to make loud noises, causing it to jump more. I ask if she likes to scare it. She nods and smiles.

In extreme cases of neglect or mistreatment, the desire to confirm his or her own sense of agency and self may impel a child to abuse an animal.[25] We can construe both the negative and the positive poles of the bond with animals as results of animate responsiveness. As the science fiction and fantasy writer Ursula K. Le Guin (1990) put it, both love and cruelty occur in the *otherness*, in "the space between us" that needs to be respected, not eliminated (p. 12). Animate connection, created through concrete bodily interaction, is the precondition, not the result, of "projective" processes.

A third subjective feature is that optimal discrepancy means *implicit self-other clarification.* The child encounters animals' differences on a concrete level where they demand immediate accommodation and interrupt the child's expectations. When multiple comparisons across animate interactants are possible, this enriches self-other clarity. These experiences may not be easily made explicit but inform the child's sense of self nonetheless. As we will see further in the next two chapters, a depth—but not a gulf—is thus added to the sense of being a human self.[26]

Fourth, recall the baby snake's meaning of "growing" for Ivy: Special *symbolism*, as introduced in the preceding chapter, stems from shared animacy. Animals are not symbolic to the child in the flat sense of representing familiar cultural concepts such as laudable or despised human qualities. Rather, because they are living animates and thus display (sometimes more vividly than do other humans) agency, affectivity, and other life processes, they embody important qualities shared in common with the child. Symbols stemming from this core commonality constitute a special category of animal symbols, ones with great subjective relevance.

One striking example of an animal's activity providing such a psychogenic symbol was provided by Yasmin interacting with the diamond doves, which she enjoyed watching. Early in the year, she would stand close to the cage and hold her hands close together, as if preparing to clap, or perhaps mimicking their positions, and then watch. In the spring, one remarkable video segment shows her silently facing the doves and their new hatchling, and seeming to carry on a dialogue in motion with them, gesturing in imitation and anticipation of their movements, sometimes remaining still in turn as they moved. She held her hands together, index fingers oriented like their heads, as they landed together on the perch. She also did twirls before them and motioned as if to rouse or encourage them. The dance-like quality of the whole episode is hard to capture in words. The episode ended with her dawning realization that the other children were already eating, at which point she herself flew off, arms flapping, to get her lunch box. Notably, Yasmin also had a great interest in flying and the character Tinkerbell from *Peter Pan*. For her, the birds' capacity of flight inspired a sense of animated agency different from her own and endowed with rich subjective meanings. It is in this sense that animals are symbolic for young children.

Finally, the animal provides an intense sense of *connection across essential difference*. This is not the same as accurate knowledge of the other, although it may initiate and motivate the search for that. Much of the sense of connection and meaning on the animate level is apprehended in an immediate manner without conscious inferences, but realized through interaction. It may later be made conscious and manifest in pretend or reflection. The fact that animate properties are possessed by both child and animal is not incidental. It means that a common reality is felt to define both the child's and the animal's experience.

The children learned that agency has a shared meaning across species by feeding bugs, beetles, worms, slugs, and so forth, to the toad. The toad would eat these only if they were moving or made to move. This was well-known by the children; animacy is meaningful for Toad, too! Likewise, the guinea pig was a continuous presence in the class in more than a physical sense. The children regarded Snowflake as a member of the class. They brought her food such as carrots, which they gave it at lunchtime. But there was more to it than just the children's actions. The guinea pig could smell the food when it was brought out at lunchtime and on at least one occasion it squealed. Ivy then fed it, and others who had heard it talked about its call. Thus, the children and the animals generated a common cross-species world, yet this world also embraced all the subtle or dramatic gradient differences that animals present.

Conclusion

Animate qualities of animals—and of other humans—are continuously present in all face-to-face interactions. Thus, the sense of animate self and other is a constant dimension of experience, carried on with subtle variability, creating connection across degrees of difference. It is this, I argue, that primarily underlies the concern for animals voiced by children in the previous chapter and that explains how the child's sense of self is constituted among the available interspecies community. I have shown that cultural frames cannot produce the phenomena I observed; that the position that children are relentlessly anthropomorphic is challenged by their response to optimal discrepancy; and that egocentric and projective interpretations must depend on something deeper. The core animate level precedes any of these interpretations. Thus, it should be given greater emphasis in our ideas about the generation of the self from human-human interaction, too. Understanding the full implications of this idea requires also considering the child's capacities for intersubjectivity and language, to which we now turn.

V

The Creature That Connects

Sharing Feelings, Words, and Minds

Many of the things children say about animals show they see them as feeling, thinking beings. Reuben had been watching squirrels outside the window when I joined him; one was turned toward us and he told me, "It's watching us." Reuben was attributing a subjective act—one that seems completely natural and indubitable—to the squirrel. Of course, since children experience animals based on core animate characteristics, the animal world is very "present" to them. The animate world is populated by subjectivities, aware of each other to some degree. But the opportunity to *express* the situation in this way stems from our intersubjective and linguistic abilities—which we acquire for the most part only in the company of other humans. Yet, once acquired, these forms of relating put their stamp on our experience of each other and of animals, although in differing ways. As on the animate level, children make distinctions based on such interactive abilities.

Children do more than see animals as subjective—they may see them as *sharing* the children's own subjective states. Dawn, for example, felt attracted to more animals than most children and was inclined to think they felt the same toward her:

> One ferret approaches Dawn, who is seated on the floor with her legs out in front of her. She draws her hands back to her sides and giggles: "He likes me."

What made Dawn think this? The ferret's keeper, more experienced with the animal's behavior, explained, "He likes *socks*." But Dawn's reaction was a feeling of mutual "liking." This example, taken from my transcripts of videotape, is like many others in the first part of this chapter. In them, interactants in some way *mirror* each other's behavior. Such episodes have special significance for how children judge three types of shared subjective states with animals: affects, attention, and intentions.

All of these kinds of sharing tap the child's understanding of others' minds—the beliefs, intentions, and feelings they guess fill the ongoing experience of the other. Consider Ivy's thought process here:

> Mr. Lloyd attempts to feed the turtle a small piece of meat held on the end of a stick. Mr. Lloyd: "Maybe if we move it a little bit." Ivy smiling: "Think it's *alive!*"

From her wording, Ivy might have meant to encourage the turtle, or she could have been describing what she guessed it was thinking. Her precise meaning is not clear. What is clear is that to her turtles have the capacity for cognition. Ivy, one of the older children, has a five-year-old's theory of mind, which will be the second major focus of this chapter. This example is especially revealing because she assumed the turtle understood animate-like motion in the same way she does—as indicating aliveness. In the mental states children attribute to animals, we find confirmation that animate qualities dominate their perception.

Shared attention and affect, the theory of mind, and, especially, shared intentions all have close ties to language development. Language makes possible many important advances in relatedness. The ins and outs of language compose a third major focus of the chapter. Sometimes, the children drew the animal into the linguistic realm with striking or humorous disregard for difference:

> Dawn helps search for bugs in the dirt, together with Cassia, Yasmin, Angela, Reuben, and the teacher. She shows me the bugs in her hand and continues looking. Cassia tells the others it's time to go. As she leaves, Dawn says to the bugs in her hand, "We're going," and runs off.

As in most cases, Dawn did not "communicate" anything of much sophistication to the bugs, but the implications of speech for our potential relations to animals are far-reaching. There are two main points. On the one hand, language is a *means of* interaction. How are children's interactions with animals affected by the fact that they have this tool? How do the essential nature and dynamics of language shape children's conduct and experience of interactions with animals? On the other hand, children's ideas about animals may come from specific meanings *transmitted by* language, thus indirectly affecting their experience of them. In this chapter, I take up the first concern, leaving the second for the next two chapters.

Young children are apt to be careless (as are many adults) in what they assume animals can understand. Indeed, to stay clear on how children make such inferences, I start with the developmental precursors to language—the nonverbal forms of intersubjectivity—and move on to examine how the structure of language depends on assumptions we must make about the cooperativeness and meaningfulness of communication. This chapter expands my analysis of children's interactions with animals to include abilities that make us uniquely human. Language has usually been seen as setting us apart from animals or, rather, above them. But, ironically, language is essential in making us the creature that connects.

Intersubjectivity

A special condition gives the child a sense of shared experience. Earlier, I discussed "complementary" moves in interaction, in which each participant responds with a different but linked action. "Reciprocal" interactions, on the other hand, occur when a given action elicits a *similar* action from the second individual (Hinde, 1976). Fewer interactions between children and animals showed this quality, but ones that did deserve special attention because of the subjective experiences they afford. When another reflects our actions, we sometimes infer a shared experience or meaning.

Imitation is a case in point. In the class, the monkey scratched itself, and Ivy began scratching herself in imitation. She was not doing it to amuse the other children; she may have meant to establish a shared feeling. In more remarkable cases, twice the monkey appeared to imitate the children raising their hands for a turn to speak. Chris noticed and imitated back, pointing at the monkey, raising his right foot approximately as the monkey had raised its, and exclaiming, "Wooo-! He raised his foot! He did this!" Although these reciprocal moves are remarkable and suggestive of subjectivity to the children, another ingredient is necessary for true shared subjectivity: confirmation from the other *that* the state of feeling or thought *is* shared.

Simple reciprocal affect, attention, and intention are evident in my data, but at most only very partial confirmation of sharing. In the last analysis, true intersubjectivity mostly depends on normal human interactants to develop and occur. Nonetheless, with affect, attention and intention, the animal fits differently than do other people into the framework of human intersubjectivity. When the children respond to the differences animals present, we find complex patterns, not a simple imposition of human schemas or socialized meanings. Each of these divergences deepens the sense in which the animal is a significant and discrepant other for the child.

Interaffectivity

Interaffectivity is an emotion that is shared and *understood* to be so. Is it possible between children and animals? Answering this question requires first determining whether a child can grasp the emotions of an animal at all. In a broad sense, this is empathy. Many definitions of it exist, but most entail temporarily taking the other into ourselves and then imaginatively comparing the internalized other's feelings with our own (see the work of the psychologist Janet Strayer, 1987). In the terms I will develop here, this combines affectively *attuning* to the other, with a more cognitive processing of information about what one observes (using, among other things, one's theory of mind—a particular animal's mind in this case). Although unavoidably imperfect, there is no doubt that empathy is important in understanding animals,[1] and also that it can be greatly improved with knowledge of the other. Of crucial importance is how one interprets signs of the other's feelings.

Categorical emotions (happiness, anger, and so on) are less likely to enter into children's interpretation of animals' feeling than are vitality affects. We infer both, partly from the series of events that lead up to an emotion, but direct cues are essential. Facial clues to animals' categorical emotions may be absent or hard to decode, but reading vitality affects (changes in intensity and quality of arousal) does not depend as much on knowledge of species-specific signals. Indeed, the children mirrored vitality affects displayed by animals, such as the excitement of the dog, the lethargy of the ferrets, and the calmness of the snake. Similarly, when the guinea pig was restless, some of the children became restless while feeding it. These cases resemble something simpler, like the mood contagion observed in infants and toddlers, or they may be unconscious affect attunement. In an exercise of more complete empathy with the turtle, Dimitri and Toby read behavior and drew on concepts of others' minds when asked to explain the turtle's actions:

> Mr. Lloyd: "What does he do when you touch his tail, what does he do?"
> All the kids are looking very closely. They pull back as Toby answers: "He puts it inside his shell." Mr. Lloyd: "He pulls it inside his shell. Why do you think he does that?" Toby: "Maybe um . . ." Dimitri (interrupting): "'Cause he's scared." Mr. Lloyd: "'Cause he's scared. He doesn't want . . ."
> Toby (interrupting): "Maybe he doesn't want us to do that."

From such examples, we can say that children can—within limits—understand animals' emotions. But does this produce the confirmed sharing of affect? To answer this question, let us look at the origin of shared feelings in infancy.

A primary—perhaps original—means of establishing interaffectivity between parent and infant is attunement to vitality affects. This process occurs when the mother mirrors back the affect contours expressed by her child, the mirroring being performed in a *different modality* (Stern, 1985). For example, if the infant hits something playfully on the floor, the mother might make a sound like "kaaaa-bam," analogically reproducing in the verbal mode the arousal contours of the suspenseful preparatory physical swing and then the hit. This is called a *cross-modal match*, and unlike imitation it necessarily carries the information that the mother registers the infant's subjective feeling, not just its external motions. Thus, it confirms shared affect, in a process that occurs largely out of the awareness of either partner. This is one of the key kinds of interactions that make intersubjectivity a domain of self-other experience among humans.

Shared affect of this sort may possibly occur between members of other species with multimodal social communication. In child-animal interaction, inter-affectivity could conceivably be created by the animal's attuning to the child (mirroring the child's affect). I did not, however, observe that happen. Indeed, the early development of the ability to share affect probably depends on the active empathy of a mature human caretaker.[2] The cases of mood contagion noted previously could be child-to-animal attunement but did not involve cross-modal matching. So we cannot say for sure, but there is no evidence from this study for true interaffectivity between children and animals.

But children (and adults) may be biased to read animal actions as conveying interaffectivity. Infants learn early that cross-modal matching signals shared feeling. This has an intriguing implication, since animals do not respond in language. Their responses to human speech (or action) are in a bodily modality or in a voice that primarily conveys vitality affect. Thus, when a child says something and the animal responds (or appears to respond), it is likely to be doing so cross-modally—by action. If the response is at all similar in vitality affect, this may bias the child (or adult) to read into it an act of attunement to the self's affect. Animals' "liking" children illustrates this pattern. Dawn, as noted, liked many animals and felt they liked her. She said the dog did; its behavior may have confirmed this. She said the ferret liked her when its behavior—approach—matched her own attraction. And this same affectively important behavior may explain yet a third case:

> The turtle crawls toward Dawn, who declares: "He likes me." Mr. Lloyd: "He likes you? He's going to crawl right under you there, huh?" Dawn backs up, spreads her knees on floor, and laughs.

Dawn probably felt a sense of mutual attraction between herself and these animals. These examples do not show true or confirmed intersubjectivity, but they do show that some kinds of affect reciprocity occur and blur into what could certainly be interpreted by participants as interaffectivity.

Important though the intersubjective domain may be, it has its limits even among humans. To compare the quasi-interaffectivity children may feel toward animals with a false conception that human intersubjectivity is complete would conceal important reasons why animals seem to share our feelings and why they are so effective as co-therapists. Because human affect attunement (i.e., parent to child) occurs only occasionally and sometimes is wrong, children probably do not base their judgments of shared affect on a perfect standard—there is always the sense that the self is somewhat opaque to others and vice versa (Stern, 1985, p. 218). So the animal's occasional response in apparent and imperfect harmony with the child's own feeling may be apprehended as more than adequate evidence of a general capacity to share affect. And since the whole process goes largely unnoticed (even in adults), it is not often open to critical examination.

Furthermore, humans are not simply imperfect at sharing affect; we do it manipulatively as well. Parents, above all, enact multiple agendas through variations in attunement. "Misattunements" occur when another attunes, establishing, for example, a shared happy affect, and then alters the situation to serve a different purpose. This ultimately motivates children to learn evasions that "keep their own subjective experience intact" (Stern, 1985, p. 214). Attunements are also used to convey prohibitions. Animals as non-attuning others do not pose these threats and thus may provide "safer" zones of interaction.

Patterns of attunement communicate what is private versus sharable. Socializing agents systematically attune to accepted parts of the child's feelings and omit attuning to affects that are not part of the public realm. This in effect creates culturally agreed-upon "private" experiences. Such "selective attunement" is especially salient in Western culture given the overlap between what is private and what is considered marginally human, or closer to the animal state. In particular, reproductive and other bodily functions and feelings associated with them are kept private and are considered "lower" in the ranks of human concerns. This convergence means children very likely feel more commonality with animals around these issues than they do with adults, who have learned to keep such matters private.[3]

For example, young children who are curious about feces face the difficulty that exploring their own is prohibited and even their interest in doing so is not attuned to by adults. But they can take advantage of animal feces and adult tolerance or inattention, as several children did during the year. The following episode captures one associated affect[4]:

> The teacher points out a pigeon, up on a ledge as the children play in a neighboring courtyard. Dimitri, Chris, and others run at it, to no effect. Toby stays longer, watching it. He says "pigeon" twice, gets on his hands and knees, and rubs his hands in the dry piled-up pigeon droppings. He gets up, steps in them, and screams—his mood interested and delighted. Then he runs off to join the others.

Since animals were used to talk about body functions and sexual anatomy in this nursery school, they acquired a special status as avenues for such interests. There were numerous opportunities to observe and talk about the genitalia and other body parts of the dog, the monkey, the guinea pig, and even the snake. The children were often the initiators of these discussions, as in the following example:

> Dawn sits forward over the dog, evidently looking at what Drew was pointing to on its belly. Joe taps Drew on the arm, saying quietly: "It's his penis." Mrs. Ray breaks in: "It's his penis, you're right." Drew turns and taps the teacher on her leg and asks: "What's the yellow stuff?" Mrs. Ray: "Maybe it's urine. Is it a drop of urine, left from last time he urinated? I bet it is . . . it's kind of wonderful that you recognized the parts of his body." Mrs. Ray to Joe: "How do you know if he's a boy, Joe? You made a discovery. How do you know if he is a boy?" Several children respond, saying "penis."

Such a demonstration with a human as the object (except perhaps for an infant) would not normally happen in the presence of non-family adults. Although no reference was made to subjective feelings that go with having sexual anatomy, the avenue is more open for children to make this mental association with an animal, whose sexual anatomy (and occasionally behavior) is at least visible, than with other humans. Since such feelings are not verbalized in the presence of children, it is unlikely that such a felt commonality with an animal would be on a level of verbal awareness either. If present, they lie outside the realm of the explicitly marked and shared, although advertisers have long exploited the connection of animals and sexuality.

Sharing Attention

Interattentionality is possible when the child can realize that self and other each have a focus of attention, that these can be similar or not, and that they can be brought into alignment. Children ascertain an animal's attention by observing what it responds to and what it watches, for example, third-person objects. Play objects included toys extended by hand to the monkey. Other foci of animals' attention the children observed were food for the guinea pig, fish, or, especially, for the toad. Toad would dramatically creep straight at a moving bug before catching it with its tongue. In object-related play with an animal, the participants shared a focus of attention. For example, in playing fetch with a dog, its attention was generally directed at the ball. If the child was focused on the ball and simultaneously realized that the dog was too, she or he could have had a sense of shared attention. But did the dog notice the child's focus on the ball? Never very clearly in my data. Likewise, although the dog might have been focused on the ball, the child might have been too focused on the dog to throw well, as was often the case. Thus, this kind of episode may not fit the conditions for true interattentionality, but it can feel very much like it.

Gaze was the children's main clue to attention. Snowflake was turned toward Drew, and I asked if the guinea pig was watching him; he said, "Yes." Drew also noticed the turtle's gaze and, indeed, experimented with it:

> Drew reaches toward the turtle: "I saw his eye turn this way, when I was touching his nose." He gestures on himself, with right hand to right eye.

Children are especially stimulated by an animal's looking at them: a situation in which the self is the object of the other's gaze and attention. Some children spontaneously reported aloud that the animal was looking at them, as did Reuben in the opening example of this chapter. He also noted, "He's looking at me," when the turtle had its head turned in his direction. In some cases, as we saw earlier with the snake, this reflected a concern that the animal might bite the child. But in others, it indicated an intense awareness that the animal was (or seemed to be) paying attention to the child himself or herself. (Indeed, such attention is probably a prerequisite to believing an animal might bite.)

Being looked at by an animal is potent because eyes convey direction of attention, *plus*, on the animate level, they shout out the interior and agentic quality of the animal. Recent research shows that adults focus on the eyes of animals to determine their emotions (Sims et al., 2005). Live animals were denoted by a special term in the nursery school: *real animal*. Ivy, in a conversation in which I used a realistic fox puppet to ask questions, explained:

> Fox asks Ivy: "Am I real?" Ivy: "No." Fox: "Is guinea pig real?" Ivy: "Yeah." Fox: "How can you tell?" Ivy: "Because he has eyes, and he can eat."

There was no question of confusing a puppet (with glass eyes) with a real animal. For Ivy, the key indicator of the animal's "realness" was its eyes. The absence of this cue could confuse the children. The point is vividly illustrated by what happened when a dead gray-cheeked thrush was brought to class. During discussion, Mindy asked, "Is that a real bird?" The teacher, as she had done before, explained that real birds can be dead or alive. But such a conceptual explanation failed to satisfy Mindy, who interjected, "Why his eyes are like that? *[sic]*" She repeated variants of this query eight times, ignoring the ongoing group effort to identify the species. The dead eyes disturbed Mindy and were at odds with the bird's "realness." To the children, eyes conveyed living otherness as well as attention, a powerful combination of domains.

Noticing the animal's attention does not alone amount to shared attention. Between humans, either party can make it fairly clear to the other what he or she is focused on, since language and gesture can serve indexical and referential functions. For example, to point to something (to index it) establishes *that* the pointer's attention is on that thing; to respond to the pointing contains the understanding that one is sharing the focus of attention. In the case of infants, the requisite abilities initially depend on the adult's capacity to share the infant's focus and mark the sharing. Before nine months of age, infants can follow the mother's line of vision. By nine months, they can follow the direction of another's pointing hand, and they can point and alternate their gaze between the object and the mother to confirm that she is sharing the focus. Mothers focus on the objects their infants are focused on and make clear that they share this focus. By twelve months, infants can discriminate the adult's object of attention regardless of other objects at different perceptual depths. They even use a person's line of regard as a clue to infer his or her behavior (Spelke et al., 1995). Sharing attention is a landmark in the development of a concept of mind and a beginning of intentional communication.

Of course, this talent is routinized and advanced by preschool age. But applying it to animals is likely to be a one-way street. Animals may notice and then reveal they share a person's focus, but this is probably rare, dependent on extensive interaction or training, and not necessarily easy to detect. The child may notice what the animal is focused on and share that focus, but the animal is not likely to notice the child is doing so or to signal it if it does notice. Thus, much of the time children "fill in the blanks" to gain a sense of quasi-shared attention. In playing "fetch," the dog responded enthusiastically when Mr. Grier retrieved a ball that had landed beyond its grasp. The dog's focus was obvious, and the game itself provided shared attention. Children can observe and share animals' attention, defining an intermediate but still compelling position for animals as social others.

Sharing Intentions

More clearly than the two previous types of subjective sharing, the confirmed sharing of intentions requires a concept of mind and depends on language-related abilities. Sharing intentions requires (1) that one attribute an intention to the other, (2) that one also know *that* the other's intentions can be aligned with one's own, and (3) that one direct an act to get the referent person to align his or her intentions to one's own. To my knowledge, this form is only rarely achieved with animals;[5] almost certainly it depends on a fully human context to develop in our young. In considering children's grasp of animals' intentions, there are two intertwined issues to address. One is how intention reading and sharing alter the flow of interaction; the other is the child's theory of mind. As before, although animals fall short with regard to intersubjectivity, the interactive possibilities they do offer are not lost on children.

It is now widely agreed that infants possess social competences that are prerequisite for interintentionality and a theory of mind. Indeed, they seem to have an implicit theory of mind by age nine months or younger, as shown by shared attention. They can tell what is intended by a communication by reading gesture, intonation, and simple utterances well before they can understand or use word meanings and combinations. Their achievements are always embedded in the here-and-now context.

The infant achieves interintentionality with acts aimed at another and intended to evoke an intention in the other. Before they can talk, infants use protolinguistic gestures to indicate their desires. These may not be initially intended to be communicative, but they become so when others treat them as if they were—for example, by delivering the cookie for which the infant is reaching. When others respond to it this way, reaching soon becomes pointing. Once used on purpose for such ends, these acts, "directed at a referent person, imply that the infant attributes an internal mental state to that person—namely, comprehension of the infant's intention and the capacity to satisfy that intention. Intentions have become sharable experiences" (Stern, 1985, p. 131). Such nonverbal interintentionality is very close to the signaling behavior of language use. Indeed, it is a prerequisite: Knowing that the other's intentions can be aligned with one's own and thus that the other can be got to serve one's own ends are pragmatic bases of language use.

Interintentionality is the third key interactive basis for the sense of inter-subjective self and other. As such, even as language and a theory of mind develop, interintentionality persists as a distinctive dimension in children's interactions with animals. Again we find a quasi-shared phenomenon. Consider a child trying to catch a playful dog. The dog must read the child's potential body moves regarding obstacles and so forth in "keep away," and vice versa. In this way, the two share a space, reading each other's intended motions. Some episodes during "fetch" with the dog showed this simple reversibility of position and reciprocity of intentions—that is, a series of moves can proceed because each participant remains a coherent occupant of space.[6] Although it is fair to point out that much human interaction depends on just such nonlinguistic intention reading, this is not confirmed intention-sharing.

Some activities by some of the youngest children I observed came a bit closer to assuming linguistic intentionality. The expectation that animals understand intentions was implicit in some of the ways children talked "at" animals:

> Toby comes to the cage and shouts, "Ha! Ah Ha!" at the birds. He leaves after about 10 seconds.

It is not clear what Toby intended to communicate, but his shouting shows a dawning awareness of, and frustration at, the inefficacy of language with the animal. Here's another case:

> Billy is making loud noises at the bugs which are in the pan for Toad soon to eat in front of the group. Dimitri asks Billy, "Why are you yelling?" Billy replies, "So they can hear."

Talking at all implicitly puts the animal in the role of language receiver expected to respond. Billy's comment, "So they can hear," reinforces this interpretation—as if talking itself should work, he tried increasing the volume when he perceived a problem!

Children only one year younger than these treat language not as a separate system but as part of a communication matrix equal with gesture, affect, paralinguistics, and other channels, as discussed by the developmental psychologists Peggy Miller and Lisa Hoogstra (1989). As with infants, action and word are not seen as separate systems. Similarly, the developmental psychologist Janet Astington (1993) suggests that very young children have only a crude grasp of the speech act as distinct from actions and mental states. They often infer the intention from the action:

> Moreover, if what someone has said does not accord with the interpretation a young child has given to the action, the child disregards what was said. Children don't interpret the words in isolation, they interpret situations, sometimes without understanding the words. . . . Their awareness of other people's mental states is an awareness of those states expressed in action, not in language. (p. 73)

The corollary—and the point—is that they also do not clearly distinguish which forms of intentional action animals respond to. It may be that the process of differentiating animals' abilities with respect to intentional communication is an ongoing task, changing as more interactive abilities develop.[7] For very young children, who do not make a firm distinction between these modes, the animal may not be apprehended as outside the "human" intersubjective realm simply because it lacks language. The children's use of exclamations in the preceding examples suggests that they consider animals part of an interintentional world but are becoming aware that language does not work equally with all intersubjective interactants.

The emergence of distinctions between intersubjective and linguistic relatedness is seen in older children, who accommodate themselves more to the animal's abilities. The children I observed occasionally demonstrated more refined and accurate attempts to communicate with an animal on a nonverbal intentional level. Several children attempted to engage the monkey in a game of give-and-take with plastic blocks or other objects. After initial presentations of a new object, the monkey usually ignored it. Benson, who repeatedly banged a block on the floor to get the monkey's attention, gave up when the monkey's attention quickly shifted. But Ivy persisted in her goal of handing it a toy monkey:

> Ivy leans forward, offering the toy to the monkey, but pulls her hand back when the monkey suddenly turns and moves in the direction of the camera. Ivy extends her hand further, but the monkey is away, by Ms. Dean's side. It scoots around, but continues looking at Ivy and the plastic toy monkey she's waving in its direction. The monkey climbs up onto Ms. Dean's lap, still regarding Ivy. Ivy drops the toy and pushes a larger block toward the monkey. It climbs up onto Ms. Dean's shoulders. A minute later it climbs down quickly and faces Mrs. Ray. The monkey is close to Ivy now; she moves closer and peers at him, her head tilted sideways, as if trying to establish eye contact. Ivy crawls closer and lowers herself, continuing to look at the monkey's face. Then Ivy claps as if to make the monkey come.

Here Ivy varied the ways she presented the toy to the monkey. In a further gesture of reciprocity, she had even picked a toy monkey! When this failed to elicit the "take" response she desired, she tried another object. Then she switched to simply trying to attain eye contact with the monkey, indicating she changed her aim to a more modest form of intersubjectivity, a shared gaze. Her sophisticated interaction shows a great deal of attunement and active accommodation to the animal's capacity.

Ivy's episode can be compared to criteria for true interintentionality. The linguist Elizabeth Bates (1979) described the evidence for it as including

"(1) alternations in eye gaze contact between the goal and the intended listeners, (2) augmentations, additions, and substitution of signals until the goal has been obtained, and (3) changes in the form of the signal towards abbreviated and/or exaggerated patterns that are appropriate only for achieving a communicative goal" (p. 36). Animals' actions were not observed that fulfilled these criteria, but Ivy's attempts to engage the monkey fit the bill. Had the monkey taken the object (as it did at times from other children), Ivy might have experienced a sense of interintentionality: The monkey would have grasped her intention and confirmed it by complying. Suppose, however (as is plausible), that her intended game was *give-and-take*. Then, only if the monkey clearly offered the block back in the same manner would she have been warranted in concluding that the monkey understood the specific intention. But on the occasions it did take a block from a child, the monkey dropped it. Feats of nearly verbal interintentional human relatedness are beyond most animals (or may depend on domestication and a close training relationship), but my aim is to give full significance to the kinds of interaction that are possible.

The Theory of Mind

Recall the earlier example in which Toby and Dimitri concluded that the turtle withdrew its head "'cause he's scared," and that "maybe he doesn't want us to do that." Their conversation moved beyond physical description to mental explanations of the turtle's behavior. We rely on the ability to think about others' minds to make sense of the social world, and here Toby and Dimitri each demonstrated the ability to attribute desires or feelings to explain the turtle's actions.

Psychologists believe children develop a "theory of mind" to interpret and predict their own actions and those of others. In general, a theory of mind, or "folk psychology," holds that people have beliefs and desires, which can lead to intentions and actions, and which interact with situations in the real world and with emotions in the self. Each of these types of mental state has certain properties and relates to the others in certain ways. For instance, beliefs may be true or false and may be held with varying degrees of certainty. Desires, intentions, and emotions may vary in strength and are not true or false. Mental states are differentiated by their relations to the real world: Desires may only be fulfilled or not, whereas intentions combine a belief with a desire and thus call for a certain action; only if that action is carried out is an intention fulfilled. We experience the emotions in relation to beliefs and the status of our goals or desires. The attribution of intentions—or any mental state—to an animal depends on a theory of mind. How do children develop a theory of mind that deals in such mental predicates?

Strong evidence of such a theory appears around eighteen months of age. Toddlers demonstrate they can think ahead and plan, and they register dissatisfaction when plan and outcome fail to coincide, as reported by the cognitive developmentalist Alison Gopnik (1982). This shows that the children can compare reality with hypothetical situations and have attained a degree of freedom from the here-and-now. Toddlers begin to pretend, can understand pretense in others, and can link their pretend play with that of others. Most researchers see this as demonstrating beliefs *about* beliefs.

By age three, according to another leading developmental psychologist in this area, Henry Wellman (1990), children can distinguish real (physical) from mental entities, but they do not understand that mental things are constructed by the mind. They have yet to achieve certain milestones in the developing theory of mind. Dennett (1978) proposed that the test of whether an entity employs a theory of mind is whether or not it can recognize that a person holding false beliefs will act in accord with them even though the subject knows that the situation in reality differs. Three-year-olds cannot recognize false beliefs either in others (Penner et al., 1987) or in themselves: They do not understand changed beliefs and are unable to remember their own earlier false beliefs (Gopnik and Astington, 1988). Also at this age, children have difficulty maintaining the appearance-reality distinction (as reported by John Flavell, Frances Green, and Eleanor Flavell, 1986), which may depend partly on the ability to encode and remember previous false beliefs.

Several further steps in children's theory of mind are evident around age four. Now they do understand false belief, they use it to explain and predict others' actions, and they remember and admit their own previous false beliefs. They grasp how someone else can believe something different from what the child knows is actually the case. This implies they distinguish a state in the mind from a state in the world. As might be expected, at roughly the same time they understand the appearance/reality distinction, and the possibility that two people may have different views of the same object. At this age, they also start to tell deliberate lies, deceiving others by creating false beliefs. A range of other abilities also becomes more enhanced: empathy, helping, and so on—actions oriented toward others' understandings of the situation. Thus, one may argue, they have a representational theory of mind. Wellman (1990, p. 118) refers to it as an "entity" concept, as opposed to adults' "process" concept: Children believe the mind is a repository of ideas and beliefs (representations) such that people take their beliefs to be how the world is.

In the years from three to six, children move to a more active conception of the mind as an interpreting, representing, understanding faculty. They distinguish desire-based versus belief-based actions more clearly. Among the developments beyond the age of the oldest children in the nursery school are ideas about mental traits (shyness, generosity, and so on) used in understanding another's behavior; these are not apparent in young children.[8] But certainly they should be capable of attributing simple beliefs and desires to animals and probably also communicative and other second-order intentions. Did they do so?

Many of the mental states children attributed to animals were wants or desires, often in close relationship to interactions. Toby's and Dimitri's attribution of fear and displeasure to the turtle reflected an awareness of its possible feelings toward them. Drew gave a simple desire as the reason for the snake's movement:

> Drew holds the snake: "He's unraveling ... he doesn't want to be in a ball anymore. He doesn't want to be in there anymore ... He opened!"

Questions such as why the bigger tarantula would chase the smaller one usually generated mentalistic explanations:

> Ms. Tanner: "Ivy had a reason why they might be chasing." Mr. Dean: "Well, let's hear it." Ms. Tanner: "Do you want me to say it?" Ivy nods. Ms. Tanner: "Maybe the big one is trying to hug the little one."

Such direct attributions are common. Less common is a first-person narration of an animal's thoughts, which Drew made while the ferret rambled about:

> Drew: "He's looking all over, woooo, 'I can't go that way, so where ... let's see can't go that way'..." During this no one is obviously listening until Billy looks at him and laughs.

The thoughts Drew attributed here imply the ferret entertained a series of beliefs that were proven incorrect as it explored. Drew, at five years and two months, applied his understanding of false beliefs to its behavior.

Thus, the children across this age range become more adept at applying mental states to animals and at recognizing the limits of intention sharing. But the lack of child-animal interintentionality may seem at odds with the strong impression, held by many who know animals, that shared intentions do enter the process of interacting with them. To take a simple case, either a dog or its owner may be in a mood to play with the other, and either may successfully initiate play. But calling this "wanting to play" obscures the mutual second-order intentionality required by "getting the other to see I want to play," which is implied. Our human bias to assume that the latter has occurred stems from the advance in our theories of mind made possible by language.

The theory of mind probably has innate origins (see the work of the psychologists Jeremy Avis and Paul Harris, 1991; and Alan Leslie, 1991), but its full development almost certainly depends on language *use*. "Speech acts" are uses of language to affect others. Astington (1993) explains their relation to states of mind: "Like mental states, speech acts consist of attitudes to propositions. However, the attitude is usually referred to as the force of the speech act. The force is how we want the proposition to be taken by the hearer, that is, as a statement, or a request, or a promise" (p. 70). Force may be conveyed explicitly, or by nonverbal aspects of language, or by types of utterance (declarative, interrogative, imperative). Thus, the "force" of a speech act corresponds with a mental attitude. Examples include the mental state of desiring and the speech act of requesting; intention and promising; belief and assertion; regret and apology; gratitude and thanks. Because these correspond most of the time, language can work as a means of sharing mental states, and so the use of language goes hand in hand with an understanding of minds—one's own and others'.

Thus, language is part of what underlies the ability we saw previously to ascribe wants and beliefs to animals, as well as to attribute second-order intentional states. Indeed, how language affects interaction is an intriguing question in itself, and one that animals—as interactants with whom this feature is absent—can help us answer.

Language and Verbal Relatedness

The themes of the animal that speaks a human language or the human who can understand animal language have long lineages in world mythologies and continuing appeal in contemporary culture. The German ethologist Konrad Lorenz (1952/1962) noted the wide appeal of a misreading of 1 Kings 4:33—that King Solomon talked *to* (rather than *of*) animals. Plato, early in the *Statesman* (272c), has the stranger recount to the young Socrates how people in the past could converse with animals and could "learn from each several [*sic*] tribe of creatures whether its special faculties enable it to apprehend some distinctive truth not available to the rest." Writer Ursula K. Le Guin (1990), putting a feminist twist on the issue, remarked that it is the myth that "civilized man" alone has a soul "which all talking-animal stories mock, or simply subvert. So long as 'man' 'rules,' animals will make rude remarks about him" (p. 10). Or perhaps, such animosity is explained by events told by the Argentine fantasist Jorge Luis Borges in *The Book of Imaginary Beings*: "Ages ago, a certain South African bushman, Hochigan, hated animals, which at that time were endowed with speech. One day he disappeared, stealing their special gift. From then on, animals have never spoken again" (Borges & Guerrero, 1974, pp. 80–81).

If animals do not speak, at least to domineering adults, some writers have imagined they might speak to children. Lewis Carroll (1871/1946) astutely imagined the outcome when the Fawn and Alice entered the meadow where things have names: "The Fawn gave a sudden bound into the air, and shook itself free of Alice's arm. 'I'm a Fawn!' it cried out in a voice of delight. 'And dear me! You're a human child!' A sudden look of alarm came into his beautiful brown eyes, and in another moment it had darted away at full speed" (p. 227). It seems that language introduced distinctions for the Fawn that were not operative before. This tale shares the spirit of our quest to understand how the nature of language disposes its youthful users to regard and interact with animals; what the animals say in return, I will not attempt to guess!

Many people believe children talk to animals a lot, although only sparse data are available. Although several writers have suggested that children confide in animals more than adults do (Serpell, 1986, p. 97), there is little evidence apart from clinical case studies. One group of children in middle childhood reported to the psychologist Brenda Bryant (1986) that they talk to pets about feelings of sadness, anger, fear, happiness, and "secret" experiences. Among ten-year-old children, 66 percent reported liking to talk to their pets, and 69 percent said they share secrets with them (Rost and Hartmann, 1994). Nielson and Delude (1989) found day care and kindergarten children directed more talk to an unfamiliar cockatiel (69 percent of the children) than to a dog (36 percent) or to a rabbit (16 percent). Others have reported the use of animals as private confidants by children (Rochberg-Halton, 1985; Hoelscher and Garfat, 1993). I did not hear my young friends talking abundantly to animals, however. More typical was silent, tactile interacting or watching.

We might expect significant amounts of talk to animals to be due to adult modeling. Adults use a special form of speech when talking to their dogs, which the psychologists of language development Kathryn Hirsh-Pasek and Rebecca Treiman (1982) called "doggerel" (perhaps as a pun on doggerel as mediocre/comic loose verse). It is similar to "motherese" used with infants. Utterances in both are short, simple, in the present tense, repetitious, and well-formed. One difference is that "doggerel" uses fewer words to point to objects; mothers use such talk to tutor children on words and names. The authors suggest that the similarities and differences in these two kinds of talk may be stimulated by the social responsiveness of the different recipients.[9] This would agree with the approach of the present study to discern how humans can adjust their social abilities to different species' interactive abilities. But adults' talk to animals can be very complex. For example, one assistant teacher said to the monkey when it crossed the line on the floor separating it from the children, "I'm sorry, but there's a boundary here." Both her words and the abstract boundary she mentioned were completely foreign to the preverbal realm of the monkey.

In contrast, the content of the children's talk to animals was simple and kept a close tie to immediate animate action. The children verbally stated aspects of concrete physical interaction, such as movements in space, as Dawn did in telling the bug in her hand, "We're going." The children marked comings and goings of animals with hellos and good-byes—often using the animal's name, a marker of individuality and coherence. Or consider again Dimitri's talk to the guinea pig:

> [Dimitri gets help from the teacher in holding Snowflake and feeding her. He then holds her a long time, carefully watching her eat. . . .] He holds her between his legs and says, "I got you." Later the guinea pig gets away and Dimitri excitedly goes to intercept it. Trying to get it to come back, he puts leaves in its cage and says, "Over here, guinea pig" over and over.

This talk simply verbalizes immediate preverbal relatedness. "I got you" expresses the present situation of contact and the boy's subjective sense of power. "Over here" indexes the pair's relative concrete positions and intentions. These children's utterances refer closely to a core level of interaction and pertain to subjective feelings generated by present events. Adults can be quite casual about the high degree of sophistication their talk assumes in the recipient animal. The point is not what the animal actually understands but how far removed adults' thoughts can be from the preverbal domains of relatedness. Children seem to be in the midst of figuring out how to accommodate themselves to the differences animals present.

Indeed, the fundamental issue is not quantity of talk or even the content. Rather, how do children's assumptions as language learners and users affect their interactions with animals? Without an analysis of the nature of language, how can we judge the significance of children's talk—and animals' silence? The interactive implications of language derive from how the structure of language allows us to use it to *intentionally* communicate. And this means attributing to the hearer a special kind of higher-order intentional state. Understanding the child's assumptions as a language user will reveal yet again how the child's interactive abilities become differentiated—and how a sense of connection develops.

Pragmatics and the Structure of Language

At this point, a somewhat technical digression is needed to lay the groundwork for the rest of this chapter and the following chapters. Our subject is how language use (pragmatics) relates to the structure of language as a system. We can pick up from where we left off in our earlier discussion of interintentionality. The main point for us—which the following aims to explain—is this: Using language imposes the demand to link preverbal meanings to the requirements of interpersonal communication. Preverbal meanings include all of the core animate and intersubjective aspects of interpersonal events, plus other practical knowledge about the world. Interpersonal communication, on the other hand, entails certain assumptions about *communicative intentions* and word meanings. The gist is that there must be a meaning meant by the language user, and language must provide a system of designation independent of that meaning.

Let us take up that last point. As noted by the Swiss linguist Ferdinand de Saussure (1959), the central requirement of linguistic communication is that signs (such as words) and rules (such as syntax) must be independent of the meanings they are used to convey. In terms of the pragmatics of the language event, this is because of the crucial role of intention in linguistic communication. Consider the prototypical language event. It involves a message sender who (1) has a goal, (2) wishes or desires to enlist another in attaining it, and (3) trusts or believes that the other party will help (Bates, 1976). What will ensure that the other party will understand that its help is desired?

This desire will be understood if the *intention* of the first party to get that help is communicated. Suppose the goal—a nonverbal meaning—is self-preservation from a threat. An animal in trouble certainly might wish to enlist others in this goal. Could that be accomplished by an alarm call? Presumably, such a non-language sign is emitted as an expression of the distressed inner state of the animal and may arouse programmed helping behavior in another. But such a call contains "natural" meaning—it communicates without anyone intending it, according to the philosopher H. P. Grice (1957). It does not necessarily communicate *that* the sender *wishes* to arouse the other and thus does not ensure that the other will respond to that intent, which could entail doing things other than the programmed response.

A word, on the other hand, does not "naturally" express the feeling of the moment. To utter the set of sounds designated by the letters *h-e-l-p* evokes not a native altruistic response but rather a learned or learnable one. It bears an arbitrary relation to its meaning. To use a word instead of an alarm call *does* require that the listener attend to the intention of the speaker, for the word must be interpreted. This is what Grice (1957) meant by "nonnatural" meanings: They depend on the other person's grasping *that* a meaning is intended. Language entails communicative intent.

How does the listener know what was intended? Partly by knowledge of word meanings. The meanings of words are negotiated between speakers, who use the words in various contexts. They are thus "conventional signs" (Mead, 1934/1962). When roughly shared meanings arise from this process, either party can use such conventions to evoke an understanding of what is intended. This is "reversibility," as described by de Gramont (1990):

> When my cat Rover meows to go out, she clearly intends to have an effect upon me. But the effect of Rover's meow is not reversible. That is, meowing does not call out a comparable response in her. If I meow to Rover, she gives me a puzzled look, but she does not appear to think to ask what my meow means; and she never attempts to open the door for me. Rover does not use signs with the understanding that they intend a meaning, so as to call out a response in the other. She cannot use signs this way because she does not have a system of conventional signs that are distinct from what they stand for. (pp. 74–75)

We can understand this relative independence of conventional *signs* from the *meanings* they stand for with the metaphor of "files" containing information, and "file labels" that tell what is in the files. The files are the preverbal (innate and learned and potentially very subtle or complex) meanings; the labels are the words—the generalized signs referring to the meanings. When I say a word, I refer to a meaning. But this referential process is not—in fact, must not be!—exact. Since the contents of a file are complex, a given word, when heard, might refer to several meanings, although the speaker intended only a particular one. Thus, the conventionality of word signs alone is not enough for the system to work! Both participants have to engage in recalling shared meanings, assessing the context, and guessing the other's point of view and intention in order to use the language system effectively. Linguistic communication requires interpretation to anticipate the hearer's frame of mind and to discern the sender's intended meaning. De Gramont (1990) summarized how language use thus fulfills the productive and receptive demands of interpersonal communication:

> The genius of language is precisely in the fact that it does not fix a reference or a propositional content. Rather, it leaves those slots open so that they may be filled by those who are communicating, based upon the setting their communication pertains to, and the assumptions they make about what they say. . . . A speaker must be capable of investing his or her words with meaning in a way that anticipates what the listener will hear. (p. 76)

So language use rests on a general ability to apprehend one's actions in a social context and to guess how one's words will be heard. It is an *interpretive* act.

Two key things are assumed in interpreting conventional signs. To infer the other's intended meaning, the listener normally *may* take for granted that what is said is relevant, orderly, unambiguous, and appropriate for some communicative purpose. This tacit assumption is the "principle of cooperation" (Grice, 1975). But since an utterance can be indirect, biased, ironic, or deceptive, assuming cooperation is not always safe. Still, the listener *must at least* assume that the words do communicate meaning if there is to be any hope of deciphering them. The upshot of this latter assumption, the "principle of communication" is that "language makes cryptographers of us all" (de Gramont, 1990, pp. 77–78). Words succeed in communicating by employing generalized signs that we assume we must "fill in" with particular contents or meanings. It would not work if we did not routinely make these assumptions.

Let us briefly look at three consequences of how language works. First, language works as a structure independent from meanings. Thus, "the generalized reality we convey with language, exists *because of language*" (de Gramont, 1990 p. 72, emphasis in original). And accordingly, "language is responsible for our ability to perceive reality as independent of our experience" (p. 19). In particular, language helps us abstract out and label our own and others' mental states from the flow of consciousness and interaction with the world.

Second, language as a system independent of preverbal meaning frees us to respond in novel ways. Because words are *about* meanings, words or labels can be detached from nonverbal meanings and compared across file contents. Metaphors do just this. The metaphorical function of language enables us to deliteralize word meanings and to realize more what meaning is *about—to* integrate the "novel implicit meanings which had been (till then) excluded from verbal meaning" (de Gramont, 1990, p. 151).

Third, because language demands coordination of preverbal meanings with the requirements of interpersonal communication (the independent structure of files and their interpretation), language creates discontinuity with the core animate and intersubjective realms. As a summary of what we have already seen, consider these contrasts:

Preverbal Domain Meanings	*Linguistic Domain Meanings*
concrete and embedded	enable abstraction
analogical, gradient expression	discrete/categorical expression
pertain to particulars	pertain to generalities
immediately meaningful	require interpretation
amodal and globally represented	separated out from sensory fusion and streams of action

Language use requires breaking the preverbal context and then productively combining word labels according to the grammatical and linear structure of spoken language. This presents young users with a formidable challenge: conveying a specific meaning using words that express generalities. For example, a toddler might repeat "eat" many times before the adult understands the specific instance (bread) from the apparent general class (edibles) the infant intends (Stern, 1985, p. 177).

This very abbreviated summary of language should make it possible now to appreciate how language—and its absence!—define the interactive opportunities offered by animals. We will look first at children's talk to animals and their interpretation of animal behavior according to linguistic assumptions.

Talking to Animals and Understanding Them

The animal that was talked to the most was the dog, but the words directed at it were mostly typical trained commands, especially "Come!" and the dog's name. Commands do make it seem as if language is effective in altering the recipient's behavior. But a command evokes only a trained and not an interpreted response. With the exception of specially trained apes, animals do not use conventional gestures. The closest the animals in the nursery school came was the dog playing fetch or the monkey accepting objects, but these do not qualify, since the animals did not use the gestures reversibly. Nonetheless, children (and adults) do not always appreciate this limitation.[10]

The children I observed expected that interintentionality and conventional signs would work with animals.[11] One older girl felt her pointing gesture communicated her intent to Snowflake:

> Cassia comes to the cage and drops in celery pieces for the guinea pig to eat. Then she holds the foil they were in over the pieces. Snowflake comes and gets one. I ask if she was pointing with the foil, and she says, "Yes." Mr. Myers: "Did the guinea pig see you do that?" Cassia: "Yes."

Children's use of language also showed they thought the animal capable of interpreting intent:

> Pogo is lying on the floor. Billy asks Mr. Grier, "Can I shake his paw?" Then he gets down, looks the dog in the face, holds out his hand, and says: "Give me your paw. Give me your paw."

That Billy did not use the command "Shake!" suggests that he assumed any appropriate set of conventional signs would work. In other words, he assumed that the dog understood words as a person does, by interpreting them. Earlier, we saw Billy yelling at bugs so they could hear him. These examples might reveal different expectations about dogs versus bugs as interactants. But Billy was also seven months older when he asked Pogo to shake and maybe better at accommodating himself to animals' different qualities. When the dog failed to respond to his words, Billy did eventually touch its paw, thus reverting to a more effective, animate level of interaction to accomplish his behavioral aim (but abandoning the aim of communicating his intent).

The children also expected that animal behavior requires decoding similar to speech. Language and theory of mind together make this possible, but it brings a subtle bias to animate experience. For example, some children "gave" animals appropriate words to "say." This tendency was most pronounced in a few of the more verbally inclined older children, one of whom was Drew. We already saw him give words to an exploring ferret; two weeks later he read meaning into the monkey's motion:

> The monkey tries to get something from its owner's hand. . . . Drew interjects, "He's like, 'What's in here?'"

These adroit words that Drew put in animals' mouths clearly relate to the concrete, animate-level activities of the animal in its environment—the most immediate aspect of the animal for children. It is not surprising he would find such meanings, but a rift has been introduced by verbalizing them. Only language as a set of markers independent of preverbal experience can denote specific intentions and aspects of the world in an objective manner. To communicate his impression of the monkey's experience, Drew had to change it.

Children attributed language-like thoughts to animals, but no example yet has shown the attribution of a specifically communicative intent to an animal's motions, sounds, or other expressive actions. It would be surprising if children did not do this, for the adult-created media surrounding children portray fully linguistic animals as cartoon and literary characters. Furthermore, the adults themselves often spoke for toy and real animals for playful or didactic purposes. Consider the snake owner presenting a baby ball python, a species that wraps itself into a tight mass for self-defense:

> Ms. Nol takes out the little snake, and explains that it's very afraid: "See, it says, 'Oh please don't hurt me, don't hurt me, I'm just a little baby snake.'"

Strictly speaking, an animal that does not use language can intend a set of affairs including that it not be hurt, but not by affecting the mental state of another—it cannot intend that you not aim to hurt it.[12]

The following transcript does show a child, again Drew, attributing linguistic intent. It also shows more children attributing core-related mental states to the animal:

> Mr. Lloyd attempts to feed the turtle a small piece of meat held on the
> end of a stick. The turtle turns toward the meat. Mr. Lloyd: "He's thinking
> about it. . . . No, now he's going to scratch his head." Drew, gesturing with
> his hand in imitation of the turtle, as if to wave something away, and
> turning slightly to one side: "Aw, no, I don't want it."

Drew repeated the motion and words several times. Rather than simply giving
the animal thoughts as in the examples before, the words, "Aw, no, I don't want
it," in the social context of feeding, carry a communicative intent directed at
the intentions of the feeder. The imputed pragmatics are clear: "I want you to
know I don't want this food so you won't offer it." In this type of case, then,
fully linguistic abilities are implicitly attributed to the animal.

Animal Language

Children thus assimilate animals to the language model they are learning—but
do they also distinguish them within it? Once, two girls denied the monkey
could understand them:

> Ms. Dean, [replying] rhetorically: "Why? Does he speak English?"
> Adrienne, Laura: "No." Adrienne: "He speaks, he speaks . . ." Laura: "He
> speaks . . ." Laura and Adrienne together: "Monkey talk."

But a dawning explicit awareness that animal communication differs from
human language was evident in one of the most linguistically sophisticated
children, Joe (five years, four months). When the dog visited, this exchange
occurred:

> Mr. Grier: "If I'm up in my apartment and he's out in this park by himself,
> I've got to know when to go get him, right, when he's ready to come in.
> So you know what he does?" A child barks. Mr. Grier: "Exactly, who said
> that?" Ms. Tanner and Drew indicate it was Joe. Mr. Grier: "Exactly, I'll
> be up in my apartment, maybe reading or something, and I'll hear from
> outside 'Woof woof woof' just a couple of times, and that means he's
> waiting right by the door outside and he's ready to come in."

Note that Joe did not answer the question in words. Rather, he demonstrated
the answer, implying that barking contained the meaning about which he was
asked. Mr. Grier's reply confirmed that barking had a language-like meaning
("Come let me in"). That evening, Joe's mother taped a conversation with him
in which he gave his account of how the dog barked to be let in. Then, Joe told
his mother how dogs talk:

> Mother: Is Pogo happy [in the city]?
> Joe: Uh-huh.

Mother: Hm. That's good.

Joe: Well, we don't know if he's happy.

Mother: How come?

Joe: 'Cause we're not him. We don't know. We're not other dogs, so we can't ask him.

Mother: Oh, do you think dogs talk to each other?

Joe: Yeah.

Mother: So other dogs would know because they'd talk to him? What did—how do they talk to each other?

Joe: Just a minute. (pause)

Mother: So when, ahh, I'd really—I'm interested in what you said about dogs talking to each other. How do they talk to each other? I've never heard a dog say anything . . .

Joe (interrupting): They bar . . . they bark, they have their own way of talking—they bark to each other.

Mother: Ah!

Joe went on to explain that wizards (which he admitted he had never encountered) can talk to animals—instances being one in a book and another in a movie he said was called *The Man Who Talked Animal* (I have never determined what this may have been, though today there are a few candidates). Joe denied what especially younger children's behavior implies, and which they seem to have assumed: that intentional human language is effective with an animal. Joe's conception of dog speech represents a further development into reflective awareness of the differences animals present in interaction. But Joe has not realized that different communication systems may be fundamentally different. Joe's version of dog language incorporates ordinary (and inaccurate) assumptions about human language: that it is both the privileged route of inner access to another's mental state and essentially a shared code. This reveals an interesting fact about his concept of communication: notions of human language form his implicit model. In this, however, he is not different from most people. Indeed, perhaps the biggest limitation in our understanding other species is our lack of awareness of our own communicative bases—and biases.

Key Assumptions

Some other aspects of language also determine the interactive significance of animals. Language is the communicative channel that usually carries the demand for accountability (Stern, 1985)—that is, it is much easier to deny information conveyed in a gradient channel such as prosody, gesture, or positioning than in a categorical channel such as words. If a nonverbal act is challenged (for example, because it caused offense), one can often deny the meaning ascribed to it. But one is held accountable for what one says. The reverse is true when interacting with an animal. The animal misses the discrete content of all but a few learned words and does not hold the speaker accountable. The effective channels are direct action, body language, tone of voice, volume, and other gradient features—features that have their analogues in the animal's own repertoire, to which a child can respond. This again leaves interaction with an animal free of a very severe social demand that is imposed almost as soon as the child can speak.

Gradient, or analogical, channels carry information that is of vital importance to social mammals—information about relationships (Watzlawick et al., 1967). As Bateson (1972) put it, mammals "are concerned with patterns of relationship, with where they stand in love, hate, respect, dependency, trust and similar abstractions, vis-à-vis somebody else" (p. 470). Perhaps, over-simply put, interacting with an animal has special salience, since children know to "read" contact and gradient information for messages about the basic status of the relationship. The animal does not present or provoke a divided or "double bind" situation (Bateson et al., 1956; recall the discussion about coherence earlier in chapter 4), since it does not present verbal messages that clash with nonverbal ones. The animal offers one message, that conveyed by behavior, which is the channel to which children (and adults) look to see what is "really" meant by what others are saying.

Although it is ambiguous and opaque (and of course nonverbal), animal behavior would seldom directly contradict the principle of cooperation by being patently deceptive.[13] In human communication, we learn to suspect the cooperative assumption by the experience of being deceived. Although people can interpret animal behavior as deceptive, the interpretation is usually very difficult to confirm one way or the other. If, as we saw, children tend to regard animals' behavior as meaningful and decodable, they may also unconsciously assume it conforms to Grice's (1975) principle of cooperation. Because animals' behavior is in the channel children trust for important information about relationships, because animals do not contradict themselves or create double binds, and because confirmed deception is a rare event, animals' activity is apprehended by children as especially "authentic," if also hard to decipher precisely.

One key conclusion about the role of language in children's interactions with animals is that it inclines them to assume that animal behavior is interpretable and therefore meaningful. Children bring the communicative principle to bear on animals' action. This may result in misinterpretations, such as wrongly attributing shared intentions, comprehension of words, intentional communication, the possession of an animal "language" with features like human language systems, or a simplicity and honesty of action. Certainly, the history of benighted human misunderstanding of animals (for example, as evil agents or as having extraordinary abilities) shows the power, universality, and potential fallibility of our biases as language users. But our interpretive habit also may lead out of these and into the realms of science, appreciation of difference, reflective practice, and concern. *Ironically, rather than setting us apart from other species, our nature as language users is what makes it possible for us to wonder about the meanings of other species' activities and ultimately to care about their subjective worlds and welfare.* Society has barely begun the task of bringing our full interpretive faculties to bear on understanding other living creatures, but many young children are very engaged by the first steps of this project.

The Animal Outside Language

We have found some ways children assimilate animals to the assumptions of language but also other ways in which they distinguish animals as existing in a separate interactive realm because animals lack language. They talk less to animals and gradually adjust their biases to fit what animals do and do not do in response to words. There are some indications children may treat animal behavior as less problematic than that of their conspecifics. But the fact that animals are outside the worlds of language has other far-reaching and non-obvious consequences.

Animals do not place demands for proper language use on children, and thus afford interactions with novel qualities. With animals, children are free from the demand to negotiate meanings. Words can be used to express exactly what the child wishes to mean without the demand to clarify; the problematic general quality of words does not interfere. The child can express her or his preverbal meanings without the constraints imposed by the phonetic, grammatical, narrative, turn-taking, and other structures of language that serve its interpersonal functions. One need not worry that the animal will tell anyone what was said, either.[14] But in contrast to monologue, in which, according to Katherine A. Nelson (1989), an expert on language acquisition, the speaker does not attend and respond to another, language with an animal is connected to the flow of the interactions and may help the child interpret the animal's behavior because it requires guessing at intentions. Herein may lie the value adults find in talking "with" animals, using fairly ordinary human talk.

That the animal does not require the child to fit his or her meanings into the forms and structures of language and yet is responsive on a core level places the animal within the preverbal, personal world of early childhood and outside the social order as we constitute it with words. These two worlds often exist in tension. Peter L. Berger and Thomas Luckmann (1966), whose work on the sociology of knowledge was so fundamental to social constructionist theory, nonetheless acknowledged that language does not seamlessly constitute all our experience. They described the experience of the tension: "I encounter language as a facticity external to myself and it is coercive in its effect on me. Language forces me into its patterns" (p. 38). The developmental psychologist John Dore described the transition when language becomes an effective mediating force between mother and infant:

> At this critical period of the child's life . . . his mother . . . reorients him away from the personal order with her, and towards a social order. In other words, whereas their previous interactions were primarily spontaneous, playful, and relatively unorganized for the sake of being together, the mother now begins to require him to organize his action for practical, social purposes: to act on his own . . . to fulfill role functions . . . to behave well by social standards . . . and so on. (quoted in Stern, 1985, p. 171)

This passage emphasizes the difficulties of a transition that is not entirely past by the age of four or five—or perhaps ever! (Recall that Stern's domains of the self persist across the life span, and thus can interact, as shown, for example, in such tensions between our core and our verbal selves.) Children are very much in the midst of being socialized at this age and still also very much in touch with the intimate, analogical, concrete, and direct preverbal world. The social order is constituted by speech acts: Others (and oneself) create action categories and enforce behaviors that could not exist without the language that denotes and elaborates them. Animals (although some are themselves intentional social products of domestication) do not compel actions through situation definitions, linguistically defined goals, adherence to conventions, demands for moral accountability, or selective affect attunements. To this extent, children may enjoy a voluntary quality in interactions with an animal—it is not out to socialize them.

Roles are one social force and product of language. Adults may impose such a schema on animals;[15] and, indeed, they use animals extensively in the role socialization of young children. But animals do not impose roles on children, and their interactions do not operate according to ascribed (or achieved) expectations or responsibilities. Role performances are subject to impartial evaluations that do not take into account the personal qualities of the actor. An animal does not judge in this way. Interaction with animals thus constitutes a domain without the conflicts typical of the socialization process. On the other hand, the child is free to imagine or impose whatever roles he or she wishes the animal to have. But there are limits to what an animal can perform or will tolerate, so such role frames may be broken before they get very far. In one example, an animal was given a culturally specific animal role: The guinea pig was placed in a vast building block maze and watched as it tried to escape. Paradigmatically for the present point, it ignored the passageways after a short time and climbed out over the walls, much to the children's excitement!

Conclusion

In summary, children gradually accommodate themselves to the fact that animals do not use language. There are ways that animals' lack of language may make children more apt to feel close to them. Animals do not demand sophisticated conformity to the structures of verbal communication, leaving children free to experience meanings and relatedness on nonverbal levels. Nor do they require accountability or draw children into the complex worlds of linguistically constituted objects, roles, morally laden evaluations, deceptions, and paradoxes. But also, the assumptions that children make as language users affect the expectations they bring to interacting with animals. In particular, children expect that animals' actions are meaningful or decodable and even especially "authentic." Thus, the child's curiosity about the meaning of an animal's behavior and experience is a key contribution of language.

In discussing how animals do not impose social roles or linguistic rules on children, I do not want to give the impression that language is only a negative thing for children. To the contrary, it also enables many uniquely human and positive experiences. My point is simply that interactive differences matter and that children respond to them. Let us consider the positive side of language. The animal does not make metaphors, which give language deliteralizing and liberating powers. The intentional worlds constituted by language offer some of humanity's greatest solaces and creative adventures. Language creates community between people. This community is basic to who we are and who we become. Speaking and listening are fundamental forms of affirmation and recognition; silencing and refusing to hear are paradigmatic of inhumanity. Furthermore, since language can mark and "hold" a meaning, with it we vastly transcend the here-and-now. We can plan and project a future. And we can reflect back, reconstructing our experience with a new grasp of its significance. We can also isolate intentions from the stream of consciousness for reflection, thus opening a new realm of autonomy and conscious choice that can guide action. With these come new forms of interaction, negotiation, and commentary that define obligation, right, and common understanding—and new forms of accountability and the regulation of social conduct.

When we share such worlds with others and when we confirm them for another by listening and discussing, we realize our humanity in a way only other humans can help us attain. Although we may grapple with the roles of animals in our intentional worlds by such deliberate reflection and dialogue—or merely by assimilating them symbolically—animals themselves do not create these worlds with us. As Serpell (1986) notes, a pet does not offer human cooperativeness, altruism, advice, or moral support; understand worries, fears, or frustrations; compare experiences, opinions, attitudes, beliefs, or goals; or comprehend the depth, scope, and complexity of human relationships. But animals also pose less potential for deceit, competition, manipulation, betrayal, and rejection. Through words, we possess and change shared meanings, opening entire new domains of connection and relatedness—and of misunderstanding and separation.

A speech-spun world implies a self. The self that I consciously think or imagine myself to be is the "self-aware" or "reflective" self. Without considering this self, our account of the role of animals in the child's sense of self is incomplete. We know who we are in relation to others partly because of how we verbally characterize ourselves—and each other—in the terms of all the kinds of talk I have mentioned here. Because the verbal self has this origin, must there not be a radical discontinuity between the child's nonverbal sense of relatedness to animals and the self-reflective sense of being a human, with roles and so on? Is the animal superfluous to human selfhood, except as we linguistically "construct" it? This is the implication of the traditional view. In the next chapter, we will explore children's pretend play both to learn the meanings children detect in animals' varied qualities and behaviors, and to explain how animals do in fact enter into the child's self-reflective sense of self.

VI

Pretend Play

Self as Human, Self as Animal

The children's entertainment industry regularly dishes up new cartoon creatures for the current crop of movie- and television-viewing kids. Whether animal or human, these figures have magnetic and dynamic personalities that hold young children's attention. In pretend play children recount and act out memorable scenes they have thus learned. While I was engaged in research for this book, prehistoric personages adapted from the animated film *The Land Before Time* were popular with the children I was observing, as shown in this excerpt from my field notes:

> Dawn attacks Joe—they butt, on hands and knees. She backs off. Kevin: "I'm Sharptooth . . ." Dawn: "Are you Sharptooth?" Kevin: "Yes." Dawn: "Then I'll fight you"; she stands, then pursues him, saying, "I'm taller than you." She runs away. . . . Dawn approaches Kevin again, who is on the floor by me. She paws the ground. Kevin turns the tables and chases Dawn and the other children, pursuing slowly with big steps, hands clawlike and elbows bent *T. rex* style.

High drama also came from the *Teenage Mutant Ninja Turtles*, another cultural animal rage. These four anthropomorphic cartoon reptiles struggling together for the good and to discover themselves were irresistible identities, especially for little boys. In one instance, somehow incited by the presence of the large real turtle, Billy and Benson pretended to be Ninja turtles in combat with it:

> The turtle, itself remarkably inert, is on the floor with the group of four younger children. Billy moves his fists in a tight circular motion, leaning toward the turtle. Billy: "Let's cut it up. I *got* your turtle, I got the turtle

119

on his back." He reaches around to show where on his own back. Benson: "*Pucchhh!*"—he thrusts his fist toward the turtle twice. Billy: "Bang!"—making a hitting motion.

Pretend play episodes provide fascinating windows into children's minds. Several issues that pertain strictly to the human world are evident in the scene above. Most obvious, the children above were completely swept up in their fantasies. In these examples, the children I observed subsumed the turtle in a cultural script; response from it was not necessary, instead being supplied by projection. Second, animal roles are an avenue for working out tough relationship issues. Dinosaurs and Ninja turtles can be helpful outlets for urges toward aggression, power, control, and heroism. Not only do children use animal pretend play developmentally, but adults exploit it this way, too—usually with a milder tone:

> Mrs. Ray talked with Yasmin while pretending to offer her worms and calling her "little bird." Mrs. Ray told her how when she grew up she would fly away and leave the nest. Yasmin was silent. Then Mrs. Ray asked if it made her sad to think of that. She nodded. Mrs. Ray said, "That's what's so nice about being a person is that you never have to leave your family, you can keep seeing them as long as you want." This did seem to help Yasmin, but she continued as a bird.

In this example, issues of autonomy and dependence were clearly central. The "little bird" identity assumed by Yasmin (recall her special interest in birds and flight) provided a distance that made it possible to metaphorically discuss the primary issue. While being dinosaurs and baby birds, these children are developing in the familiar psychosocial sense.

But these examples—and this way of looking at them—confirm the traditional views of animals: that they are important to children only secondarily whereas human factors are primary. What is mainly happening is projection, or rehearsal of a linguistically created cultural script. The animal is just conveniently appropriated, or reappropriated in the case of cartoon creatures. Or perhaps, as some researchers hold, the function of pretend play simply is to give practice in human roles; it serves socialization goals. Corsaro (1985), in an important study of young children's creation of their own culture, discussed two pretend episodes in which children played animals. These involved the roles of pets—kitties—with other children playing husbands, wives, and children. Corsaro's analysis touched on power and control and the fact that lack of language limits the possibilities of the kitty role. But his key foci were children's concepts of human social roles and the ways status is conceived of and negotiated through the language children use. In fact, Corsaro excluded roles that children "cannot reasonably be expected to enact or encounter in later life" (p. 78). Thus, despite the ubiquity of animal pretend play in nursery schools, the only episodes considered important were those that illustrate family roles.

Let us consider another example, much like those just discussed but with an element that helps distinguish a more unique developmental role of animal pretend play:

> Yasmin, "meowing," is a kitty. Solly is "a dog, a space dog" on all fours and making "arfing" noises. Both are crawling about in the doll/play house area, and near the block play area. I help Solly with his suspenders, which are coming loose. His role as a dog is not greatly interrupted by asking me for help: He spoke, but continued his posture and noises. He pulls away, goes to the play house door, and looks in. His pose evokes a dog's alert "sitting" posture. Mindy, evidently "mother," is in the house. She tells him to get out; he butts at her. Yasmin comes over and sides with Mindy, telling Solly to get out. Solly gets in a play scratching fight with Yasmin—she is still a cat. Mindy intervenes, chasing him out with a saltshaker. He retreats a bit and meets up with Joe. They agree to "go after that kitty" and crawl to the doll corner. Mindy shakes the saltshaker at them again; they scratch at Yasmin, who is seated in the high chair. Then Solly and Joe play with the telephone cord, holding it in their teeth and stretching it. Yasmin likes that and does it too. At about this time, the teacher announces that it's snack time, but Solly continues a mild attack on Yasmin. Solly tells the others, "I'm playing ruff ruff superdog and underdog." . . . Later, I ask Yasmin what she was—no response, so I add, "A kitty?" She meows affirmatively.

Again, we see the assimilation of animal roles to the human "household." But it is the role of the body to which I want to draw attention. Consider the scratching, pulling of phone cords with teeth, and Solly's sitting pose. Solly was leaning on extended arms, his "tail end" on the floor, knees down and pointing ahead, lower legs turned out on the floor to either side, back straight, head up. Solly's body is not a dog's, but it offered possibilities for translation to a dog's. As with other examples here, the fidelity of his posture to a dog's suggests attention not just to the appearance of the pose but to its inner "feel." In the dinosaur scene, Kevin's *T. rex* pose and motion were unmistakable. As Yasmin received worms, her neck reached up in imitation of real baby birds she must have seen on television or in real life. And as Corsaro (1985) astutely observed, use of language is also unusual. Yasmin faithfully avoided verbally responding even when questioned directly. In animal roles, children do sometimes talk, but the talk is truncated and fits closely with the actions: Yasmin told Solly to leave and followed up the words with scratching. Solly formed an alliance with Joe, wherein, as dogs, they verbally agreed to attack "that kitty."

This interpretation centers on the meanings of the interactive features of animal roles. If pretend play reveals (among other things) what animals mean to children, it confirms what we found before: The preverbal domains of animate and intersubjective relatedness are primary in children's connection to animals. In this chapter, I develop this theme, using pretend play as a window on children's meanings. But I claim it is more than just a window. It is also an important contributor to the development of the self-reflective sense of self.

Intentional pretending and imitation enhance the sense of self in relation to the nonhuman animal in two respects: The child sees himself or herself as being like the animal and thus feels *more connected* to it; at the same time, accommodation and differentiation are required, and so the sense of what it means to be human and not the other species is *clarified*. Although advance via differentiation and integration is a broadly observed pattern of psychological development (for instance in Piaget, 1963; Jordan et al., 1991; Csikszentmihalyi, 1990), when applied to bodily imitation of animals it results in an important—even unorthodox—conclusion. The implications go far. The aware sense of being a human self that pretend animal play produces is not a sense of being *categorically* human. Pretend play creates and preserves *continuity* between animal and person *and* between the preverbal and the self-conscious realms of selfhood. Thus, it provides insight into larger problems of psychology, including certain discontinuities of experience and the mind-body dichotomy. Leading the way to a view of the full contribution of child-animal relations to social development theory, pretend play and the self—as developed in this chapter—will provide us with a model for looking at continuity of concern, interest, and community in the next chapter.

Language, Imagination, and Self-Reflection

The attentive reader may have noted that my assertions here raise an issue alluded to at the conclusion of the previous chapter. It is unusual to propose that self-reflectivity arises from nonlinguistic sources, such as pretend play. But here, the most fundamental issues about the role of the animal body—ours or another species'—are ripe for rethinking. To tie things together, an excursion into the idea of self-reflectiveness will be helpful.

In the predominant theory that self-awareness depends on language, the audible character of the word and the organization of social roles play special parts, and the body is dismissed as incapable of contributing to a self-reflective self. All of these presuppositions are questionable, and for our particular purposes such a basis for human self-awareness is inadequate, since it leaves animals entirely out of the picture. On the face of it, this exclusion is implausible. Do we not have a self-aware feeling of being *human* exactly because of the cross-species comparisons available? Granted, with language we can construe those differences flexibly. But we know now that children make distinctions between themselves and animals on other than cultural and linguistic bases. Indeed, they do so on interactive bases, where the animal contributes. Let us try to look beyond the constraints the earlier view set on our understanding of the self and see how children's cross-species interactions extend into self-awareness.

Our thoughts on the self have been greatly influenced by the work of the pioneer social psychologist George Herbert Mead. We need to examine his thinking here because he specifically denied that pretend play and imitation contribute to the self-reflective self. Why did he think so, and was he right? Mead (1934/1962) proposed an exclusive mechanism for how William James's objective "me" came into being: "I know of no other form of behavior than the linguistic in which the individual is an object to himself, and so far as I can see, the individual is not a self in the reflexive sense unless he is an object to himself" (p. 142). Two points are made in this passage: First, only language can objectify the self. When I speak or use a sign-language sign, my meaning is symbolized simultaneously to both the other and to myself. I have an inner response to my own gesture and *can confirm it by seeing the other's response.* In this way, a verbalized meaning *about me* lets me stand outside myself. The result is the "me," an object: the self that is perceived, known, and described with attributes much as another would use.

The second point in Mead's passage above is that such an objectified version of myself is required material for self-awareness. Self-awareness is a capacity of the "I"—the subjective self, the actor, the knower. But the "I" slips from grasp in the very act of grasping: The "I" is not *what* I can be self-conscious of but *the faculty I use to be* self-conscious. I can have self-awareness only indirectly, when the "I" creates (based on words) an objectified image of itself in the "me." The whole self develops from the back-and-forth of the "I" and the "me": A new self-concept (me) can shape the next choice and action (of the I), and so on, dialectically. In general, this portrait of the process seems plausible.

But Mead (1934/1962) gave language a role it cannot fulfill. He said it is the simple audibility of the spoken word that provides the person a way to identify with or have access to the perceptions of others.[1] There are problems here, for actually we do not hear our own words exactly as others do—due to anatomy, physics, and differing perspectives on what is meant. Words have to be interpreted; they do not work automatically, as we saw. With words, we can express ourselves, or something characteristic of the self can be summed up—but if this is how the self becomes available then it is in a different respect than mere audition that language makes the self reflexively available.

The more important factor that Mead left out is imagination, as the philosopher Karen Hanson (1986) has argued. We need imagination—the Cambridge philosopher Ludwig Wittgenstein called it "*seeing* (something) *as* (something else)"—to take the other's viewpoint on ourselves. This accounts for how words can express something characteristic of the self but not simply due to the broadcast nature of speech. In terms of its perceptual basis, analogy-making is dependent on the general preverbal ability to apprehend one's own actions in a social context, which is a sense carried through the life span. But Mead assumed an incoherent body and an asocial starting point, from which this should not be possible.

Mead (1934/1962) said the self must be distinguished from the organism. The eye can see the foot and thus objectify it; but only the self unifies the body. Hanson (1986) says Mead came close to denying the body's basic integrity. Consider his denial of self-coherence: "The individual organism, without the socially generated self, responds only to parts or separate aspects of itself, and regards them, not as parts or aspects of itself at all, but simply as parts or aspects of its environment in general" (Mead, 1934/1962, p. 172). Today, we have strong counterevidence. Daniel Stern (1985) examined two four-month-old girls who were "Siamese" twins born facing each other. Before separation surgery, they were observed to occasionally suck each other's thumbs. Stern tried pulling thumbs from mouths. As he did so, he found that when twin A was sucking on B's thumb, A's head would strain forward to maintain sucking, but B's arm offered no resistance. But when A was sucking her own thumb, the arm resisted. On occasions when the twins were simultaneously sucking each other's thumbs, Stern pulled on both arms, and observed: "The results indicated that each twin 'knew' that one's own mouth sucking a finger and one's own finger being sucked do not make a coherent self" (p. 79). Indeed, Mead had it exactly backward: Only with language can anything be conceived of as truly independent of the self. Bodily coherence is first.

Of course, imagination and the self-reflection it supports take more than bodily coherence. Comparing, or *seeing* (x) *as* (y), is founded on the innate ability of infants to detect invariants and patterns of experience. It is further developed by the metaphorical capacity of language that deliteralizes meanings. And imaginative reflection on the self is rooted in the social world. As Hanson (1986) puts it:

The self may not be given in a response which is immediately shared
by others [as Mead had contended] . . . but there must be a foundation
of shared responses to support the vault of imagination. The whining
complainer, for example, must share the winces of others. He need not,
of course, now or ever react with a wince to his own tone. *Pace* Mead,
we need not duplicate the behavior of others at the moment of sighting
ourselves in reflection. (p. 102)

Granted these prerequisites—basic self-coherence, comparison making, and
shared social responses—imagination enables the kind of perspective taking for
which Mead (1934/1962) was looking. Such perspective taking occurs in pretend
play, which thus would seem to contribute to the child's growing sense of self.

But no, according to Mead. Only organized social roles, for example in
games, are alleged to be sufficient. Mead (1934/1962) claimed that only the
internalization of the "generalized other" enables the individual to objectify
"the whole self" to himself or herself in reflection, and only the organized
perspectives of other players in a game create this paradigmatic social self.
Hanson (1986) concedes imagination enables the apprehension of only *a* self,
such as a role (a complainer; a leader); it does not seem to produce one single
definitive self. Why did Mead argue so strenuously for the experience of "the"
whole self? Hanson suggests his concern was autonomy and self-control (pp.
86ff.). For Mead, the "generalized other" enables the individual to *not* be ruled
by the particular other people present at a given moment.

But Hanson points out the contrary implication of truly internalizing
the "generalized other": "An individual who comes to be the incarnation of
all the common attitudes might well be thought to have abdicated individual
integrity" (1986, p. 88). Thus, the "me" is too rigidly given by Mead's concept
of how language objectifies the self. Indeed, Mead was mindful of this danger
of the overly conventional person. In effect, he conceptualized the "I" so as
to supply spontaneity, and he stressed the unpredictability of its actions by
excluding habits from the "I." But, Hanson rejoins, habits are very much the
sort of thing that becomes incorporated into the person in the dialectic of the
"I" and "me" that forms the self. Habits are also among the things of which we
occasionally become aware through reflection, and which seem essential to a
description of actual selves. This last point about habits emphasizes the fact that
self-reflection is not as automatic as Mead would make it seem. It may happen, but it may not—much as would be the case if it depended on occasional
imaginative insight! So it may be that Mead's requirement of reflection on
"the" whole self is unrealistic, at once too mechanical and too ideal. Reflection
on "a" whole role of the self-in-context is more like life.

There are other reasons to doubt a too linguistically oriented view of the objective self. Development of the objective self is signaled by several roughly simultaneous events at about eighteen months (Stern, 1985, pp. 165–166). At this age, the use of pronouns ("I," "me," "mine") to refer to the self occurs. So, too, does touching the face when the infant sees a surreptitiously placed spot of rouge on his or her face in a mirror. We also observe early acts of other-directed empathy, and this is the first age of pretending and of planning. Given the diverse inputs implied by all these achievements, it would be presumptuous to give any one input causal primacy in the emergence of self-awareness.

The need to explain "the" whole self led Mead (1934/1962) to focus on the organized qualities of games and to dismiss pretend play as a developmental means of achieving a reflective sense of self. Now that we have rejected his argument that the vocal gesture uniquely underlies taking others' roles, pretend play "is easily assimilated to an account of the self which places imagination at the core of reflexivity" (Hanson, 1986, p. 78). But precisely how is it a route to understanding how the child's self-awareness as a human person is expressed and clarified by the enactment of animal roles?

Mead (1934/1962) admitted that the child pretending must, to guide his or her performance, "take the role of the other." But, he said, "the latter phrase is unfortunate [here] because it suggests an actor's attitude which is actually more sophisticated than that which is involved" (p. 161). The child in pretending is not so advanced as to be deliberate but is "simply exhibiting responses characteristic of the other because the other's attitude is also in the child, 'ready for expression'" (Hanson [paraphrasing Mead], 1986, p. 80). But could the child really *inadvertently* enact the part of the other? To the contrary, pretend is an intention-dependent concept.[2]

To knowingly play the role of the other requires a delineation of self and other. Hanson (1986) illustrates this point with an example that is coincidentally harmonious with our focus:

> The child playing bears, pretending to be a bear, knows he or she is not a bear. That is just why pretense and imagination are necessary. If the child simply had growling among his usual repertoire of reactions, if growling were just among the responses "ready for expression"; if he were as likely as not to drop to the floor and pad about on all fours; then this growling, padding behavior would not be thought—by him or anyone else—to constitute a specific role-play. But the (normal) child who growls and pads and swipes with a hand held stiff from the shoulder, the child pretending to be a bear, does not normally exhibit this behavior, and that is just why it is appropriate to this pretending play, why the child has, so to speak, chosen it. (p. 83)

This concept of pretend play, unlike Mead's (1934/1962), involves conscious contrast between self and other. Although Mead intended to find in pretend play some contribution to self-other differentiation, his formulation of it as unintentional had the consequence of ruling out that possibility, and he let the important work fall on games. Hanson (1986) elaborates the achievement necessary in pretend:

> The child can be discovering which bits of behavior are most appropriate to the other and which are most characteristic of himself, for he must evidence or emphasize the former and suppress or disguise the latter. A more coherent sense of both himself and the other is thus obtained. Hence, as engaging in this sort of play does further demarcation of the self, it is reasonably cited in an explanation of the development of the self. (p. 83)

Language is still a part of the picture here—to see animal behavior as meaning-laden may depend on the child's assuming the communicative principle. And the formation of the very intention to pretend may also depend on a language-related theory of mind. But what we now can say is that the development of self-reflexivity is not the product of language exclusively. Nor is it an achievement possible only in relation to other language users.

Pretend Play and Imitation of Animals

What can we tell about children's concepts of self and other from their pretend play? Pretend play shows the differences children consciously perceive between themselves and animals. This might be revealed in the content of the pretend episode (what the child does) or in the deployment of different media (how language is used, for example) in enacting the episode. So long as the child must be deliberate in his or her action, either pretending or simpler imitation meets the criteria discussed previously. Accordingly, the imitative acts we will consider are all performances addressed to a (*usually* human!) audience.[3] The most important thing that is revealed by pretend animal play and imitation is that the alterity, or "otherness," of the animal is preserved and represented. We find this in three aspects of pretend play: orientation to social forms, use of language, and use of the body.

Orientation to the Social World

In pretending to be an animal, the child's orientation to the everyday human social world is changed, even more so than in other pretend roles. First, the roles enacted typify animals rather than humans. This was not always the case, as when an "animal" occupied a human role such as "baby," but more often pretended animals were predators, prey, combatants, pets, or working animals. These different roles are enacted by movement, the occupation of space, forms of activity and passivity, and so on that are uncommon in children's other roles.

Children's orientation to space and time while being animals is altered from normal patterns. In everyday life, space is patterned by social convention and cultural objects. For example, tables are not just physical objects; certain rules surround their use, as children know. But in pretend play, space is correlated to the "animal's" own shape.

> Mr. Lloyd, the turtle owner, asks Katra, "Would you like to be a turtle?" At first she seems not to have heard him, but then begins pretending. Katra: "I'm going in my shell." She hunkers down into a turtle position, arms and legs tucked in. Both she and Angela tuck down, turtle style. Mr. Lloyd tries to address Katra: "Miss, dear . . ." Katra: "I'm going to my shell." Mr. Lloyd: "Oh, you're going, okay, you're playing the part of the turtle." Katra moves toward the corner and climbs into the blanket shelf, a tight spot a bit bigger than herself. Then she rejoins Angela, and they both go off to the corner, Katra still intent on the blanket shelf.

I had never seen any child crawl into the blanket shelf before, but for a "turtle" it became an obvious option. Time also may be altered, as when Yasmin became so absorbed in nonverbal "dialogue" with the doves that she failed to realize lunch had begun.

Certainly, children's sense of time and space are not fully socialized to begin with, and many activities besides animal role play find their unique tempos. But the children's comments make it clear that identifying with animals frees them from social pressures. Sam and other children responded very positively when asked whether they would like to be monkeys and why:

> Sam: "I would stay in trees and never climb down." Mr. Myers: "Really, how come?" Sam: "Because I don't want to come down," slapping his leg for emphasis.

Children perceive animals as not being subject to socialization pressures. Billy said he would like to be a monkey:

> Billy: "I wish I wouldn't have a mommy so I could just do whatever I want to." Mr. Dean: "You wish you didn't have a mommy?—Do you think monkeys have mommies?" Ivy and Billy reply, "Yes." Ms. Dean: "Yeah, do you think their mommies tell them what to do?" Billy, Ivy, and Benson all answer, "No!"

Nor are animals burdened by school demands. In a different small group, I asked Solly if he would want to be a monkey:

Solly: "Yeah." Mr. Myers: "Yeah." Ms. Dean: "How come?" Solly: "Because
they can swing by their tail, and they wouldn't have to go to school."...Ms.
Dean: "You think their moms make 'em go to school?" Smiling, Dimitri
and Solly answer, "No."

This perception is an added plus of pretending to be an animal: The child acts
in a space that feels free of, or in opposition to, social structures. Rules that
apply to children may be relaxed for "animals":

> Mrs. Ray notes that the slugs which the children and she are holding have
> no legs but can move. She asks, "Do you know other animals like that?
> How about a snake? How does it do it? Watch and see if you can figure
> out." Mrs. Ray calls Ivy over; she looks a moment at the pill bug, and then
> leaves, seeming not too interested. . . . But not long after watching the
> slugs, Ivy, Cassia, Yasmin, Katra, Dimitri, and others get on their bellies
> in the sand area and squirm across it. Dimitri calls out, "Look! Tracks!"
> Ivy adds, "We're making tracks behind us!"

The children delighted in this activity, which had the special appeal of being
normally discouraged, since it made them dirty.

Socialization teaches children to evaluate behavior. "Good" or "bad" can
also be applied to animals, but they, like other pretend identities, offer freedom
for exploring this evaluative dimension:

> Yasmin and Laura want me to watch while they are kitty and witch. Yasmin
> is the wicked witch's bad kitty, and scratches (gently) at me. I wonder out
> loud if she might not really be a good kitty, and she switches to be one. But
> preferring the bad kitty, she switches back. They both growl. Yasmin: "But
> they eat persons. But bad witches eat persons." . . . Laura: "Why would
> anyone want to be bad?"

Yasmin found it more acceptable to be a bad kitty than a bad person; she used
the animal role to explore and express "badness" without threat of censure.

These examples indicate children perceive pretend animal identities
as affording an orientation distinct from the ordinary human world with its
structured time and space and its roles and rules of conduct. This confirms my
earlier conclusion that because the animals differ as interactants on the verbal
level, children perceive them as independent from role pressures. Children
represent this contrast through pretend play. Correspondingly, the child's human
self must be experienced as engaged in such roles and social patterns.

Use of Language

Pretend animal roles may or may not involve talking. Corsaro (1985) observed
that as an animal, a child cannot talk. Is this true in the following play?

> Rosa and Yasmin were playing in a cozy corner behind the "space capsule."
> The play was primarily pretend, and Yasmin alternated between being a
> guinea pig, making squeaking noises, and a kitty, meowing. In either
> case, the animal could make ice cream. . . . Rosa asked, "Do you want
> to go in a big cage?" When Yasmin didn't reply Rosa said, "Little kitties
> can't talk." Yasmin: "How can kitties talk?" Rosa: "Can big kitties talk?"
> Yasmin explained: "They can go 'meow, meow.'" The play continued,
> focused on objects and less on roles. . . . Later I asked Yasmin if kitties
> talk. She said, "No." "Can they talk to each other?" I asked. Yasmin
> said, "Yes," but offered no more explanation.

Here Yasmin broke the pretend play frame in which she, as a cat, could not talk, in order to explain that fact. While in a role, the children generally observed this interactional constraint of pretending to be an animal (notably, anthropomorphized cartoon animal models do not suffer this constraint). Yasmin's responses to my questions make it clear that this is her conception of being a cat. But her responses also indicate that she considers the meowing she does as a cat to be far from meaningless: It signifies effective communication between cats. This is as we would expect based on my earlier discussion of children's assumptions about animal action and vocalizations.

As with other pretend role play, some talk in and around animal roles marks the pretend frame and confirms the play is a performance: It is metacommentary. This kind of talk is used to negotiate roles and plot. With human roles that involve speech, some in-role talk adds indirect definition of the role—for example, saying the things a mother would say indicates that one "is" a mother. So do animal roles require more out-of-role frame-establishing talk? As "animals," children are aware that their behavior needs a frame to be interpretable:

> Today at lunch, Abeo sits next to Angela and Ms. Tanner. She announces
> to Ms. Tanner, "I'm a beaver," and takes a bite from her apple, which is
> sitting on the table—without holding it with her hand!

Normally such behavior at lunch would be corrected. Abeo's play here illustrates exactly the intention essential to pretense. At lunch, pretending even for a moment to be an animal requires deliberate distinction from her normal behavior.

But when the context can serve to mark the shift to pretend, children may dispense with verbal framing. Recall how Joe barked in answer to the question of what the dog does to get in. In contrast, Reuben then gave a mixed verbal-barking reply: "He goes, [three barking sounds]." But neither boy simply said, "He barks." Where humans talk, animals simply act—or bark; this contrast obviates the need for frame-establishing talk.

Talk within animal pretend roles revealed a variety of ways children exploit the freedom the animal role gives from the constraints of language. Talk may merely call attention to the nonverbal role-play:

> After looking at a beetle with other children, two or three boys, who before had been chasing and tackling, play at being the beetle. They repeat, "Beetle, beetle, beetle" and crawl over each other in the sand and on the grass.

Words spoken in most pretend play may stand in a flexible, open, and non-literal relation to action. One of the attractions of animal roles is that children are even freer from the demands of reciprocity and accountability that come with use of language. Occasionally this can cause problems:

> Out on the lawn, virtually everyone is a shark, or at least is chasing around. Ms. Tanner asks the sharks, "What do you want?" The reply: "Bones." Mindy dashes about, hands raised, fingers gripping, and growling continuously. Toby grabs her; she screams and lashes out in protest. The teacher admonishes her, "It's not fair for you to grab others but they not you." Mindy smiles. Mrs. Ray: "That's silly."

Mindy was enjoying the shark role as a chance for aggressive play but did not see it as a reciprocal and accountable kind of action. But the teacher imported non-animal standards into the pretend frame. Reciprocity is more inherent in language use, and fairness is more typical of the formal and impersonal nature of social roles than of the animal activities Mindy pretended to perform.

"Animals" need not endure the demand to match meaning and word; action can mean just what one wants. Baby role play offers a similar safety, allowing the "baby" to fuss and intend the most indecipherable meanings toward its "mother." The following episode shows how baby and animal roles can blend around this common trait:

> Two pairs of "pet owners" and their "animals" leave the rug for the doll area: Reuben with Mindy as dog, and Angela with Abeo as cat. Each animal has a necktie around her waist and crawls on all fours behind the owner who tells her what to do. . . . At the doll house, Abeo gets in the crib but won't talk to me—she only meows somewhat threateningly.

Far was it from me to tell precisely what the cat-baby meant by this!

In sum, the role of talk in animal pretend play does not vastly differ from its role in human-role pretend. Talk is still necessary to negotiate the play episode, and can also be used in role. But children sometimes avoid language and use animals' nonverbal nature to jump into a pretend animal role, and sometimes children strongly avoid talking in an animal role. The lack of talk in an animal role affords a freedom from demands and constraints of language, confirming the interpretation that interactively defined differences are salient to children, providing ways that children clarify the difference between human self and animal other. Arguably, this is *realized in awareness* through imitation and pretend play.

Embodied Meaning: Translation of the Body

To imitate or pretend to be an animal, children embody it, as when Solly translated a dog's qualities of motion into his own body. Words may help label the role, but the intelligibility of the play depends on fidelity to the constraints of the particular creature. In this play, the child must clearly *see* her or his action *as* that of the animal. It is possible to thus reflectively grasp the otherness portrayed, because the child has not only her or his own sensations and perceptions but also the responses of others. Children in complementary play roles hone each other's enacted agency, affect, and coherence, such as the aggressiveness of "cats" fighting, or the friendliness of a panting and attentive "dog." Or feedback can be more direct:

> Dawn crawls forward facing the turtle, crouches down on the rug, and tucks her head down.... She rises up suddenly, saying, "I know how to be a turtle in my shell." Mr. Lloyd: "Is that how it would be, like that?" Dawn: "Yeah." Mr. Lloyd: "But you couldn't see anything then." Dawn brings her head up to disagree: "Huh huh." Mr. Lloyd: "But the turtle stays in his shell and he sees things." Chris disagrees: "Yeah, and ah, I can." He is in "turtle" position, crouched down over his legs, but holding his hands by his face and pointing his head forward rather awkwardly.

In response to Mr. Lloyd's challenge, Chris modified his pose to meet the objection. This gives us confidence that the play is a conscious self-other differentiation.

But these children are also telling us that the externals of the performance are not the essence of pretending. Their acts are not only physical, but are imaginatively and subjectively charged. Chris and Dawn first denied their action was incorrect, suggesting that an important dimension of pretending to be an animal is not just how it looks but how it feels to the child—they felt they could see just like a turtle. The dimensions of embodied action together with subjective experience constitute the animate otherness of the animal as described in chapter 4. Reflective portrayal of these properties, complete with their species variations, is at the heart of children's pretend play as animals.

Animate Properties. Children translate the animal's body movement into their own in creative ways that analogically reveal core or animate properties of the animal being pretended. Core agency is revealed in movements, implicit intentions, inhabiting of space, and uses of objects of a pretend animal. A child may use just a part of his or her body to show how an animal acts:

> Yasmin is asked what she liked about the dog. Yasmin: "He blows the wind on my hand with his tail." She gestures, waving her right hand over her left palm. (Earlier she held her hand on the floor below the dog's wagging tail.)

Careful observation led Ivy to notice how the dog chewed on its ball:

> Ivy bends down, looks into Pogo's mouth, sits up, and says to Mr. Grier, pointing at her mouth, "He moves his, he moves his tongue over here [she points to her right cheek] so the ball can fit over here." Ivy points to her left cheek.

Ivy interpreted the dog's implicit intention, but this required referring to her own face to show what the dog did. Just a little earlier, Ivy had shown why a dog could not pick up the ball with its paws, again making gestures that captured the bodily limits of the dog's agency rather than explaining it with words—which would have been quite difficult to do precisely.

Such translation of the animal's actions to one's own body goes beyond using parts, to the possibilities of the whole body:

> Ms. Nol asked, "Can you see why it's a 'ball' python?" Benson: "Ball." Ms. Nol: "It wants to roll up in a ball." Benson says immediately, "Like this," and quickly curls over, head to knees. Ms. Nol: "That's right. When it's afraid it rolls up into a ball to try and hide itself."

We have seen many other such examples in episodes already described.

The animals' divergent animate coherences were shown by portrayal of the animal's body as *a different kind of whole* from the child's own body. An animal's appendages—or lack of them!—can be a hurdle in pretend play, but the lengths to which children go reveal their faithfulness to the animal's different self-coherence. Several interesting techniques were used to illustrate the snake's body, as in this taped session at home between Abeo and her mother:

> Mother: The snake came today?
>
> Abeo: Yeah, there was a baby snake and a momma snake.
>
> Mother: Oh, there were two of them.
>
> Abeo: Uh-huh.
>
> Mother: How did they interact, how did they react?
>
> Abeo: I'll show you, I'll show you.
>
> Mother: Oohh, they were creeping like that, oohh, did you try to do that while they were there?

Abeo: No.

Mother: Oh I bet you like creeping like a snake. Abeo is creeping up and down. You like to creep?

Abeo: Yes!

In class, Dawn took a similar approach:

Mr. Myers to Ms. Nol: "How fast can a snake like this move?" Ms. Nol: "Not very." Just after my question, Dawn inconspicuously backs away from the group, then extends on her stomach on the floor. She comes around behind Chris and Joe, pulling herself slowly along on the floor by her hands.

Sam offered a different possibility, using part of his body:

Sam taps Chen on shoulder and shows him a snake motion with his arm in the air. Sam: "Chen . . . makes a 's'—Sssssssss." Chen puts his hand on Sam's to make him stop, then makes a snake motion on the floor with his own hand. Sam takes this up also.

The turtles elicited much imitation, but of course entirely different embodiments than did the snake. Sometimes, children portrayed the animal's shell with their backs and head movements. Solly and Joe explored a different approach to being a turtle:

During a whole class discussion of the turtles, Joe walks on his knees to the back of the group and falls forward on all fours facing Solly. Immediately, Solly places both his hands on the back of Joe's head and pushes it down in an exaggerated nodding motion three times. Each time, Joe brings his head back up by himself, to look toward Solly. Then, Solly grabs Joe's shirt, prompting Joe to try pulling it up over his head. Solly helps, but Joe's shirt only comes to his nose, and he pauses to look at Solly. Benson sees this activity and immediately begins pulling his shirt up also. Solly reaches for Joe's head, encircles it with his arms, holding him. Ms. Wick interferes at this point, first by calling, "Solly," and then by reaching out to touch him. He crawls away behind Joe. Joe desists and listens for half a minute to the discussion of the depths at which fish versus turtles swim. During this interval Solly leaves him and comes around behind on all fours, putting hands and knees down deliberately and emphatically. This stroll lasts a full 27 seconds.

This example also shows how animals' vitality affects are conveyed by qualities of motion in pretend play. Toward the end, Solly's turtle walk perfectly captures the characteristic slow, plodding "feel" of the turtle's gait.

The dog's vitality affect was effectively embodied when Mr. Grier elicited pretend behavior in the presence of the dog:

Joe crawls around by the camera, "woofing." Dawn moves her legs as if to get up, but then crawls over by Joe.... Mr. Grier asks the group, "If you had your choice, do think you'd like to be like a dog, like Pogo?" Chris: "Yes." Mr. Grier: "Yeah, you'd like to be?" Joe and Dawn both come toward Mr. Grier, "panting," and assume sitting positions facing him with animated expressions. Cassia gets down from her chair and joins the others, dog-mode. Mr. Grier looks at them, smiles, and watches for several seconds. Pogo lies on his side, wagging his tail slightly. Mr. Grier: "Pogo's going to think you're a dog." They move closer. Cassia barks, then Dawn also. Then they sit back up.

Here, the calm but eager and friendly demeanor of this dog—or of the dog the children want to be—is reflected in the children's dog imitations. Apart from their actual inner states, different species' simple qualities of motion can strongly suggest affects to children. Vitality affect is a discernible aspect of the core other that children embody in pretend play or imitation. The vibrancy and lively quality of the children's performance in these examples is hard to convey verbally, though it is something we all recognize and understand. Indeed, these are two main points of this theoretical discussion! It seems that among the most salient things embodied in animal pretend play is a sense of vivid animate aliveness itself.

A sense of core self-other continuity, or history of interaction, might be expressed in pretend play by a child's presentation of the same particular animal identity over time. Parents were asked, "Does your child like to pretend to be any animals?" and, "What animal identities does he or she take on, and when?" Parents of roughly half the class listed between one and seven animals their child liked to pretend to be. Two-thirds of these included a cat or a dog, probably the animals best known to the children.

Interestingly, favored animal roles were unrelated to the animals children had at home. In fact, the four children who most avidly practiced pretend animal identities at home had no pets in the house: Yasmin's parent listed her being a "cat almost every day. If not a cat, she pretends different animals"; as we have seen, at school Yasmin had two of the most enduring animal identities of any child: cat and bird. Chen's home list included lion, crab, wolf, and dinosaur. Billy was lion, dog, cat, ape, frog, snake, and dinosaur at home; and Rosa was reported to pretend to be dogs, lions, and alligators. Taking the whole class, I found this relationship statistically significant: Children with no pets were more likely to have two or more pretend animal identities than were children with a pet.[4] A factor that might explain this relationship is siblings: Single children are known to fabricate more imaginary social interactions. But there was no relation between pretend animal identities and lack of siblings. Pretend animal identities may substitute for real animals rather than being stand-ins for human relationships.[5]

Animals taken collectively were prominent among the roles the children took on in pretend play. A very wide variety were enacted: The children were alligators, an ape, bats, beavers, beetles, cats, crabs, dinosaurs, dogs, doves, ducks, elephants, ferrets, fish, flies, frogs, lions, mice, monkeys, rabbits, sharks, sheep, a shrew, slugs, snakes, squirrels, spiders, a swordfish, toads, turtles, a wolf, and more. These constitute a full and ever-available cast of divergent identities into which the children readily stepped.[6] Although there surely are cultural influences on animal pretend play (see discussion later in this chapter), the animate qualities of actions like comings and goings, holdings and chasings, mutual presences, and the range of vitality affects and so on are the material out of which more complicated cultural scripts can be enacted. Animal pretend play offers the special advantage that the child's meanings can be consciously felt and experienced as being of a piece with his or her actions, without the difficulty of aligning preverbal, global meanings with conventionally appropriate verbal symbols and syntax.

Consequences for the Self. Every time a child intentionally imitates an animal's divergent space-time reality or variations on core agency, coherence, affectivity, and continuity, she or he must objectify the self. Language is not necessary for that. In the process of embodying meanings in pretend, the child imagines what it is like to be the animal and thus feels closer to it. The process also enhances the differentiation of the self from the other. The differences children depict in pretending to be animals are the same ones we found to be salient in their interactions with animals. This supports our overall interpretation that direct interaction is more primary in children's concepts of animals than other factors such as culture, psychodynamics, or anthropomorphism. It is evidence that children see and represent animals in a manner consistent with our view of core relatedness.

Pretending to be animals clarifies children's sense of what it means to be human. The key point is that it is not a rigid kind of human-animal distinction that is experienced but one underlain by deep animate commonality. This is different from the emergence of a categorically human self. And here is a larger implication of the commonplace episodes we have witnessed. The behaviors children act out in pretending to be animals carry meanings; some the children express verbally, others by animal-like vocalizations. But most meanings they convey implicitly in action—in complementary interactions and in the ways the child bodily translates the animal's core agency, coherence, affect, and continuity.

In pretend play, these meanings are made self-conscious, but note an important difference between this and the old view that self-awareness is only possible through language. Language requires the separation and encoding—and by the recipient, the interpretation—of preverbal meanings into discrete, general, abstracted "labels," or words. By contrast, pretend play *preserves continuity* between the preverbal realm and the self-conscious. Using language, it would be nearly impossible, or at best very difficult, to present to self and to others a comparable sense of the otherness of the animal. Pretend play and imitation do not entail as much opposition or tension with preverbal modes as does language. Imitating lets the awareness of being a human self develop in more continuity with animals as core and intersubjective others—that is, as embodied beings like ourselves. Thus, children's relations with animals point to a resolution of the old and general problem introduced in chapter 2—the relationship between the animal body and the self-aware human mind.

Continuity Between Preverbal and Verbal Experience

What does the insight reached in the previous section mean for development? Answering this question requires some further steps of theory, but the upshot is that it is *discontinuity* that needs explaining. Again, our habits of thought—the high evaluation given to the linguistic mind and the low status of the animal body—have led us to overlook normal continuities.

Many thinkers have stressed the dichotomy between the nonverbal and the verbal, and we saw that language makes possible a generalized reality that would not otherwise exist. We compared how language works to a system of verbal "labels" on "files" containing nonverbal meanings. The ability of a label to act as a placeholder for a meaning makes self-conscious thought possible. This underlies, for example, the linguist John Searle's (1983) distinction between deliberate "prior intentions" versus nonreflective "intentions in action"[7] Certainly, this is an important distinction. But to the extent the difference is conceived of as a *discontinuity*, the linguistic pole is usually granted greater importance in our higher mental functioning. It is more closely related to abilities we regard as uniquely (and thus we suppose essentially) human. The linguistic side is also simply more accessible for study, and as a result its importance in the meanings, plans, and memories by which people lead their lives is easier to demonstrate.

But much of human life is actually led by "intentions in action"—that is, without prior reflection. Fully conscious self-reflective deliberateness may be the exception, as the English philosopher Alfred North Whitehead observed:

"From the moment of birth, we are immersed in action, and can only fitfully guide it by taking thought" (quoted in Ingold, 1988b). But how much are our abilities really divided against each other? Interplay between conscious and preverbal forms of thought occurs in artistic and scientific creativity, in psychotherapy,[8] and in problem solving. The psycholinguist David McNeill (1992) has shown that a unitary process of meaning creation underlies words and gestural communication (see also McNeill, 2000). As evidence of the development of this fundamental capability, the language acquisition researchers Cynthia Butcher and Susan Goldin-Meadow (2000) revealed that the ability to coordinate gesture and words emerges during the one-word speech phase of development. Earlier, Martha Alibali and Susan Goldin-Meadow (1993) showed that children's hands tell more than they can say as they attempt to solve challenging math problems, evidence of cognitive processing that can be symbolized in alternate channels (see also Evans, Alibali & McNeil, 2001). Indeed, children must always be able to bring preverbal and practical-experience knowledge of their world into conjunction with language. This fundamental ability should make us wary of assuming too great a discontinuity.

Despite some social theorists' heavy emphasis on the constitutive power of language, if we trace this emphasis back to its origins, we find earlier writers who stressed continuity centered on the immediate face-to-face social situation. Even the founding theorists of the social construction of knowledge, Peter Berger and Thomas Luckmann (1966), so impressed with the "coercive" power of language, nonetheless also noted that "the other ... becomes real to me in the fullest sense of the word only when I meet him face to face" (p. 29). Their predecessors, sociologist Alfred Schutz and philosopher Maurice Merleau-Ponty, also granted the nonverbal a foundational role in communication and society. Both drew on a tradition in European philosophical biology that was more friendly to the idea that the animal body is pre-prepared to find meaning in the world, and especially in interaction, than was the American behaviorism followed by Mead. An alternative to either behavioristic or physiological explanations of behavior was provided by the animal behaviorist F.J.J. Buytendijk:

> On the level of behavior there is an original identity of perceptibility and intelligibility. . . . For although there are realities which are perceptible without being intelligible, such as colors and figures, and realities which are intelligible without being perceptible, such as mathematical and logical relations, we believe that we have here singled out a level, behavior, on which, strictly speaking, perceptibility and intelligibility are given inseparably from one another, so that behavior cannot be perceived without at the same time being (although possibly wrongly) interpreted. (quoted in Grene, 1968, pp. 124–125)

As an analogy, we might ask, how do we understand music and dance? Their intelligibility is given immediately with how they sound or appear to us. These theorists are saying behavior, on the most basic level, is like these arts. Music and dance share with interaction the additional trait of entailing a duration of time. The founder of ethology, Jakob von Uexküll (1940/1982), spoke of the "melody of movement" (pp. 62ff.). Schutz (1951) used the "mutual tuning-in relation" between performing musicians to illuminate interaction. This relation is "established by the reciprocal sharing of the other's flux of experiences in inner time, by living through a vivid present together" (p. 96).

More simply put, in our ordinary attitude we immediately "interpret" qualities of behavior. For example, we cannot precisely say all that it is about someone's greeting that tells us it is friendly or not, but we normally receive and respond to others' behavior with such information already "included." This is simply a phenomenological description of our findings on children's sense of connection to animals: The animal is a subjective presence because of its united agency, coherence, and affectivity in interaction. We do not experience action in its mere "behavioristic" minimum of physical motion in time and three-dimensional space—a minimum to which we must then establish connection through the use of word signs. Rather, the preverbal sense of meaning and the verbalizable meanings blend into each other. The two functions are not really separate.

This should not surprise us, because of what we already know about infants' abilities. Of special importance for the development of a reflective sense of self through pretend play is the ability to "*see* (x) *as* (y)"—to make comparisons and find invariants or patterns. This ability precedes language; we saw it in the infant's ability to detect invariants across sensory modes. Very early imitation might employ this ability in generating a sense of self. The psychologists Andrew Meltzoff and Alison Gopnik (1993) suggest, "Infants are launched on their career of interpersonal relations with the primary perceptual judgment: '*Here is something like me*'" (p. 336, emphasis in original).[9] This perceptual judgment is rooted in an innate ability to find correspondences between self and other, as revealed in imitation. According to Meltzoff and Gopnik, "The work on early imitation shows that even newborn infants recognize some equivalences between externally perceived behaviour—that is, perceived body movements—and literally internal proprioceptive states" (1993, p. 339; see also Meltzoff & Moore, 1995). Similarly, Mitchell (1997) attributed imitation and pretend to "a capacity for matching between the kinesthetic ... sensations of one's own body's position and one's own bodily feeling, and visual images of ... others' bodies" (1997, p. 43) or what he calls visual-kinesthetic matching.

These authors are arguing that from infancy forward, when we see others move we can map how those motions roughly feel in our own bodies, through our proprioceptive sense, the sense that we use to feel our own body's position and motion. This suggests some kind of neurological connections that would correspond to the phenomenological descriptions of earlier social theorists, such as the mirror neuron system that has recently been described.[10]

The comparison-making abilities of infants are later given a huge boost by the metaphoric mode of language. The ability to "detach" the "labels" (words) from the "files" (clusters of preverbal meanings) and compare them across different files deliteralizes word meanings and enhances our sense of what meaning is *about*. De Gramont (1990, p. 94) illustrates this with the phrase "I am an American." If taken literally the person is saying he or she *is* the state or entity referred to—thus, it is a statement of categorical identity. Figuratively or metaphorically, on the other hand, the phrase suggests many associations of history, culture, and so on—meanings of being an American towards which one might have a variety of different attitudes. Overt metaphors and language play evoke the comparison and crossing of different realms of meanings, as when one says "love is a rose": the compared object elicits one variety of meanings of love, just as a different object ("love is a trial") generates another. Meaning is about our complex and sometimes inchoate preverbal knowledge of the world, ourselves, and words. In this mode, language is not discontinuous with world experience but enriches it. The child engaged in translating the body to *see* himself *as* a cat is doing something similar to both invariance-finding and metaphor. He enacts comparisons that are perceived and immediately intelligible (and interpretable through more sophisticated metaphoric and logical processes) by both himself and others.

Understanding Discontinuity

If continuity is the primary relation between verbal and nonverbal, why should animal pretend play, which enhances continuity, be so important in our account? The answer, while not immediately obvious, lies in the prevalence of certain forms of *discontinuity*, at both the individual and societal levels. One hint comes from studies of the complex enigma of autism: Discontinuity may be explained as the result of some *obstacle* to a normal process. Interestingly, children with autism often have fairly intact language, but they lack a normally developed theory of mind. They also are unaware of their own mental states, do not distinguish between appearance and reality, and do not pretend. The Swedish child psychiatrists Christopher Gillberg and Peder Rasmussen (1994) reported a case of an autistic girl with symptoms of Williams syndrome who would be a dog from time to time. Her mother says she did not "pretend" to be a dog like another child might do: she would be a dog. If the family entered a shop, she would do so on all fours . . . barking and nosing, completely oblivious of other people (and of 'other' dogs). If anyone tried to stop her in this ritual she would tear down the shelves. In spite of her excellent performance as a dog she cannot participate in mutual imitation games. (p. 387)

One explanation, offered by the psychologist Alan Leslie (1991), is that these children lack the ability to represent their own representations. Normally, such meta-representation underlies the theory of mind and certainly is vital to metaphor. More broadly, the psychologist Uta Frith (1989) sees in autism a pervasive cognitive inability to integrate information into larger meaningful wholes, a lack of cohesion-making (reviewed in Astington, 1993, chap. 9). The key point is that autism demonstrates a deficit in the abilities needed not just for metaphor but for even more basic forms of continuity between parts of experience. The consequence is impairment of social abilities and compromised self-awareness.

More recently, an intriguing case of autism has emerged which suggests an underlying deficit that might explain the general patterns described above. A severely autistic boy from India, named Tito Mukhopadhyay, was raised with exceptional patience by his mother to communicate by typing in English. He has been examined extensively by neuroscientists, but more importantly, has been uniquely able to express himself and provide insights into his disorder. Tito "seems to lack a sense of his own body, the kind of internal map that normal children develop in their first few years," according to Dr. Michael Merzenich of University of California at San Francisco Medical School (Blakeslee, 2002). In Tito's own description, "when I was 4 or 5 years old, I hardly realized that I had a body except when I was hungry or when I realized that I was standing under the shower and my body got wet. I needed constant movement, which made me get the feeling of my body. The movement can be of a rotating type or just flapping my hands. Every movement is a proof that I exist. I exist because I can move" (quoted in Blakeslee, 2002).

Other scientific findings indicate that some autistic children have scrambled body maps, the dynamic brain patterns that process the parts of one's own body. Lacking such a map could cause an impairment in visual-kinesthetic matching, and thereby in understanding others. Studies of autistic children further reveal they have difficulty integrating sensory information. Tito, for example, is not able to perceive both a beep and a flash on a computers screen unless the light follows the sound by a full three seconds (Blakeslee, 2002). The ability to integrate information across sensory channels, which as we have seen is so fundamental to normal infant development and sense of self, may be compensated by atypical brain patterns in autistic children like Tito. The drawback to the varied ways autistic brains come to compensate is that higher neural circuitry that ordinarily builds earlier integrated centers may be compromised. While we are far from understanding this spectrum of disorders, the new research points even more strongly to the importance of the bases of a sense of connection emphasized here. It also highlights that it is discontinuity between body and mind, or between self and other, which calls for explanation by the general idea of an obstacle or deficit.

Normal children do not have the basic deficits of autisitic children as obstacles to development. But language can pose an ordinary but important obstacle to continuity when its generalized reality is confused with concrete reality. Patrick de Gramont (1990) analyzed moderate, specific, and indeed common forms of the breakdown of metaphorical ability caused by this confusion. Language, because of the independence of sign and signified, carries the risk that the person will not realize that a word is about a meaning and will thus treat the word meaning as thing-like. He or she may thus "reify" a meaning, losing the ability to "detach" the "label" from the "file" contents and perform a metaphorical comparison.

This poses a developmental challenge. Young children can be trapped by confusing the sign for the signified—that is, they can reify meanings in their learning of language. Such distortion occurs in language learning because words start off as induced labels (the child is taught by being told which words correspond to which things, actions, or events) and may thus taken to *be* the things they name, according to de Gramont (1990, p. 93ff)[11] The metaphorical function develops with the realization that words stand for things without being them. The child then can have flexibility about word meanings, and is less likely to be trapped by them.

Two broad classes of reification, however, may afflict us all: "capture" of meaning by affect, or by ideology.[12] Both forces—emotion and unmovable dogmatism—are known for their ability to make us lose touch with the concrete and treat a person as an object that fits only our emotionally charged construction of them, or treat an abstraction as reality. "Distortion occurs not as a result of regressing to a preverbal mode, but of collapsing the metaphorical mode that emerges with language into a literal meaning that operates like a preverbal meaning" (de Gramont, 1990, p. 138). A vivid example of such a literal meaning is a clinical phenomenon called "glove anesthesia." It is characterized by numbness or pain occurring according to a location as designated in verbal thought (the whole hand from wrist down), not according to the body's nervous structure. A more prosaic example is the polarized and hardened way some ex-spouses come to view each other: the positive portion of the full meanings of the other person have been "captured" by emotionally flooded judgment.

Affective or ideological capture can create confusions of the self with others—including with an animal. For example, mental illness often involves affectively motivated distortions of identity. The influential American psychologist Erik Erikson (1958) noted that people with schizophrenia may become "dehumanized, and eventually even de-mammalized. These patients can feel like a crab or a shellfish or a mollusk, or even abandon what life and movement there is on the lowest animal level and become a lonely twisted tree on the ledge of a stormy rock, or the rock, or just the ledge out in nowhere" (pp. 103–104). The psychologist Hendrickson and colleagues (1990) describe examples of alternate "animal" personalities in cases of multiple personality disorder. The pioneering psychologist of human relations to nature Harold Searles (1960) pointed out the occurrence of animal imagery and self-perception in schizophrenic symptoms. There are also psychiatric syndromes involving the delusion of being an animal. One specific type with an old history in Europe is *lycanthropy*, the belief one is a wolf, usually a dangerous one.[13] Possibly demonstrating a related social pathology, a number of the German Nazi elite had powerful identifications with predatory animals. Hitler had especially close attachments to dogs. They were constant companions, including one named Wolf that belonged to his landlady in the 1920s. Indeed, when he was young, he used the name Wolf. In the 1920s, with a woman who played the role of his foster mother, "Hitler would often sit at her feet and lay his head against her bosom while she stroked his hair tenderly and murmured, 'Mein Woelfchen'" (O. Strasser, quoted by the sociologist Arnold Arluke and historian Boria Sax, 1992, p. 16). Given the Nazis' ability to completely distance themselves from the feelings of other humans, it seems likely this evidence points to both affective and ideological capture of identity meanings.[14] In all these examples, the self is taken not just to be *like* an animal in a metaphorical sense but to categorically *be* the animal. The underlying dynamic here is not so fundamental as that afflicting the autistic child who believed she was a literally dog described above, but its origin—a breakdown of metaphoric ability—does not make it less troubling, partly just because it may be more widespread in society.

Continuity Between Self and Animal

Although the cases discussed here of the human self's becoming reified as an animal are clearly pathological (albeit perhaps common in certain historical situations), it is possible that reification of the human self as *human* is a typical ideological capture of meaning in some cultures. That is, whereas early experience revolves around continuity, a culture may dictate human-animal discontinuity. In Western culture, this may have roots in the classical opposition of the simple animal body versus the human mind, defined historically by spiritual superiority and in modern times by a high standard of self-reflective thought. Ironically, we now reify language itself as a discontinuity between the body and the mind and between the animal and the human. One important implication is that in this culture there may be a complex set of affective and linguistic meanings (explored in the next chapter) that encourage individuals to draw the human-animal boundary *categorically* and that weaken metaphorical human-animal continuities.

We are now in a position to counter this particular reification in our psychological theories. First, animate commonality is primary. Second, it is ironic that language is reified as difference because *it* is what lets us wonder about the meaning of behavior—actually enhancing our sense of continuity. Its potential to help us do this is basic to its nature, but also open to much greater cultivation. In light of this chapter, self-reflection and language can be employed *within* their matrix of bodily interaction, imagination, and metaphor; this is the third key theoretical point. We have seen that for the young child, at least, the gap between the human self and the animal interactant, although real and intriguing, is far from absolute. And we have seen that this is based on self-consciousness in continuity with the interactive human animal body. This kind of difference-within-continuity *can develop further* rather than suffering reification. Let us examine this final point in more depth.

What would development that fostered continuity look like? I will address several aspects in what follows. First and most simply, it could involve developmental trends in pretend play among young children. A bit more broadly, I will ask what kind of longer-term potential for understanding animals generally can be hypothesized. Finally, generalizing much further, how does the perspective here inform our thinking about the relations between psyche and culture?

What about developmental trends in animal pretend play? Children in the older half of the group I observed (over 4 years, 4 months) accounted for the majority of incidents of animal pretend play. But focal-child observations in the spring, when I observed a subset of children more intensively, showed no age-related difference in tendency to pretend, and the four children reported by parents to have the most pretend animal identities at home were among the younger ones, including Yasmin, who accounted for thirteen of the twenty-four instances of pretend animal play by the younger half of the children in the fall. These three contrary indications support at most a conclusion that individual differences are important in preference for pretend animal play, as discussed earlier. On the basis of general developmental trends in pretend, we might expect a decrease from early to middle childhood, and a shift towards other forms of fantasy identification, such as imagination while reading. Lacking data on older children at present, however, this is only rough speculation.

Development of a skill can be unrelated to age, but rather related to practice. For example, differences in the quality of pretend animal performances were evident between children who did it less frequently versus those who did it more, regardless of age. Some children very seldom imitated or pretended to be animals. Chris, Adrienne, Dimitri, Irvin, Toby, and Reuben were among those showing low levels of animal imitation or animal pretend play in class, but they did not show less interest in animals than other children. Frequent pretenders included Drew, Dawn, and Yasmin. We have already seen a plenitude of creaturely enactments by them. These frequent pretenders suggest developmental advantages from pretending to be animals such as exploring the meaning of animal behavior, as when Drew imitated the turtle wiping its paw across its face, an action he repeated several times, giving it the words, "I don't want it." Another gain for those children who avidly engage in embodying animals may be a generously bestowed identification with them, as with Dawn, who was the only child observed to imitate all the animals brought to class. We saw Yasmin's long imitation/"dialogue" sequence with the doves. As noted already, being a cat was her other most constant role; in the following, she adorned herself for it:

> Katra helps Yasmin make a 6-inch masking tape cat tail. Katra asks, "Do you need a bigger tail?" Yasmin answers, "No." Yasmin tells Katra that "cats have 'em, you know, those things that scratch with claws." Attaching her tape "claws" by the bathroom, Yasmin tells Reuben, "I'm a dog. No, a cat." She has lines of tape spanning from her nose to her cheeks for whiskers, and is busy mounting little pieces on her toes and fingers. Katra helps by supplying pieces of tape, which Yasmin cuts with scissors. Yasmin: "Once, my grandma, she has a kitty, and I'm going to visit her, and . . . she has . . . [we] went to visit her and she has a cat, and ah it scratched me and that's its claws doing it. Sometimes it puts out its claws when it's playing 'n it accidentally scratches you."

Her observation and experience with a "real" cat informed the ways Yasmin modified her own body for the role of a cat, suggesting another dimension of development enhanced by pretend: the positive motivation to seek and enact knowledge of animals.

More broadly, on the basis of my argument in this book, translating the shape of the animal's body into one's own, the key continuity, may extend well beyond childhood and provide a life-long route to understanding animals. Some suggestive evidence for life-long imitation of animals comes from cultures in closer contact to, and dependence upon, the animal world than our modern urban one. Consider such examples as the old Kwakiutl ceremonies (recorded by the ethnographic photographer Edward Curtis in the 1916 film *In the Land of the War Canoes)*, in which animals are vividly enacted by masked dancers. Traditional Asian martial arts derived from a system of "animal forms" whose embodiment was primarily an "internal work"; later these became the external forms of snake, crane, monkey, tiger and so on that characterize the versatile forms of self defense (Loren, 2001). Or consider the unusual imitative talents of one member of the Bushman group in the ethnographic film, *The Hunters*. The role of a bodily felt dimension of the animal is highlighted in this account of Bushman hunters by the anthropologist Guenther:

> . . . the hunters would attune themselves spiritually to one animal species or another, and in the process, attempt to gather whatever presentiments they could about the impending hunt: the animals they might encounter, the direction they could come from, the likely dangers, the duration of the hunt. These presentiments . . . activated the hunter's entire body; they were felt at his ribs, his back, his calves, his face and eyes. His body would be astir with the 'antelope sensation,' at places on his body corresponding with those of the antelope's. (Guenter, 1988, p. 199, quoted in Serpell, 2000)

These cultures seem to have supported a specialization in animal imitation. While one can readily identify many hunter-gatherer cultures where identification with animals is documented, I know of no compilation of cross-cultural evidence for imitation of animals. But the practice was no doubt common. For example, Fernandez (1986) reported pretend animal play in the Fang of Africa, and among children in the Asturian region of northern Spain. There is wide-open ground to explore here. One fruitful avenue may be to look at culturally elaborated successful human-animal performances. We could study systems in which humans interact with animals such as dogs or horses (Hearne, 1986; Irvine, 2004; Millot and Filiatre, 1986; Mitchell, 1987a; Shapiro, 1989; Sanders, 1993a, 1999; Brandt, 2004), cats (Alger and Alger, 1997; Turner & Rieger, 2001), old world primates (Strum, 1987; Goodall, 1990), new world monkeys (Cormier, 2000) and other primates (Fuentes & Wolfe, 2002), bears (Burghardt, 1992), elephants (Hart, 1994; Hart & Sundar, 2000) and other species. For example, in a study of people with intimate knowledge of wild black bears (biologists, trackers, bow hunters, and hinterland old-timers), graduate student Ann Russell and I found that the bear experts revealed elements of overt or implicit bodily translation in how they understood bear behavior (Myers and Russell, 2004).

Speculating further, we should consider the possibility that animal-role pretend play emerged because of the selective advantage it afforded early humans. Shepard (1996), attempting to ground human cognition in the interspecies context of our evolution, comes close to this claim in his explanation of the role of such play in development. Anticipating a prey's or predator's movements would benefit from the same abilities as pretend, including kinesthetic-visual matching, and thus might have been selected for in evolution (Mitchell, 1994). But if this is true, we should expect the same result in the case of any predator, as well as their prey, who would gain by understanding the movements of the predator. It does seem that there is a behavioral-ecology premium on reading others' motions, and it might form part of a gross cross-mammalian choreography. Whether such a universally intelligible predator/prey dance exists, how far it extends, and whether other animals use visual-kinesthetic mapping and imitation are questions beyond the present scope. Supposing it is true even minimally, then early humans would have built upon a deep mammalian legacy. But the proclivity for pretend that has been built upon it drew on humans' sophisticated mirror neuron system, plus emerging intra-human higher-order intentionality, self-consciousness, and later on linguistic abilities. These capacities, however, must have emerged in our ancestors' highly complex social groups.[15] If all these speculations were true, then on evolutionary grounds we might expect the animal-imitative bent of the human psyche to have affected cultures universally.

If there are universal roots to this fundamental route to understanding animals, we should expect it to be expressed even in cultures that seem biased against it, such as our own. The children in this study can attest to its presence early in life, and indeed, there are examples of concerted efforts in our own culture to understand animals in their own terms that deserve attention. Clinton Sanders and Arnold Arluke (1993; 1996) suggest sociologists and others should explore this area, taking their cues from those who work and live closely with animals. They go on to say people can go much further to "learn to speak in the animal idiom" with animals by exploring the "least human role," reproducing as much as possible the animals' own repertoire of movements and sounds in context (Sanders & Arluke, 1993, p. 383). An outstanding example is that of Kenneth Shapiro (1985, 1989), who used a pioneering method to understand the subjectivity of his dog, Sabaka. It is worth examining for its advanced use of the kind of the bodily translation we have seen children do. He first considered how social constructions of dogs—popular and scientific—affected his preconceptions, and he became "a historian of the individual animal . . . under study." The principal method, however, was to recover meanings implicit in the dog's activity through "kinesthetic empathy" in which the investigator "attempts directly to sense or empathize with the motor intention or attitude or project of the animal" (1989, p. 185). Combined, these three methods provided interesting insights. Sabaka "is embedded in a lived rather than an objective space. It is a space shaped and oriented by his own position, interests, and projects." Shapiro concluded that space is fundamental to Sabaka in the way that time may be for humans: "He can just lie there for hours because he is not primarily waiting, he is not primarily anticipating, he is not thinking in our sense; he is already arrived, he is at home" (p. 189). A third central concern of Sabaka's is his relationship to Shapiro. After Shapiro reprimanded the dog, he reflected, "I directly sense his searching for my bodily attitude to him. He is, as it were, studying my kinesthetics." (p. 190).

Shapiro's bodily empathic attitude has much in common with animate relatedness and its elaboration through imitation and pretend play. Bodily empathy involves "the meaningful actual or virtual imitation or enactment of bodily moves" (Shapiro, 1989, p. 191). Its potentials with nonhuman animals demand sensitivity to a shared "prelinguistic region where meaning is and remains implicit, embedded, and more consistently enacted directly" (p. 192). Self and other are not assumed to be originally isolated, a conception that could only arise with linguistic distinctions. And this process does not necessarily mean a more limited access to the other's subjectivity than that available though explicit means, since "the comportment through which an animal's intention . . . is embodied is less deceitful, more visible, and therefore more directly inhabitable by us" (p. 192). Shapiro was describing a disciplined phenomenology of visual-kinesthetic matching.

What might we achieve by stretching our human powers of understanding, including not just the cognitive and historical but also the bodily empathic? Children do something quite like Shapiro's (1985, 1989) practice spontaneously, and the knowledge of the other creature which it provides is brought into consciousness via pretend play and imitation. Noske (1989) noted with regret that authentic feral children were not studied for what they might have known about their animal "foster parents." I would suggest that "principle investigators" in future ethological studies might best begin their research in infancy, with parents who nurture their relations to animals in addition to their normal human attachments. Having spent the period of greatest behavioral plasticity in a mixed species community, such individuals might, much later and upon further disciplined study, come to unanticipated insights into animal behavior.

Conclusion

On the most general level, continuity between preverbal and verbal experience has very broad relevance. It reinforces a deep understanding of the creative process and reframes the problem of knowing and understanding other subjectivities—human and otherwise. The dynamic whereby continuity can be blocked sheds new light on development and socialization, which we will explore in the next chapter. My findings have implications for our collective self-understanding, including as it is formalized in psychological theories. Perhaps, we should not be too proud of the things we achieve uniquely as humans, for our creative abilities depend on the foundation we share with many other species. Although we can never become other than human, what makes us essentially human is what we have *in common* with other creatures. Important values are at stake in our relations to nonhuman species as well as to our own human animal bodies. How these values are played out in the culture of the American preschool is the subject that occupies us next.

VII

The Animal in the Cultural Context of Development

This is the age of cultural diversity—many now appreciate how each culture's beliefs and institutions shape its members' views of the world. And animals are clearly part of those cultural worlds; the variability in how animals are used, regarded, and symbolized across cultures is vast. In this chapter, however, I suggest that the variability in the meanings of animals (at least for young children) is not merely the result of arbitrary cultural invention. Instead, its patterns reflect the early developmental potency of core animate relatedness. Culture shapes important aspects of mind and self. But just as we discovered that animal-role pretend play fosters *continuity* between human self and animal other and between body and self-reflective awareness, so, too, do children's relations with animals reveal important dynamics in the realms of morality, cognition, and identity. Our interest here will be in continuity of three aspects of the self: *continuity of concern* for other living animals; *continuity of interest* in understanding them; and *continuity of community* between self and animal other. The cultural context of childhood has much to do with the realization of these potentials, but such achievement happens only to the extent the culture *works with* the patterns of connection already operating on the animate level.

So strong is the consensus about the force of culture, however, that this proposal may appear quite radical. Admittedly, people appropriate animals in symbol and flesh in so many ways and to so many ends as to give reason to believe that the meanings of animals *are* wholly social constructions. Consider the social historian Keith Tester's (1991) look at the history of the animal rights movement. It has roots, he shows, in the "invention" of animal rights in the nineteenth century through the animal rights activist Henry Salt's juxtaposition of humans' similarity to animals with humans' perfectibility. These principles made it possible to believe in a natural source of obligations to animals. But Tester believes the invented nature of these concepts was systematically obscured. Their proponents ignored the sea of evidence of human cruelty, and they fetishized "rights." In truth, he writes, "animals are only made the site of moral worries to the extent that they are useful in establishing social definitions of the properly human" (1991, p. 195), and the task of reading meaning into the "blank page" of animals' pain "takes skill, know-how and subjectivity ... abilities which only fully social human individuals are said to possess" (p. 197). Thus, we are to believe, adult humans seamlessly construct all meanings of animals; and children, lacking the requisite subjectivity, passively absorb them.

In developmental studies, a culture-centered approach akin to Tester's is familiar. It assumes culture makes the child. The mechanism, socialization, is the reproduction of occupants of social roles and statuses, of believers and speakers of the native discourses. Certainly, all the adults in the children's lives—and the children themselves—are immersed in cultural networks of belief and practice. But it is not just that morality, cognition, and identity cannot be complete without the cultural context; the claim being advanced is that culture mainly determines them.

To accept such a one-way model of socialization, however, ignores children's influence on socializers and on each other, not to mention any deeply entrenched or inherent dynamics of psychological development. More immediate doubts are raised by evidence presented here of real interaction with animals, which proceeds with intricate accommodation to the animals. Contra Tester, far from not "possessing subjectivity," even infants have the capacities to form a social sense of self. Young children retain and flexibly employ these same core abilities with other species. We saw how pretend play confirms this. Animals' living subjective presence makes them powerful symbols for parallel matters in the child's own life—symbolic in a sense both psychologically richer *and* more determinate than cultural constructionist studies typically detect. These patterns hardly paint a picture of one-way socialization in which childhood is a blank slate or primitive animal body to be shaped and formed by culture (cf. Gendlin, 1987). Indeed, other-than-human creatures themselves turn out to be important in our becoming who we are.

The relations of language, cultural messages, feelings in the body, and individual subjectivity in development are complex. We can take as a clue the *continuity* of connection-within-difference that the child experiences by pretending. Rather than assuming that the preverbal and self-reflective selves are necessarily at odds, we found evidence for a particular dynamics of continuity and discontinuity. In this chapter, I apply these insights and locate similar patterns in different domains—patterns, that is, whereby some cultural practices promote or harmonize with an aspect of the individual's unfolding subjective experience and others that thwart or distort it. In this search for wider implications, we will look in three domains—moral development, cognition, and socialization—for conditions of continuity in experience.

The Animal in Moral Development

We have seen many examples of young children's concern for animals' wellbeing. It would be odd to claim that this concern arises from cultural messages, for in fact nursery schools are pervaded by *conflicting* moral messages about animals. We will look at several facets of this, and then come back to the events that children themselves react to in ways that are nascently moral. The importance of the patterns we find can be seen in light of several perspectives on moral development. These patterns indicate the conditions that allow *continuity of concern* for animals.

If children do absorb moral messages in adult-designed cultural media aimed at them, there is no dearth of input. Children's literature and cartoons are full of animals participating in morally loaded narratives.[1] The writer Margaret Blount (1974) noted several varieties of morality in children's animal tales, including didactic animals whose natural behavior is used to make a moral point; instructively amoral characters like Brer Rabbit; "people-with-animal-heads" enacting typical social situations; and animals used satirically to show the human race to itself, as in *Gulliver's Travels*.

Besides the various such moral animal messages in books, the nursery school I observed was not isolated from the wider culture's conflicts over the moral status of animals, as data from my videotaped conversations and other observations showed.

> Joe: "Can you make him [the monkey] talk?" Ms. Dean: "Do you think I can make him do anything he doesn't want to do?" Several kids answer: "No." Ms. Dean: "How come?" Joe: "Because he has his own rights."

Animals' rights came up again with a species at the opposite end of the anthropomorphism continuum:

> Ms. Dean: "[Would you] squish a spider in your house?" The children respond, "No." Ms. Dean: "No, how come?" Solly: "Because it has to have its freedom."

In both these examples, the questions posed by Ms. Dean had a rhetorical and highly suggestive tone, making it clear what answer was expected. In turn, their answers had a rote quality—the very picture of inculcation.

Indeed, Mrs. Ray provided strong indoctrination of human rights to the classroom, indirectly providing the opportunity for children to extend "rights" to animals. But her same principle worked in an opposite direction as well: In another instance, she related how people in other cultures eat snake, monkey, and turtle meats. Implicitly, tolerance and the interests of people can take precedence over extension of "rights" to all species.

Another tradition countervailing that of animal rights is the motif of ecosystem as impersonal economy. Pests like bugs fit well in this frame, and the teachers sometimes tolerated ill-treatment of them, as once when Mindy, Rueben and Dawn were at the classroom's side door to the outside:

> On the floor, Dawn says: "Uh-oh, a bug's coming." They look at it together. Reuben tells it, "Get out, little bug," and he pushes it under the door. As they look for more bugs they inch their way outside. Mindy says, "Here's one," and she reaches out. Ms. Tanner brings them back inside. Mindy continues to stand and look out, sights more bugs, steps on them, and says, "That one's dead."

Intruding flies or collected bugs—food for the toad—were excluded by the teacher from the compass of moral concern. Once the fate of a beetle was put up for a vote; eight children wanted it to be toad food, five wanted it left outside, and nine wanted it kept in a jar in the classroom. In the end, it stayed in a jar until it was dead. Food chains and science justified the suffering of some animals.

Although some bugs did not matter, others were worthy because of their beauty or usefulness to people. Mindy was about to squish an ant, but Sam intervened, insisting, "*No*, don't kill it, he's a *good*, he's a good insect." Thus had lessons about good-citizen bugs been internalized.

Of course, human meat-eating can also be assimilated to the nature-as-smorgasbord image. Once, a hunter talked to the class about his sport:

> A man comes in with an elk antler. He says his guide found it while they were out hunting deer and elk in Wyoming. He shows a magazine cover with a picture of an elk on it. Mrs. Ray asks him why they shoot elk. He replies, perhaps too fast, "Food." He tells what they do with an animal: They use the hide for a blanket and cut up the rest for meat. He asks the kids, "Do you eat meat? Do you eat hamburgers?" Reuben nods, smiles open-mouthed and starts screaming quietly and crawls excitedly off the rug. The man adds that meat comes from cows and chickens. Mrs. Ray says that a long time ago everybody got their meat from animals by hunting, and some people still do, but many prefer to get it at the supermarket.

Killing animals and meat eating is officially okay, even though a deer is a much more immediate other than a bug.

But the children also learned the other side of the issue:

> Mrs. Ray says that when she grew up, her mother didn't let her eat pig meat, illustrating that "Some people are not allowed to eat certain foods. . . . And some people eat no meat at all." Kevin: "They're vegetarian."

Some children knew such people, such as Laura's uncle. But two-thirds of the parents said meat eating had not been raised as an issue or that it had but there was no disagreement. They conveyed acceptance of meat and justified the choice with nutritional and ecological reasons. None of the parents actively advocated vegetarianism to their children, though several said they would allow the children to make their own choice when older. Shortly, we will look at the children who *did* have reservations about meat, but what is clear from all these mixed inputs is that simple internalization could not explain the concern children felt for animals' welfare. The culture speaks in many conflicting voices about the issue, and the children are exposed to all of them.

To the contrary of the cultural absorption hypothesis, the children expressed moral sensitivity to harm, sometimes in contradiction to adults' attempts to directly construct the children's reactions. One series of such events began to unfold as the turtle presenter told about turtle reproduction:

> Mr. Lloyd: "They lay [their eggs] in the sand and then they forget about them." Billy: "Why?" Mr. Lloyd: "They never—they never see their babies. That's the way reptiles are. Turtles are reptiles and they do not take care of their babies." Billy: "Do the babies die?" Mr. Lloyd: "Some—a lot of the babies die. Because so many things eat them and they've nobody to take care of them. See when you're born, your mommy and your daddy take care of you. A little turtle doesn't have anybody. So the turtle gets eaten by other animals and that's important too because if all the baby turtles that hatched out of eggs lived, we'd have far too many baby turtles, so some of them have to die to feed other animals and that's part of what we call the food chain. Everybody in the wild kind of eats everybody else. But a few of them survive. This [adult] one survived, and this [baby] one will survive."

This was clearly a challenging concept for the children. Being eaten violates core self in every aspect; in addition, here it was reported happening to vulnerable young creatures. This convergence of factors made the baby turtle's fate a vivid symbol for the children's core concerns. The teacher stepped in to try to soften the blow:

Mrs. Ray: "I had a question that I wanted to know. If they had many many many eggs that means that they don't expect all of them to live." Mr. Lloyd: "That's right." Mrs. Ray: "You know what? Some big animals have only one baby, and they're the kind of animal that take care of their young, but when an animal has many many many many babies like a mosquito or like an ant or like a bee, they don't take care of them, and some of them are *meant* to be food for other animals. Wow, that's wonderful to know."

Nonetheless, the sight of *this* individual baby turtle was impressive to the children, *it* had received much attention from a caregiver, and it *would* survive. Despite the teacher's help, the baby turtles still carried a large symbolic load for the children, as reflected in later behavior. Particularly, several children, including Mindy, Katra, and Billy, told their parents about the baby turtle. Only core-animacy issues such as this were so common in these child-parent conversations:

Abeo: And you know what, um . . . um, the turtle has a baby and the mom was still at home, was still at home and the raccoon came into the yard, into the owner's yard, and ate up ten babies.

Mother: *Really?* Who told you this story?

Abeo: The owner.

Joe also discussed the turtle with his mother. He had been attentive during the class discussion, and the teacher's rationalization evidently stuck with him, although his intonation in this passage was a blend of curiosity and dismay:

Mother: So then you were going tell me about the turtle and the ma . . . baby, the baby turtle and the mother turtle.

Joe: There's no mother. There's—the turtle's name was Flattop, because he had a flat shell. And Flattop's baby . . . survived, but some of the other babies had to be eaten by other animals.

Mrs. Ray's explanation of the babies' deaths seemed to calm Joe, but the supposed necessity of the deaths was prominent and bothersome. In a later discussion:

Mother: You told me that some of the babies, that there were some other babies but they died?

Joe: Don't—I don't want to talk about that.

Mother: You don't want to talk about it? . . . How come?

Joe: 'Cause it makes me sad.

Mother: *Oh,* the other day I asked you if it makes you sad, and you said "No." Do you remember what you said? I said, "Why wasn't it sad?"— Remember what you said?

Joe: Yeah, but now it *is* sad.

Mother: Now it is sad. Yeah, I can understand why it's sad.

Joe: Don't—don't talk about it.

Mother: Well, I just wanted to ask you not about it being sad, but when you *weren't* sad about it, you told me why you weren't sad. You said it wasn't sad because, why? Do you remember that? You taught me something . . . I remember you said, "It isn't sad because it's part of life." I thought that was interesting . . . that you said that.

Joe: Well, now it is, it *is* sad.

Mother: I see. Okay, well, let's not talk about it then.

The teacher's reconstrual of the animals' deaths had at first been repeated by Joe, but it appears now that it only superficially buffered the sense of loss symbolized by the baby turtles' deaths. In this second talk with his mother, Joe was overwhelmed and clearly could not mitigate his feelings with the teacher's words.

This set of examples reveals a definite contribution from the child, which bears the familiar mark of core-relatedness: concern about self-other continuity and the symbolization of core issues that are personally meaningful to the child. This was even clearer when the animal involved was known personally. Indeed, although nothing threatened Snowflake directly, threats to the guinea pig were discussed. One day, Drew wanted to know why the animals were called "guinea pigs." I looked through a book with him and we found an explanation, but the passage also mentioned that people in Peru eat guinea pigs. He said little but seemed visibly disturbed. Later in the year, when the ferrets visited, several children guessed that they were carnivores. But this took on a concrete meaning:

Mr. Myers: "Today I did something and I didn't think what I was doing, but Ms. Collins pointed it out afterwards. I took that ferret carrier with the ferret in it and I set it next to Snowflake's cage, to put it out of the way for a while . . ." Ms. Collins: "I said 'I bet that guinea pig's going crazy.'" Mr. Myers: "And Snowflake was hiding under newspapers." Ms. Collins: "He smelled the ferret." Mr. Myers: "And in the wild . . . In the wild the ferret might be something that would eat a guinea pig . . ." Mrs. Ray broke in immediately: "So guess what, in this room we would not let that ferret get next to our guinea pig. We would protect Snowflake, right?"

This incident was reported at home by Drew:

Drew, whispering: 'Cept those kind of animals do eat guineas.

Mother: They eat *guineas*? Uh, so did you, what'd ya do, keep the guinea covered up?

Drew: No, we didn't put it near the guinea.

Given Drew's response to this event, one might guess that people eating guinea pigs was an *entirely* foreign idea. Drew's sense of self existed in a connection with guinea pigs that would never conceive such an act.

Nascent moral feelings are strongest when several factors emphasize the animate needs of the animal, as in the case of pets. Pets' moral status is over-determined for children, but not only because of cultural meanings. Granted, pets are assimilated to the family and treated as training ground for responsibility taking and being gentle. And caring for them is gender-role consistent for girls and not gender-role discordant for boys (Melson & Fogel, 1988). But deeper relational factors are more important.

Pets fit into two universal features of young children's experience that the psychologists Carol Gilligan and Grant Wiggins (1987) say constitute the seeds of moral development. One universal is that the child is relatively powerless compared to his or her caretakers. This experience is the root for later concerns about independence, equality, and the injunction not to treat others unfairly—in other words, for an orientation toward justice. Simultaneously, the child is also dependent on and attached emotionally to his or her parents. This can generalize to a care orientation centered on responding to need, preventing harm, and the injunction not to turn away or abandon another. Gilligan and Wiggins's framework applies to pets in a particularly salient way. With a pet animal, the child is in the parental position in both respects. The child may be more powerful than the animal, and it is dependent on her or him. In this circumstance, the child's own emerging experiences of justice and care moralities may readily generalize to the child's sense of moral obligation toward the pet.

Consider, for example, the time Mrs. Ray trimmed Snowflake's claws. The day before, she prepared the class by telling them that the guinea pig would not like being held tightly but the operation was really just like cutting our fingernails, which does not hurt. The children were very interested. Ivy was clearly worried, and received reassurance. The next day:

> Mrs. Ray begins by saying that guinea pig will not like it. She holds its front paw and it struggles and whines. "Hey, wait," she says to it. The children smile. She tells it to be quiet, and notes it didn't understand her words. She compares the whole thing to taking a baby to the doctor.... "It's important to let the guinea pig know that we aren't going to hurt it," so she'll just clip one today so it won't get upset.... One claw is clipped; and then three more.... Mrs. Ray: "Nobody really likes getting hurt."... As she clips more the children crowd in to see. Ivy is very concerned and says out loud: "It won't hurt; it'll only take a second."

The teacher's response to the children's concern was adept. She helped them assume the caretaker's morally active position in a relationship like one in which they were usually the patient. Ivy overtly identified with the caring role.

In the examples of the baby turtles, the guinea pig-ferret issue, and the guinea pig claw-trimming, adults responded very carefully to soften the emotional impact on the children. But they are not just shaping the children's morality in these cases; they are responding as they feel they must to respect and support the morality implicit in the sense of connection the children express toward the animals involved. Mrs. Ray's analogies helped the children contain their concerns—and sometimes failed to help, as in Joe's case, discussed previously. The children are working though these early moral issues in their own terms, but they are not doing so from an arbitrary base, including any constituted only by culture.

Perhaps it is not surprising that children have the early moral responsiveness to animals we have observed. A critic might argue that this is because such values are common in the American middle class, and are taught by parents. Evidence for this view is summarized by Ascione (2005, pp. 76–77), based on the extensive naturalistic observations of young children and their parents by Zahn-Waxler and colleagues (Zahn-Waxler & Smith, 1992; Zahn-Waxler et al., 1992). The researchers found that certain kinds of parental responses to a child's causing of distress in another (including examples with animals) were associated with the children's showing more empathy and prosocial behaviors.

I do not want to deny the force of parental example, prohibition, rules, encouraging of perspective taking, and other important ways of teaching consideration of animals and other humans. There are, however, two problems with the argument that these are the only roots of the moral-emotional responses I observed. First, the sample in my study was not uniformly American nor middle class; the parents came from various countries (see the list in the appendix) to the affiliated university. And some children were from the neighborhood, attending on scholarship. Secondly, but more importantly, other studies suggest concern for animals occurs in children across cultures. Bexell (2005) has found that both U.S. and Chinese four-year-olds understand what is harmful to animals, what animals need if in distress, and the positive feelings helping would engender. Röver (1996, cited in Nevers et al., 1997) found that German children as young as six years defended animals'"interests" on the basis of their being living things. The developmental psychologist Peter Kahn (1999) and colleagues have studied moral reasoning regarding nature by children in urban and hinterland Amazonia (Brazil); in Portugal; and in poor African American neighborhoods in Houston, Texas. Using structural-developmental interview techniques, they identified the forms of reasoning children used to justify judgments of the rightness or wrongness of acts such as polluting a waterway. Kahn reports that in each culture over 89 percent of children cared that harm to animals (birds, specifically) would result from pollution. Substantial majorities of children cited harm to animals as a justification for why they judged acts of pollution to be wrong (1999, chs. 6–10; p. 188).

More evidence corroborating the universal importance of harm to animals and the links between early empathic feelings and morality also comes from a very different theoretical point of view than that of Kahn. Relativistically inclined cultural psychologists Richard Shweder, Monamohan Mahapatra, and Joan Miller (1987) declared that "the abstract principle of harm" (p. 19) is one of a few mandatory features of any rationally appealing code of morality. Indeed they found that "kicking a harmless animal" was one of only a few items that Oriya (Indian) and American five- to seven-year-olds agree is wrong (p. 61).

Core relatedness may underlie this apparently universal constraint, which even these vying developmental paradigms acknowledge. The American psychologist Jerome Kagan (1984, 1986) has pointed to the emergence of morality around age two, and noted, "The capacity for empathy is inherent in children. . . . Since WWI, American psychologists have declared you've got to teach children morality. We use the term psychopath, referring to a person who never learned a moral sense. *But one can only lose a moral sense*" (1986, pp. 87–88; emphasis added). A sense of morality itself is an expectable outcome of a normal early childhood, and it appears to extend to animals.

I suggest that discontinuities in concern must be the result of some interfering factor, causing a loss, in Kagan's terms. Intriguing evidence comes from the children's attitudes about eating meat. According to the parent surveys, two children did not like meat because of how it tastes. Four children had asked for information and three of these were hesitant to eat meat once they had learned where it came from: Mindy, Yasmin, and Joe. Mindy said, "Yuck, I don't want to eat cow meat anymore." Joe once told his mother he did not like to eat dead animals. Thus, despite the parental acceptance of meat eating, there was some resistance to it, especially when the origin of the meat was clear. One reason may be disgust, but another is probably the children's recognition that killing animals violates the valued animate properties of the other:

> Cassia, Ivy, Adrienne discuss meat eating at the game table. Cassia: "Do you know people eat animals?" Ivy: "And animals eat people." Cassia: "And animals eat animals." Adrienne: "*You* eat animals!"

The children felt conflicts over eating meat; although this may be un-avoidable, it may also signal the loss of continuity of concern. The abstract quality of these three girls' talk should not be missed; the issue feels somewhat vague to them. Indeed, they have no contact with the reality discussed. The nursery school culture helps keep it out of the way; for example, children's books idealize farm life.

Not only do children's media sanitize meat production, so does the larger society. Serpell (1986) suggested that humans' empathic responses to animals require that people distance themselves psychologically when they exploit animals. Society thus provides means to reduce the conflict between emotions of connection to animals and reactions to harm linked with meat eating. Agnew (1998) advanced a theory to explain criminal abuse of ani-mals—a situation that highlights the same sort of distancing, only in extreme individual behavior. Specifically, Agnew drew on the social psychologist Albert Bandura's (1990, 1999) theory of moral disengagement. Bandura suggested that several mechanisms may be at work when inhumanities are perpetrated: 1) mentally reconstruing the actions as good by moral justification, drawing advantageous comparisons, and euphemistic labeling of harmful conduct; 2) minimizing, displacing, or denying personal responsibility; 3) disregarding or distorting harmful consequences; and 4) marginalizing the victims by blam-ing or dehumanizing them. Psychologist Scott Plous (1993) hypothesized similar factors in the case of general acceptance toward animal exploitation: conflict reduction, animals as an out-group, detachment, concealing the harm, misrepresentation, and shifting the blame.

These psychic mechanisms obscure or misrepresent exploitation, thus relieving the discomfort we might otherwise feel. The net effect is what psy-chologists Susan Opotow and Leah Weiss (2000) term moral exclusion. These mechanisms appear to be ambient in our culture, as suggested by some scholars[2] and as shown by empirical research testing a model based on Agnew's and Bandura's theories by Vollum and colleagues (2004). Studying a context where a premium is placed on the ability to distance, Melson (2001) interviewed youth and parents involved in 4-H about how they "disattach" from animals they care for but raise specifically to be sold for meat. These children's words revealingly describe the distancing mechanisms employed (Melson 2001, p. 69). The children in my classroom, however, had not acquired—or were in the course of acquiring—these methods that adults use to reduce the dissonance of harm to animals.

This particular kind of cultural acquisition is not arbitrary but plays a particular function in development. In a study about children's identification of the self with a variety of animals (Myers, 2002), I found that children declined to identify with two animals, a cow and a lamb, which occupy the status of exploited in our society. Their reasons for repudiating (often disdainfully) these animals related to our use of them for food. Tellingly, the youngest group (4 to 5 years) was more positive than the older groups (10 to 11, and 17 to 18 years), suggesting the acquisition of a distanced psychology by the older children.

Children's concern and unconcern about animals thus reveals the inherent and self-organizing psychological dynamics of moral functioning. It does so more vividly than does their moral development toward other humans, because in the case of animals the culture encourages a discontinuity—or, at best, a complexity that is hard to navigate with moral sensibilities intact. If moral dilemmas are to be optimally resolved, then the fundamental role of core relatedness must be acknowledged and means of continuity fostered.[3]

The entire mixture of cultural messages places animals at the center of a complicated set of moral sentiments. We are tied to animals by bonds of social relating, emotion, and by the ways (whether truly necessary or not) they serve our needs. For the young child, the emotional bonds are strong. Add to that how the animal can symbolize the self's vulnerabilities, as well as the self's needs for self-perpetuation, defense, self-assertion, coherence and so on. With such various pulls, maintaining a continuity of concern is challenging.

A reader interested in application might reasonably ask at this point what the practical implications of this perspective are. Where possible, the real conflicts posed by exploitation should be removed by ceasing the exploitative activities. Otherwise—or rather in addition, for we shall probably never escape conflicts between our and animals' interests—what can be done is to acknowledge and embrace the conflicts and sustain an open but critical dialog about our use of animals. Moreover, we should reflect on and own our own vulnerable connectedness. This means acceptance of our mortality and physical and psychological frailties, thus emphasizing our kinship with other beings, and our fallible morality. It also certainly means helping children appreciate animals' needs through observation, interaction, nurture, and reflection.

The Animal in Cognitive Development

Animals are relevant for many concerns of cognitive development, including topics I have touched on such as the child's understanding of causality, mind, biological categories, and social roles. But what about the unique intersection of the child's concepts and experience of animate relatedness? In particular, how do we understand a child's *continuity of interest* in the subjective worlds of other species?

The answer necessarily blends cognitive, affective, and evaluative elements, as we will see here in examining children's sense of wonder and what adults can do to encourage (and not discourage) it. I will begin by revisiting the classroom and some of the teacher's most effective practices. We will also consider the impact on conceptual development of cultural practices and representations featuring animals as a center of interest. Since cognitive development advances when second-order representations of experience are available (i.e., how we help children to think about their experiences), a key question is, What forms of representation best facilitate the sense of connection? Finally, I will speculate that intelligence in relation to the natural world, and to animals in particular, constitutes a special kind of cognitive-affective skill that we might better understand and foster.

One of the hallmarks of children's interactions with an optimally discrepant animal is the emotion of wonder. Animals present ambiguous and challenging properties for children to interact with and understand. To the young child, they must appear as beings with somewhat mysterious inner qualities, and as frustrating but also gratifying interactants. Perhaps Toby best expressed the feeling the time he exclaimed he was "amazed" by "you funny birds." Behavior or physical appearance can spark wonder:

> Ms. Collins brings out the other ferret, which is a lighter color. Chris: "He's *different*."
>
> Ms. Collins: "Yeah, see he's a different color." Dawn: "Yeah, that's what I was saying . . . Hey, but they are two different eye colors."

Toby exemplified the attitude of wonder. Consider some of his remarks about the turtle:

> "I, I got a chance to touch his shell. . . . That feels so funny. . . . I just touched, I got to feel one of his claws. . . . Hey, do ya wanta feel his shell?" Toby touches the turtle, pulls his hand away very quickly. . . . "Hey, this feels very funny, feel it. Feel this part right there. . . . Hey, look-it, he has a tail! Tail! Can you believe it? There's his tail." He puts his hand by the turtle, pointing. He, Rosa, and Mindy look closely. Toby: "I didn't know a turtle has a tail." Toby lies on his stomach, looking closely at the turtle.

In this case, the adults simply listened and helped him sustain safe interactions without overshadowing the animal with their own input. Toby showed he had benefited from such opportunities when he stopped Mindy from chasing pigeons:

Mindy moves toward them a step or two, and suggests they chase or scare them. Toby, a bit behind her, reaches forward, grabs her coat, and says, "No, let's just watch."

Toby had learned to restrain even Mindy's urge to provoke an animal's reaction, valuing more the chance to observe.

The teacher supported this attitude by encouraging appreciation. She did so by modeling, near the end of the tarantula visit:

Mrs. Ray raises her hand to talk: "I thought they were ugly, and I thought they were scary, and I thought they were frightening, and I thought they felt wonderful, and I liked them after I knew them, so: another animal that I didn't know about at first, and when I knew it, I really liked it."

Other times, she directly encouraged the children to observe:

Joe continues to look at the monkey more closely: "Hey, he got three fingers and um, one thumb." Mrs. Ray: "Look carefully Joe, look carefully." Joe and Dawn continue close inspection of feet, hands, fingers. Joe: "One thumb, one thumb—oh, that's his pinkie?"

Less directly but with equal effect, the teachers used questions:

Cassia shows Ms. Tanner what the visiting rabbit was doing: "This is what he was doing"—she puts her tongue out and makes a lapping noise, then lifts her foot up. "He was licking his shoe—yuk!" Ms. Tanner: "Does he have shoes?"

This got the children to look at its feet again. Open-ended questions, on the other hand, do not verbally select a focus of the child's attention. Another practice was offering information about animals that highlighted the discrepancy between expectation and actuality. The tarantulas had a number of surprising features:

Mr. Dean: "Who thinks they have more than three eyes?" Toby exclaims: "Three eyes!?" He bends over to look with surprise into Billy's face.

Its ability to molt was another new thing:

Ms. Dean: "They have a skeleton on their outside, and what they do, is they actually walk right out of their skeleton. Now this [showing an old exoskeleton] is from this guy. . . . That's a spider skeleton." Billy: "He just walks out of his old skin?"

Stories about animal behavior also had the capacity to reveal the divergent subjective world of the animal:

Mr. Lloyd: "One winter . . . my wife was making a sweater. . . . And this turtle thought that that yarn was a worm, it was green, and it went over and it started to eat the end of the piece of yarn. And when we found him he had eaten over ten feet—that's almost as long as this wall—of yarn. We had to carefully pull it out again, because if it would have continued to eat, it would have eaten about a hundred feet. And it wasn't bothered by the fact it didn't taste it."

Several children mentioned this story to parents later; the power of narrative in human cognition is widely recognized (Bruner, 1986) and of course applies to experiences with animals.

Given some near-at-hand animals, children express their interest in various ways: Joe, for example, expressed his interest in his ability to focus on animals, ask questions, and spin ideas about them; Toby, in his intense desire to watch animals without disturbing them and his concern for their autonomy; Yasmin, in her vivid bodily identifications; Drew, in wanting to see what unconfined animals do; Ivy, in her closely attuned nurturant attitude; and Solly, in his style of observing closely and quietly. For each, cognitive and affective factors enhanced each other, but an adult would have to be quite attentive to the individual's style to best promote and expand it.

What larger cultural factors or attitudes affect this developmental potential? Some of our habitual attitudes to animals do not help. A list of possible candidates includes the belief that animals are okay for children but unimportant to serious adults; overly sentimental feelings toward pets, coupled with dismissal of animals we exploit and indifference toward other wild species; utter skepticism about attribution of subjective states to animals; insistence on clinical sterility in talking about the body and reproduction; and unreflective rejection of moral reactions to events in nature.

Some of our actual practices with animals objectify them or turn them into mere spectacles for detached observation and entertainment or crass curiosity. These include confining animals; training them to perform on command (especially for mere entertainment value); restricting their agency, innate species social groupings, interactivity, and access to chances to fulfill evolved-in environmental needs; reducing them to mere means (especially for nonessential human aims); and explaining them via reductionistic scientific doctrines to the exclusion of other ways of representing life processes. Each of these attitudes and practices prejudicially devalues some element of the child's (and adult's) total reaction to the animal world. Adolescents' and adults' awareness of the tendency to sentimentalize animals too often leads to off-hand or deliberate devaluation.

Alternative practices that honor a child's experience of animals can be occasions for creativity. Upon recently viewing a superb documentary of the lives of wild emperor penguins, for example, my young children reported they had not liked it. The reason turned out to be because of the number of deaths endured by the population. At first I found myself explaining this as "just how it is in nature." But upon reflection, I fetched two stuffed penguins and two other favorite animal puppets and suggested the girls design a ceremony to express these penguins' feelings over the film. With my help lighting a candle, they said their wishes for penguins, and grieved the loss of the ones in the film. They had been allowed to create a psychological space where their feelings—and the realities—could be maintained, a space where moral reflection was then possible.

There may be no great economic gain to be had by an appreciation of other species in their natural state, but they are arguably some of the most intriguing and complex phenomena on this planet, and non-economic values are clearly at stake.[4] Ironically, since animals are considered part of the child's domain, they are an area where children can be the relative experts. This is good, but we also need to build support and acceptance for animals' being a lifelong passion for more people. Several things can help. Observation, as encouraged by traditional natural history, stresses pattern detection and sympathy with the subject of study. In the school I observed, most of the teachers' talk about animals reflected a very respectful attitude and was pitched right at the children's level. While sentimentality is not helpful, there is a distinction between objectification and critical yet appreciative observation. Science lessons can strike this balance; one important movement is toward providing substitutes to animal dissection in schools, while also conveying the wonder of learning about animals' insides. Animals should not be something to be left behind as children become more focused on peer groups. Pioneered at the San Francisco Zoo, and now available at others, are career ladder programs that help adolescents maintain and increase their knowledge about and connection to animals and their identities as conservationists.

Continuity of interest is encouraged by respecting children's expression of wonder at animals and by helping them explore how the meanings they discover can be conveyed. This is the issue of second-order representations alluded to earlier. Finding ways to re-present animate relatedness on a higher-order symbolic level without distorting the experience is a challenge but also facilitates continuity. One medium is the body. In the preceding chapter, we saw that mimetic or theatrical representation of animals can be culturally supported. Teachers' appreciation of dance and other artistic expressions and of children's own idiosyncratic symbolic meanings fosters the conscious realization of connection. Part of the problem is that we may simply not have developed the vocabulary to articulate the feelings we have in relation to nature. In the process of piloting a study on adults' emotions in response to viewing zoo animals, we found we had to use phrases like "sense of special privilege" to offer people the right categories for their experience (Myers, Saunders & Birjulin, 2004).

A related problem is how we talk about animals so as to honor the interest children have. The children in my study used the word "real" with a special emphasis when they meant an actual, living animal, as opposed to a dead or artificial one. Abeo, her older sister Ifama, and their mother talked about chicks they had recently hatched at home:

> Mother: Abeo, do you like the chicks?
>
> Abeo: *Yes!* I *did.*
>
> Mother: How come?
>
> Abeo: Because! I got to pet one of them…
>
> Mother: Oh, Abeo's jumping up and down at the thought of the chicks! You really like the chicks then.
>
> Abeo: *Yes.*
>
> Mother: Is it because they're really nice and cuddly?
>
> Ifama: They're real.
>
> Mother: Because they're real.
>
> Abeo, interrupting: *Yeess!*

Real carried an affective load far beyond its dry logical meanings. Can this be merely a cultural construction? Postmodern critic Donna Haraway (1989) deconstructed cultural notions of "encounter" with wild nature, and John Berger (1980) said that modern experience makes it impossible to "centralize" animals' alterity. Yet, for young children, encountering living animals has a compelling, centralizing quality that shapes thought and culture.

Real animals interrupt easy anthropomorphism; they are familiar but also unknown. Too often, humans' (including social theorists') level of understanding of animals stops at particular symbolic meanings and misses the complexity and ambiguity that made these possible. Also missed are the affective dimensions of what a *living* animal means.

Interestingly, understanding animals may tap—and contribute to—what the psychologist Howard Gardner (1983) has called "interpersonal" intelligence. Relating with animals might fit Gardner's framework for an intelligence in these respects: (1) It might use specific brain areas (used also by interpersonal intelligence), which would be those associated with the processing of information about movement, including proprioceptive sensation, and about the expression of arousal and affect, perhaps associated with the limbic system. Evidence for humans' extending their ability to read faces for information on social interactants to animals comes from Blonder and colleagues (2004), whose MRI scans showed that many of the same parts of the brain are active when looking at human faces as when looking at the face of a dog (cited in Sims et al., 2005). Further, people with difficulty recognizing human faces also have difficulty recognizing animal faces (Bornstein, Sroka & Munitz, 1969). New evidence also suggests that other aspects of biological concepts may have innate bases. (2) The ability to relate to animals can be selectively spared when other faculties are absent or deficient, as in authenticated cases of feral children who adopted the social behaviors of their animal foster parents. Some syndromes (discussed earlier) show a related specific deficit having to do with a discrete mental module serving empathic and theory-of-mind functions. (3) It can be developed to a high degree of virtuosity, as shown in human-animal partnerships of various sorts. (4) It is supported by cultural systems, such as those enacted by zoo animal care-takers, ethologists, wildlife biologists, participants in culturally specific working animal systems enumerated earlier, and other such phenomena.

Gardner later added the "naturalist intelligence" to his list of intelligences. According to Gardner, "a naturalist demonstrates expertise in the recognition and classification of the numerous species—the flora and fauna—of his or her environment," and he names several prominent naturalists who, he concedes, "could not readily be classified in terms of the seven . . . intelligences" he previously defined (1999, p. 48). Gardner demonstrates that this form of intelligence does meet the eight criteria for an intelligence laid out in his earlier work (Gardner, 1983), including a plausible evolutionary history; specialized mental abilities that are distinct and isolatable from others, as demonstrated by brain damage case histories, idiot savants, and exceptional people; definable developmental pathways; support from psychological experiments and measures; and susceptibility to encoding in symbolic systems that are used by specialists within living cultures. In the latter connection, Gardner notes, "the naturalist is comfortable in the world of organisms and may well possess the talent of caring for, taming, or interacting subtly with various living creatures" (1999, p. 49). Gardner also suggests, however, that the basic categorizing operations of naturalist intelligence may be applied exclusively to distinguishing between art styles, consumer goods and brands, or scientific patterns of any sort. This suggests that the naturalist intelligence alone would not account for the capacity for connection to animals elaborated in this book because it does not tap social abilities, though it may play an important part.

Whether knowing animals is a subset of interpersonal intelligence or its own unique area of mental excellence, many other capacities contribute to the sense of connection. Linguistic ability, for example, is probably essential for grasping the intentionality of animal action. There may be no part of us that cannot be engaged by our animal cousins. Connection itself is metaphorical for intelligence, as suggested by a character in a story by Ursula K. Le Guin (1990): "I know that sentience or intelligence isn't a thing, you can't find it in, or analyze it out from, the cells of a brain. It's a function of the connected cells. It is, in a sense, the connection: the connectedness. It doesn't exist. I'm not trying to say it exists. I'm only guessing that [one] might be able to describe it" (p. 142). Animate relatedness retains a central place among our capacities throughout life. The richer the field of other entities it integrates, the greater our potential for locating the self and acting appropriately within that field.

Animals in Socialization

What is regarded as "human"—in the sense of being sharply and preferentially divided off from the "nonhuman"—is a matter of cultural definition carried out in language, evaluative attitudes, and action. Such socially constructed distinctions cut across the human self, across body and mind. They function differently from the developmentally earlier connection-within-difference. When meanings become reified around a particular contrast between humans and animals, that is, when the human becomes a discrete, separate and superior category, then the metaphoric movement between human self and animal other may be curtailed. In the previous chapter, we saw pathological examples of the breakdown of metaphorical ability in which the human self is mistaken for an animal. Far more common and normative is ideological and affective capture of "human" to mean emphatically "*not* animal."

At stake here is *continuity of community*—the sense that one's identity bonds one with others in an interspecies community sharing a common fate. Although the children's capacities, including language, inclined them to experience such identification, the nursery school reflected both wider human-animal boundary disputes and emotionally laden and culturally specific evaluations of "proper" behavior. What were these disputes and evaluations, and how did the children respond to them? We are here looking at how the discourses reviewed in chapter 2 are played out within the psychosocial dynamics of development. I found that the children did not just automatically adopt or fit in with these schemes. Nor was the result a simple additive acquisition of arbitrary and otherwise equal cultural attitudes. Nonetheless, some children displayed a discontinuity with animate relatedness and the formation of a more rigidly categorical human self.

The Contested Human–Nonhuman Boundary

We have observed that animal contrasts are used to mark the human boundary across cultures and, indeed, in developmental theory. So it should be no surprise to find them in everyday life, too. Language makes categorical distinctions across what are continua on the preverbal level. Members of a culture may treat these distinctions as if set in reality, making expression of similarity—whether by pretend or theatrical play, metaphorical comparison, or language—more difficult. The instances of talk about animals we will see next reveal the presence of old cultural traditions. Through them, the categorically human self's specific similarities with and differences from other species are negotiated.

Animals have long been key benchmarks for surveying the human-nonhuman boundary. The exact location of that boundary is a preoccupation of Western culture, and these debates even entered the nursery school classroom I observed. Broadly, humans and animals are in the same group:

> Mrs. Ray: "There are lots of animals in the class. Some are human animals—the people. Others are little animals like Toad." As she feeds the toad she notes how he wipes grass off his mouth, just like a person would wipe some food.

Continuity is recognized, but part of her statement begs the question because larger size does not set a clear boundary. But what does? Taxonomy seems to simplify the matter. Recently, biologists have pushed the divide to somewhere between humans and nonhuman primates; this has reached five-year-olds:

> Ms. Dean calls on Joe. Joe: "Are people related to monkeys?" Ms. Dean echoes the question back: "[Do] you think people are related to monkeys?" Ten children raise their hands; seven feel people are not.

We adults want to know, can apes talk, use tools, plan, remember, have culture?—all purported key criteria of humanity. Children focus on other features. Joe had one idea:

> Joe: "Hey, I know why they're related to people." Ms. Dean: "Why?" Joe: "'Cause they have the same nose."

Joe's thought seems derived from fresh observation and comparison. But of course an adult picks differences that relate to more profound philosophies:

> Joe: "His hands are his feet." Dawn: "And . . . he only has four fingers." Mr. Dean: "And how many do we have?" Dawn and Joe reply: "Five, five." Joe: "No, we have—no, we have eight and two thumbs." Joe holds his hands up,

turning toward Mrs. Ray, behind him. Mr. Dean: "So what is he missing?" Dawn: "Two thumbs." Joe: "A thumb." Mrs. Ray: "[Remember what] we talked about—[he] cannot do this"—she pinches thumb and forefinger together several times. Joe, Chris, Dawn do the same.

Mrs. Ray did not explain the rationale for pointing out *this* feature instead of, say, having fur all over one's body. But the opposable thumb is the paradigmatic anatomical characteristic (and thus symbol) of *Homo faber* and his or her technology. Stressing it calls on the popular belief that human inventiveness makes us what we are.

What happened next was revealing. Joe transformed this abstractly important anatomical fact into a concrete and intentionally communicative gesture. He made an "okay" sign with thumb and forefinger and proclaimed, "[He] can't do this!" Joe's interest in categorical differences gravitated toward the interactively and communicatively relevant!

We know Joe had a theory that animal languages are like human languages. But adults went out of their way to be sure the kids were not thinking animals talk or understand language:

Drew: "Why is the turtle talk[ing] in the microphone?!" Mr. Lloyd: "Do turtles talk?" Kids: "No." Drew: "What if it just made noise in the mike?" Mr. Lloyd, interrupting: "No, turtles don't talk."

Joe contested this philosophically critical categorical boundary also, even against adult incredulity:

Ms. Dean: "Can he understand English?" Chris and Dawn answer: "No." Joe: "Yes." Ms. Dean: "Yes?" . . . He repeats this, nodding for emphasis to Chris and Mrs. Ray behind him. Ms. Dean: "Do you think he can hear what we're saying and understand exactly what we're saying?" . . . Joe nods: "Uh-huh, because he's *related* to us." Ms. Dean: "Because he's related to us? So he would automatically know English—but how about Japanese people? Would he understand what Japanese people say?" Joe: "Nooo!" Chris: "Only Japanese monkeys." Mr. Dean: "You mean he'd have to be a Japanese monkey?" Chris nods. Ms. Dean: "He'd have to be a Japanese monkey to understand Japanese people?" Joe: "Uh-huh." Chris: "Yes."

At a risk of over-interpreting this humorous exchange, the children's belief that, to the extent a monkey will understand, it will only understand the tongue it has already heard seems reasonable. But Joe's rationale would not wash. From the adult point of view, monkeys are not *closely enough* related to us to understand. For Joe, there is continuity of intentional, meaningful communication—a belief that comes from seeing animate activity in the light of his assumptions of language use and a theory of mind.

Cultural assumptions of human-animal difference are subtly communicated; what we have seen are just the most obvious parts. But they are not merely communicated; as we saw, these categorical distinctions are negotiated. Joe articulated his own experience of human-primate *continuity*—an experience that emphasized interactively important features. A child need not, however, be exposed to explicit philosophical rationales. Human-animal difference is implicit in many practices, and it is conveyed in the form of judgments about what is desirable, admirable, and good versus what is unacceptable, despicable, and bad. As we shall see, this fault line runs through evaluations both of humanity and animality, and of the mind and the body.

Animals in Cultural Evaluative Perspective

Another entire set of categorical features attributed to animals by words has great relevance for continuity of community with other species. Language makes possible the evaluative marking of behaviors as good and bad, and animals are appropriated as symbolic markers of desirable and undesirable—as exemplars and antiheroes. Antiheroes—deviants—are either physically or symbolically annihilated by being appropriated to serve in a culture's practical and symbolic universe. Exemplary animals are made to stand for good traits.

Children are quite well attuned to this dimension, as I found in interviewing children from five to eighteen years about which of several symbolically laden animals they most wished to "be like." The children tended to identify with animals whose cultural meanings were appropriate for the age and gender roles they occupied or were moving into, and not those whose meanings were inappropriate. Of six animal photographs, young children universally favored the vulnerable bunny; ten-year-olds picked animals by gender-appropriate connotations (lions and eagles for boys, rabbit for girls); and late adolescents valued the independence of the lion and bear and especially the omniscience of the eagle (Myers, 2002). More generally, the human-nonhuman distinction itself is heavily value-laden (cf. Midgley, 1988). We will look at animal symbolism in two typical nursery school issues: unruly behavior and bodily taboos.

Animals stand ambiguously outside the social order; many of their behaviors set bad examples to be corrected. The teacher went so far as to censure aggressive bird behavior:

> Mrs. Ray notes that one bird is pecking another: "That bird needs to learn
> to be gentle"; she adds that some people are like that and need to learn
> also. Birds are like people sometimes, "or is it people are like birds?"

Ms. Wick once asked some rambunctious children, "Did a wild beast get you?" She may have mistakenly thought they were pretending to be animals, or else she saw children as roughly like wild beasts at times—certainly a familiar cultural theme!

Children do identify with animals' freedom from socializers like mothers and school. Perhaps in response, adults sometimes remarked on animal actions that are disallowed to children. For example, the monkey crawled over to the table and ate cracker crumbs off the rug:

> Ivy: "He's eating the crumbs." Drew: "He's eating the crumbs." Ms. Dean: "He's eating the crumbs. . . . Those must be good crumbs, do you think those crumbs are pretty good?" Several kids: "Yeah." Ms. Dean: "How come, would you guys eat those crumbs?!" Some kids: "Yeah." Solly: "No!" Ms. Dean: "You eat those crumbs before?!"

Ms. Dean's tone of voice and repetition conveyed a good-humored disapproval. The analogy between child and monkey socialization was even made explicit:

> Drew: "Does he break your stuff, in your house?" Ms. Dean: "We can't really tell him 'Koko, don't break that because I like that, I like that plate, or I like that special glass or that special vase." Joe: "You have to train him." Ms. Dean: "We have to make sure that we keep a very close eye on him." Joe: "Why don't you train him?" Ms. Dean: "Well, that's the thing about monkeys is they're not very easy to train. They decide what they want to do because they have their own mind to think about what they want to do, so if I tell Koko, 'No,' sometimes he'll listen to me, but sometimes he's not too happy, just like when you guys, when your Mom says, 'No, I don't want you to do that,' sometimes you listen and sometimes you don't? Is that true?" Mr. Dean: "Because if you don't want to do something, sometimes you just don't want to do it, right? Same with a monkey." Ms. Dean: "Same with a monkey."

Monkey as child: disobedient, willful, unsocialized. Independence must be tolerated, but both creatures would ideally be tame. This analogy was exhibited in practice. On the one hand, children witnessed adults controlling animals' behaviors, physically or by command; on the other, children were the recipients of adult dictate:

> Billy complains about not having enough blocks, or particular ones which others have. Mrs. Ray tells him: "Look around you!" He does so and sees that there are plenty. She says his behavior "tells me you need a nap so you can be in control."

Caregivers enforce behaviors and justify doing so with such appeals to the child's own good, and they use animal keeping as a metaphor for explaining such child-rearing strictures.

Thus, not surprisingly, adults are not alone in aiming for socialized outcomes. It was Joe who offered the obvious socialization procedure for Koko: training. Here is an additional alliance, not between the children and the animal but between the children and the adults, on the side of socialization. Children generally do not want the disapproval that misbehavior brings, even if they cannot control their behavior. And they may be given some responsibility for disorderly animals. Thus, it is not surprising that in the end children side with the social world. And to the extent that they see the animal world as opposite to that world, their sense of a categorically human self may exclude the animal.

A second evaluated issue is the body. Besides misbehavior, animals openly use and display their bodies in ways not allowed to humans. In the classroom, animals are used as didactic tools, particularly for nonverbalized issues or for feelings to which caregivers do not attune—that is, those that are private. Among humans in Western culture (and many other cultures), such functions as defecation, urination, masturbation, intercourse, and childbirth are considered private. Parents socialize these functions as private by not attuning to the subjective experiences that go with them. Earlier I suggested that this may make such bodily experiences seem to children to be more subjectively shared with animals.

But adults' intention is the opposite: Eventually children must identify with the socialized position. The practice of using animals' behaviors as examples of what is undesirable, messy, and private hastens this. The teacher of this classroom used animals as a vehicle for modern, open talk about functions that are less "appropriate" to talk about (or certainly to observe) in people. Dogs were a vehicle for discussing male and female anatomy; so were some other animals:

> Mrs. Ray says that with a guinea pig you can press its belly, and if it's a male you can see its penis show. Does that mean it's a boy or a girl? Kids: "Boy." She says that if it's a girl it has a vagina. Mrs. Ray explains it's the same on birds, though the parts are inside where you can't see them, and there's no way to tell about the toad.

Animals are clearly safe and public for talking about what is problematic between humans. Steps toward embracing this distinction can be traced in a series of examples involving animal excreta. Toby delighted in rubbing his hands on pigeon droppings; Mindy only admitted to a past in which such delights were acceptable:

> Mindy and I are at the guinea pig cage. She wants to touch its "poops," but says they're "yucky."

Her fascination was a step more restrained than Toby's. In the following case, three boys discussed the guinea pig's droppings:

> Drew advises Joe that the thing Joe is handling is a "BM." Joe denies it.
> Joe and Solly talk about whether it's guinea pig food or guinea pig "BM."
> Joe holds it in his fingers, firmly disagreeing. Solly tells him it's a "BM";
> again he denies it.

In either account, a "BM" (Mrs. Ray's term) was obviously repulsive; the debate was only over whether the object was one. These boys seem to have fully accepted the social messages about excreta; the next step might be aversion to anything even resembling it.

In her talk, Mrs. Ray used animals as a safe way to talk about body functions and was careful to not be too loaded in what she said:

> Mrs. Ray: "Well, did you ever notice that our guinea eats a whole lot?
> And some of the food that all creatures [eat] becomes part of what your
> body needs for growing and some of it is extra and it's called waste, and it
> comes out of your body like a BM, and that—we use toilets but animals
> don't. I never saw a dog go to the toilet, did you?" Solly: "I have on TV."
> Mrs. Ray: "Really?" Solly: "Yeah." Mrs. Ray: "Well, I never have. And
> so, if our guinea pig is down on the rug, then he's, she's liable to leave
> droppings on the rug."

Although animals and humans are biologically similar, and no strong value judgments were made about body functions, the socialization message was clear.

Children of course grasp that growing up involves control over bodily functions, and they draw parallels between maturing humans and animals. For example, when the turtle's and toad's spontaneous way of urinating was discussed, Dawn was reminded of how her baby brother sprinkled on her. Thus, children again are in alliance with adults over the issue of their own socialization. After all, they want to grow up, and be on the human side of the boundary, if a boundary there must be.

Thus, accompanying the moral and practical dismissal of animals and the ideological reification of the human-animal divide discussed previously, highly motivating affective valences are communicated by cultural agents. It would be no surprise if a felt connection to the nonhuman succumbed to these captures of preverbal connection.

The Categorically Human Self

We have discussed two sorts of cultural discourses and practices. One is the setting of conceptual human-nonhuman animal boundaries. The second involves evaluative exclusion of animals by aligning them with negatively valued behaviors or with publicly unacceptable aspects of body and feeling. These cultural influences eventuate in a strong force against close identification with animals. They provide content and motivation for the formation of a categorically human self. In contrast, preverbal interactions and pretend-mediated senses of self entail only degrees of difference within continuities. Little exists there to inform or motivate such a strict division. But when differences are discretely marked and preferentially ranked and an evaluation of certain differences is communicated by selective attunements, misattunements, and language, then fluid identification becomes problematic to the self. The categorical self is an experiential integration like the other senses of self, but it is based on an abstraction from the full set of features of the self. The categorical human self—both a reification as discussed in chapter 6 and an ambient defense mechanism as introduced above—is unequivocally *not* an animal self.

Toward the end of each small group session with five of the animals in the spring, each child was asked whether he or she would like to be that animal.[5] Most children said they would like to be a number of the animals; only ferrets were significantly less popular than monkeys, the most popular. But some girls responded quite differently. The data show a sex difference in identification with these animals, but most of the statistical weight changes when age is considered also. The *older* girls account for much of the difference. Three of the four oldest girls in the class, Cassia (5 years, 8 months in the spring), Ivy (5 years, 8 months), and Adrienne (5 years, 6 months), showed an interesting pattern suggestive of a categorically human self.[6]

To *none* of the five did Cassia answer, yes, she would like to be the animal—she gave an ambivalent response to the monkey and said no to the other four. Ivy said yes to the monkey, although qualifying her answer with "only for a day," a weak yes for the ferret, and no to the turtle; she was ambivalent about the others. Adrienne said yes to the monkey and no to the tarantula; she was ambivalent toward the thought of being a turtle, a snake, or a ferret. Interestingly, these girls enjoyed interacting with animals, and each of them readily pretended to be a dog during the dog small group sessions. But they showed markedly less self-other continuity with the animals than did the other children.

What might be causing this? These were the three we saw earlier intently discussing meat eating; perhaps some moral distancing and superiority is working as a defense against this discomfort. Ivy was exemplary in the taking of nurturant, mother-like roles in relation to the animals. Although quite positive, such roles are complementary rather than reciprocal, and are thus less conducive to a sense of shared experience. Gender socialization might be reflected here to the extent that it encourages this kind of role. Perhaps most likely, misbehaviors typically associated with being "animal-like" (aggressiveness, rough-and-tumble, dirtiness, the "grotesque" body, and so on) are more at odds with young girls' developing gender identities than boys'. "Don't be an animal!" may carry a greater warning to one gender than the other. Although these data constitute no proof, they strongly suggest that toward the end of the age group studied, at least for girls, a sense of categorically human self is developing.

An instructive exception, however, was Dawn, who at 5 years, 6 months was the third-oldest girl. Dawn said, yes, she would like to be four of the five animals; she was only ambivalent about such identification with the snake. Dawn even found it strange that Cassia, who was in her small group, was so hesitant to express identification with animals:

> Mr. Myers: "I'm asking Cassia a question—did you want to be a ferret?" Cassia shakes her head. Mr. Myers: "No. How come?" Dawn: "You didn't want to be a dog, turtle, ferret." Mr. Myers: "It's okay not to want to be one. I'm just wondering why."

As we saw, Dawn often felt that the animals "liked" her, something she read from their approach behavior; and it was she who took her baby brother around the class, introducing him to its animal members. She was also the only child to imitate all the animals brought to the class, an indication that this activity may encourage a child's continued sense of connection on terms that do not threaten animate relatedness. Taking a cue from the power of imitation and pretend play, perhaps we could propose that other activities that encourage continuity of community are ones that encourage metaphors and analogies, affective expressions of commonalities, finding degrees of difference (not categorical ones) and animate relatedness.

Another factor that differentiated Dawn from the other older girls was that her father took a keen interest in animals and shared it with her. The other girls' parents expressed mild interest or indifference about animals and their role in the children's lives. Asked "What, in your opinion, are the benefits your child derives from the real or fictional animals in his or her life?" Dawn's father stressed concrete contact and letting the child discover how the animal felt—revealing his sense of the importance of core connection with the animal. In contrast, the other girls' parents stressed abstract socialization goals couched in terms of the animals, such as: "[through stories] develop sensitivity to the needs of the animals" or "love, caring for another." Adrienne's mother simply wrote, "I don't see many [benefits]; as a result we don't have many pets."

Probably no deficit in normal development would be detected with these girls; as A. H. Kidd and R. M. Kidd (1987b) have said, a lack of interest in animals can be normal. But this does not negate the possibility of unrecognized (or theoretically unformulated) developmental potentials. Until the work of Ross et al. (2003), researchers thought that young children lacked a common biological category for humans and animals. But if we look at pretend play and identification in most of these young subjects, we do not find a rigid separation. Categories can work in different ways in relation to felt, preverbal meanings—we need this way of thinking about concepts, in addition to their logical meaning or cultural referents. In particular, word meanings may be reified and function as if literal when we lose track of the fact that words are *about* meanings, not identical with the preverbal contents to which they refer. The younger children's sense of being a human self does not have this static quality; they take their bearings in a fluid continuity with a community of other animate subjectivities. But the older girls do have such clarity—perhaps rather rigidity—of self-concept, echoing Western culture's high evaluation of the mind and of the human over the body and the animal. Considering the multiple encouragements in this direction surveyed in this chapter, this result is hardly a surprise. The alternative, a developmental goal of a human self connected by concern, interest, and community to the other living beings of this planet, is a possibility we desperately need to better understand.

VIII

Conclusion

Our species evolved not only in the social environment of other humans but also in the nonhuman natural environment in which we continue—uneasily—to exist. Although this ancient history has left its enduring marks and although various individuals and cultures demonstrate the human capacity for a finely attuned relation with the elements of this environment, a capacity for connection is not treated by the social sciences as a fundamental dimension of human potential or development. Rather, to the extent it is even considered, this capacity has too often been seen as an epiphenomenon of various putatively more basic processes. But the children in this book have demonstrated a constellation of developmental processes that account for animals being central to their sense of self. Far from these underlying dimensions of animate relatedness being secondary, there is a strong case that they constitute and constrain psychological, social, and cultural phenomena. Thus, basic issues about what makes us who we are come up for reexamination when we take children's relations to animals seriously.

Writing of feral children, Malson (1964/1972) asked, "Now that it is generally recognized that the dominant, fundamental role in the shaping of man's personality is played by his social environment, should one be surprised that a non-human environment produces semi-human children?" (pp. 35–36). In turn, we can now ask, Can a child, provided with a human social environment but deprived of nonhuman others, develop her or his full humanity? Thinking back over what we have learned, I can suggest a number of things that would be lacking in such a scenario. There would be no rich sense of different interactive styles, no quasi-social domain free of the pressures and deceptions of the human realm. There would also be a sense of isolation rather than of being in the company of other creatures who confirm one's sense of going-on-being, agency, affectivity, coherence, and history; fewer perceptions of other ways of being, of seeing oneself-as, and of pretending to be in alternative concrete and subjective realities. The possibilities of the self-reflective self are reduced to the extent the community of animal others is impoverished in diversity.

The great social psychologist George Herbert Mead (1913) felt that ethical choice and action were possible when the person could represent internally every "element" or perspective in the situation. In his theory, these perspectives were limited to those of other humans. But at least at an early age children themselves show that a much wider inner theater of moral deliberation is developmentally probable. Moving away from social psychology's fixation on language as the privileged route for knowing others, we can see that the more analogical and imitative modes of identification can include every element—every species! This has important implications for the possibilities of a society-wide ecological ethics.

The sense of connection to the animal and by extension to a subjective ecology is a *telos*, or end, of development. It is a pre-potent potential, and we might do more to recognize its value. Its value derives from our experience of the animal and its ecological world as something more than human. Just as animals offer children patterns of optimally discrepant social responsiveness, so, too, has the natural world value to us because we sense that it connects with but stretches beyond what is humanly identical, controlled, or created. That value is realized through our sense of connection to this realm. Thus, the sense of self is clarified and deepened by engagement with animals and thereby might ultimately extend to be a truly "ecological" self.

A sense of connection to the nonhuman also serves values beyond quality of immediate experience. Across the life span and across cultures, we must choose to make the changes that are required of us by ecological constraints. Choice and desire stem partly from our sense of self. To *the extent the self is experienced as connected with the systems by which it is in fact constituted, so much the likelier the needed changes.*[1] Environmental problems are quintessential human problems, yet the social sciences have not striven greatly to contribute to adaptive change. Especially, they have not examined how their own foundations might be part of the problem. Like any other value that has such intrinsic and extrinsic appeal, we should seek to cultivate our sense of connection, although we have a long way to go.

To cultivate this value means first to understand it. Helping children develop to care about animals, their local habitats and wider ecologies is not straightforward. This is because as children draw animals into their developing selves, important cognitive, emotional, and moral responses to the welfare of animals develop also. These bonds have inherent dynamics that must be respected if continuity of interest, concern, and community are to be possible.

To the extent an ecological self is developed and inclusive, it enables the person to maintain a sense of connection despite loss and necessity. Hunter-gatherer cultures maintained continuity of connection despite exploiting animals because they believed in a spiritual realm that continued after death and that made it imperative to respect their prey. We have no such meaning system intact, but we still have the psychology of what Paul Shepard (1973) called the sensitive carnivore who experiences the animal as a social other.

Children need acknowledgment and support of their feelings about harm to animals. A sense of connection creates psychological and spiritual challenges in dealing with loss and violence to those to whom one is connected—and related challenges are in place regarding those one already excludes or opposes. If society were to really grasp what is at stake in child development, we might well reduce exploitation of animals to a minimum dictated by a stricter sense of necessity. But the aim of development cannot be the elimination of all conflicted relations and feelings. Vulnerability, loss, the taking of life, are constants. Rather, the aim is continuity of psychological openness and inclusion.

Such emotional support is needed even more for the extension of concern for animals beyond the familiar, near-at-hand, tame mammals children most commonly encounter directly. With development, care can extend to wild animals and to those minute creatures far from the human scale that play vital roles in ecosystems. This may require greater imaginative reach. An integral extension of care is to realize that animals' environments are important to them and that in some cases the protection of species must take precedence over individuals, and yet seemingly paradoxically we must simultaneously maintain our care about the lives of individuals.[2] These are not trivial challenges psychologically or intellectually, but we have created these choices and must decide them.

On the societal level, continuity depends on complex feedback relations between our representations of ourselves (are we separate from or part of nature?), our forms of thought (do we value artistic and metaphorical ways of affirming our connection?), and our practical action (do we care for, respect, and preserve other life forms?). Our "rationality" needs to be expanded to embrace the inherent values that we learn from the sense of connection (cf. Plumwood, 2002). The philosopher David Rothenberg (1991) urged a conception of "a nature which includes us, which *we only understand to the extent which we can find a home* in the enveloping flow of forces which is only ever partially in our control" (p. 245, emphasis added). Finding a *home—and our place in the family of creatures living there*—is at once a cognitive and an affective task, and one my young informants have shown us they are prepared for. Without this, our unalloyed instrumental rationality—our pursuit of efficiency to the exclusion of higher ends—will ruin the very conditions of our self-in-relation to other species in a defeating feedback of ecological and cultural-psychological destruction. Ultimately, no "transcendent" mind can lift us away from our body on the earthly world from whence both grow. This in turn suggests we should reconsider our self-image as a species, as a separate "humanity."

Appendix

Methods, Setting, and Subjects

Much of this book relies on my research in one nursery school classroom. This design was the result of my search for optimal conditions in which to explore the patterns in children's relations to animals. By taking an ethnographic and interpretive approach to a single group, I gained a depth of understanding of child and context that would be hard to match any other way (see the work of the childhood ethnographers Thomas Rizzo, William Corsaro, & John Bates, 1992; other notable landmarks include Corsaro, 1981 & 1985; Corsaro & Streeck, 1985; Denzin, 1982; Fine & Sandstrom, 1988; Mandell, 1988; Tammivaara & Enright, 1986; and Waksler, 1986). My research involved an extended series of interactions of many kinds, which I sought to structure so as to answer an evolving set of hunches and to test out an emerging pattern, which this book presents. For readers who want to know more about my methods this appendix gives more on methodology plus a more concrete sense of the settings, the actors, and my techniques.

Methodologically, this book is a grounded-theory case study. Case studies are an indispensable component of the scientific method, but their nature, purpose and strategies are not as familiar to many as more canonical quantitative theory-falsification methods. So a brief introduction may be in order. As argued by Donald Campbell (1975) and others (Yin, 1989), a case study contributes to its field of knowledge by analytical generalizability, through a procedure of pattern-matching between the case and applicable theories. In grounded theory, the analogous term, theoretical generalizability (Glaser and Strauss, 1967), highlights how, rather than aiming to make generalizations from a sample to a population, one aims to work within a specific situation to propose and test a whole series of (eventually) interlinked hypotheses (constructs, outcomes, etc.). The emphasis is theory generation more than falsification. Although theory generation involves many steps of formulating and testing ideas, one just doesn't go the additional (large) step of generalizing to a population.

In such generalizability, the key question is: What is it a case *of*? In my research here, the unit of investigation is the inter-individual interaction, where the individuals are children and animals. And the constructs I was concerned to test about these units are social interactive processes and the social capacities of the child, generally derived from the developmental literature. I came at this problem steeped in major frameworks from human development, which posed additional interpretations that I tested against examples and consistent patterns in my observation. As it turned out, the variety presented by animals as interactants worked quite well to produce further articulation of the constructs about social development derived from observation of children with other humans. Some may want to contest some of the conceptual extensions to which I compared my observations, and that is to be expected. Many more ideas are presented in this book than are rigorously tested. The strength of the book, nonetheless, rests with the degree to which the concepts I worked with were networked and grounded in data.

A description of the case study "sample" and setting will help make my methods more concrete. The nursery school classroom where I spent a year in the early 1990s was part of a complex of gray stone buildings laid out in a figure eight, serving multiple school grades. The class regularly used the inner play yards and occasionally portions of the neighborhood. The classroom itself was divided into three large areas for different activities: a rug-covered area used for meetings, block play and other sorts of play; an area with tables for art, activities, and lunch; and, furthest from the entrance, an area furnished with tables and shelves stocked with materials for carpentry, fantasy play, games, puzzles, books, and so on. This area had the most open feeling because of windows and glass doors to the outside.

The teacher, Mrs. Ray, was a tall, vivacious woman who had been teaching young children for over twenty-five years. She brought tremendous experience, energy, insight, and affection to her relationships with the children. She was equally welcoming to me, willing to throw the doors open and let me get to know her children. Mrs. Ray encouraged science activities and equipped the room richly, including many things from nature. Among these were the resident animals—goldfish, Toad, Snowflake the guinea pig, and the diamond doves.

The classroom housed a two-year preschool program, after which the children go on to kindergarten. The children's ages in the fall ranged from three years, five months, to five years, four months. Of the twenty-five children, fourteen were boys and eleven were girls, but because two half-year children were boys, the ratio was always thirteen to eleven. Facts including age, sex, ethnic background, and whether the child was in the class for his or her first or second year are given in table A.1. Although few patterns related to ethnicity arose in my analysis, the classroom was diverse, reflecting the international draw of the associated university. As a result of high tuition cost and modest financial aid, there was only moderate variation in socio-economic status. Most parents were in (or preparing for) the professions or business; a few were working-class or tradespeople. In many families, both parents were busy full-time.

Table A.1 Basic Information on the Subjects (by age)

Name	Sex	Parent's Ethnicity	1st/2nd Year?	Age in Fall (Years:Months)
Chris	M	F: African-Amer.	1	5:4
Kevin	M	Caucasian	2	5:2
Cassia	F	Jewish-Amer.	2	5:1
Ivy	F	Caucasian	2	5:1
Dawn	F	M: Mexican	2	4:11
Adrienne	F	Caucasian	2	4:11
Joe	M	Caucasian	2	4:9
Benson	M	Caucasian	1	4:8
Drew	M	Caucasian	2	4:7
Abeo	F	Nigerian	2	4:5
Angela	F	Caucasian	2	4:4
Solly	M	Jewish-Amer.	1	4:4
Irvin	M	Chinese	2	4:4
Sam	M	Chinese	2	4:4
Yasmin	F	M: Middle Eastern	2	4:2
Chen	M	Taiwanese	1	Not in class (4:9 in May)
Dimitri	M	F: Middle Eastern	2	4:2
Laura	F	Caucasian	1	3:10
Katra	F	Slavic	1	3:10
Mindy	F	Caucasian	1	3:9
Toby	M	Caucasian	1	3:8
Reuben	M	African-Amer.	1	3:8
Billy	M	Jewish-Amer.	1	3:8
Rosa	F	F: Mexican	1	3:6
Scott	M	Middle-Eastern	1	3:5 (in class Fall only)

My activities in the room were varied, but I avoided taking some adult responsibilities. After a period of observing and "gradual field entry" (Rizzo et al., 1992), I began to partake in play, ask questions, and learn from the relationships I developed. I obtained school and parental permission for the research and have preserved the anonymity of all subjects in this book. Whenever I conducted a special activity (such as individual play-interviews), I let each child know what we would do and allowed him or her to choose whether to do it then, later, or not at all.

I used many strategies to learn about the children. I observed for all activities with resident animals, and I observed a subset of children systematically (focal-child sampling). I organized joint play sessions and interviews, and I collected children's stories. All parents completed a questionnaire, and parents of focal children kept home journals recording animal-related comments and activities. Mrs. Ray provided further family background information. Finally, I arranged visits by the animals listed in chapter 1. All animal presenters were expert animal keepers (except for the dog owner, Mr. Grier, a graduate student). Time was spent with each animal briefly as a class, then in groups of four children, and then a longer session with the whole class; all of these were videotaped. I instructed the presenters on the outlines of the session, and how to respond to children's questions—mostly by reflecting them back so as to probe for their ideas rather than by introducing information that would probably vary across the groups. I also asked them to let the small groups have the maximum permissible free interaction between child and animal. Interaction was followed by questions designed to tap the children's perceptions of, and identification with, the animals. My detailed transcriptions of action and speech in these tapes serve as a major source of data I discuss in this book.

This book, then, works from a thickly contextualized understanding of the roles of animals in the development of particular young children, towards broader patterns drawing on the social development literature. It is my hope that the patterns I describe will be both rich enough to be convincing and general enough to be provocative. I hope others will find here departure points for investigation as well as convincing reasons to believe children's involvement with animals is worthy of such attention.

Notes

Chapter I

1. See, e.g., the work of the cognitive scientist Francisco Varela, the philosopher Evan Thompson, and the psychologist Eleanor Rosch (1991).

2. Shortly after the first edition of this book, entitled *Children and Animals*, psychologist Margot Lasher (1998) also proposed the use of Stern's theory, including the concepts of core self and other and attunement, as of potential use for the study of humans and animals.

3. For a philosophical discussion of the field of self and of a subjectively attuned biology, see the work of the philosopher Neil Evernden (1993).

4. The perceived unimportance of animals' roles in the field of child development is illustrated by examining the indexes of Damon's (1998) *Handbook of Child Psychology*, 5th edition, for references to animals in any role in development, pets, or animals under social relations or development. Volume 3, on social development, showed no references, nor does volume 4, on practical applications including therapy. Volume 2, on cognition, perception and language, gives three entries on the recent topic of biological knowledge; in that case, however, the fundamental concerns are the organization of knowledge and mechanisms of developmental change in knowledge and reasoning, not relations with animals per se. Symptomatic of the situation in psychology broadly, animals are indexed only once in Ramachandran's (1994) *Encyclopedia of Human Behavior*, in a brief discussion of animal phobias. Recent years have seen the formation of human-animal studies sections in the American Sociological Association and a parallel effort to create such an interest group in the American Psychological Association.

Chapter II

1. The exact nature of this process of symbolic human-animal comparison-making, although something we cannot yet answer, is an important

question and a venerable one in anthropology. Many cultures have elaborate systems of *totemism,* often identifying a social group with an animal. Anthropologists report that the Amazonian Bororo, for example, claim to *be* red macaws—or, at least, to be metaphorically like them—as opposed to the totem species of other groups (J. Christopher Crocker, 1985; Lucien Levy-Bruhl, 1966). The famous founder of structuralism in anthropology, Claude Lévi-Strauss, described totemism as a manner of thinking based on a parallel between *"two systems of differences,* one of which occurs in nature and the other in culture" (1966, p. 115). But in which direction does the parallel making move? Some theorists, such as the early French sociologists Emile Durkheim and Marcel Mauss (1903/1963) and the anthropologist A. Irving Hallowell (1960/1975), argue that social or psychological distinctions are extended to the natural realm of species. Another possibility receiving attention recently is that the human mind has a proclivity to create biological species categories of an especially rigid or "essentialist" sort (entities are what they are because of inner unchanging properties or essences) and that this type of category is then extended by analogy to human social groups, thus accounting for totemic divisions, and also perhaps for prejudice (see Hirschfeld & Gelman, 1994). In either case, animal analogies employ the diversity of local fauna to interpret the particular social order (see also Urton, 1985; Malamud, 1998).

2. See works by the cultural critic Donna Haraway (1989) and the cultural historian Harriet Ritvo (1995).

3. On feral children, see chapter 5, note 2. Robert Kidd (1986) has discussed other themes connecting animals and children in culture.

4. The most striking authentic example I am aware of, of a child thus standing up is the statement of Severn Cullis-Suzuki, at age 12 to international representatives at a plenary session of the 1992 Rio U.N. Conference on Environment and Development. One transcript of the speech is at: http://www. thespeechsite.com/famous/SevernSuzuki-1.htm.

5. For an engaging and critical set of perspectives on empowerment, animal, and nature themes in recent and classical children's literature, nature magazines, music, *Sesame Street,* and other media, see Dobrin & Kidd (2004).

6. Johnson (1995) discusses primitivism in Hall's recapitulation theory.

7. For other early works by psychologists on children and animals, see W. Fowler Bucke (1903); C. F. Hodge (1902); Susan Isaacs (1930); Arthur Jersild and Frances Holmes (1935); and Mabel Marsh (1902).

8. For recent critical examinations of this history, see the volume edited by Craeger and Jordan (2002).

9. A considerable portion of the recent flourish of animal studies scholarship may be guilty of not adequately critiquing its own language- and symbol-centric assumptions, for example some essays in Rothfels (2002), and some work on animals in story and legend. For a spirited rejection of social constructionism of animals, see Dombrowski (2002); for a balanced structural-developmental critique of deconstructionism, see Kahn (1999).

10. I discuss the problem posed by Sarles and its significance at greater length in Myers (2003).

11. Key questions here have been developed by the psychologist Eugene T. Gendlin (1962, 1987, 1992); for several points of view on the significance of Gendlin's work broadly, see *Language beyond postmodernism: Saying and thinking in Gendlin's philosophy*, edited by David Michael Levin (1997, Northwestern University Press).

Chapter III

1. To briefly elaborate my position vis-à-vis the biophilia hypothesis, I agree with Kahn (1999) that an adequate conception of biophilia must be developmental, because the activity of the person negotiates the intervention of environment between genotype and phenotype. Although some aspects of biophilia may echo specific ancient adaptive preferences for biotic environmental features (water, views, refuges, interest in moving things, etc.), the simple genetic concept of biophilia cannot do the work asked of it when theorists want it to explain relations characterized by truer, other-oriented *"philia."* Rather, an account of fuller biophilia needs to be grounded in our species' social and cognitive development. Our pattern of development itself is a complex life-cycle adaptation, and the environment of development (the small human group) was therefore a powerful environment of recent human adaptation. Our species-typical sociality, docility, cognition, language, morality, and the life-cycle development of these arose in response to selection in a complex ecological *but more importantly social* environment. That infants and children must solve basic survival problems almost solely within the fluid, interactive, reciprocal, and conventionally ordered context of the social group is of paramount importance in our species' ethology. The infant must reliably understand and interact well with significant others early. As Humphrey (1984) argued, the leap in complexity of social interaction as hominids evolved to *Homo* called forth a leap in the psychological understanding of self and others. This entailed the de-coupling of some instinctive responses from their social stimuli and brought behavior under greater psychological and social mediation. The example of greatest importance in this book is that the early social responses

of our species are not tightly targeted to only conspecifics. My perspective on biophilia is thus that social development imparts universal roots and dynamics to relations to individual animals, which can contribute uniquely and irreducibly to our development, including a potential for fuller biophilia.

2. Preference for interacting with animals was clearly demonstrated by kindergartners studied by the psychologist Barry Brucklacher (1992); these children made significantly more and longer visits to a live guinea pig than to a stuffed one.

3. My procedure was to observe any animal-related activity by the children, but my sampling was not sufficiently focused to catch all guinea pig-child interactions. Thus, the data must be taken as merely suggestive. I also cannot rule out an age explanation, since the average age of the "new" group was seven months less than the "second year" children.

4. Other psychologists have argued that increased empathy or role-taking skills are possible outcomes of children's involvement with animals (Cindee Bailey, 1987; Vanessa Malcarne, 1983; Robert Poresky & Charles Hendrix, 1990; V. Vizek-Vidović et al., 1999; Paul, 2000). Notably, Martin Hoffman (1987) and Ervin Staub (1986) have linked empathy with moral development. A recent study by Beth Daly and L. L. Morton (2003), however, provides contrary evidence to the predominant view: They found that children owning pets did not score differently than non-pet owners on a measure of empathy. When dog owners were examined separately, however, they showed higher empathy, whereas cat owners showed lower empathy. Daly and Morton suggest further research into personality, animal-bonding, and related constructs.

Chapter IV

1. Alternate parsings are suggested by Watzlawick, Beavin, and Jackson (1967, pp. 54–56).

2. Bregman's findings anticipate recent work by Öhman (1986) and Ulrich (1993) on the resistance of conditioned "biophobias" of spider and snake stimuli to experimental extinction, among adults.

3. In the following sections, I will discuss children's experience of subjective properties of animals on the assumption this is valid, even if children (or adults) may sometimes be wrong in their attributions of specific mental states to animals. Thus, I affirm that agency and so forth *are* attributes of animals (indeed, Stern, 1985, also notes some animals may have "core" selves; for a recent social interactionist case that cats and dogs have selves, see Irvine, 2004). The questions of anthropomorphism, and animal consciousness, feeling, and thought are being discussed in many forums, and a full treatment is beyond the

scope of this book. Indeed, this question constitutes both an urgent social issue and a frontier of science and practice. Provisionally, I take this fairly cautious position: At a minimum, all animals can be described as what the philosopher Daniel Dennett (1987) has called "first-order Intentional systems," that is, they can be validly regarded as agents with beliefs, desires, feelings, and other mental predicates. In science, the idea of animals' subjective worlds goes back at least to founders of ethology such as Jacob von Uexküll (1940/1982). The philosopher Gareth Matthews (1978) and the animal experimentalist Jerry Garcia (1981) have even avowed the strategic employment of such assumptions by behaviorists! Second-order intentionality (e.g., beliefs *about* beliefs) is a much harder question (related issues, such as the child's explicit belief in animal mental states, are discussed in the next chapter). But I disagree with assertions like that of the philosopher Donald Davidson (1985) that "a creature cannot have thoughts unless it is the interpreter of the speech of another" (p. 25). In an excellent discussion of Davidson's position, the philosopher John Fisher (1987) provides this paraphrase of Davidson: "Beliefs only arise in the process of interpreting the utterances of a linguistic community." But this confuses first- and second-order systems. In a milder version of his argument, Davidson said it is inaccurate to attribute to animals thoughts containing distinctions embodied in our linguistic expressions, but that there are thoughts that cannot be formulated in words, and animals might have these (Fisher, 1987). I would leave even more open, on methodological grounds. Sentiments such as those just cited seem overly concerned with marking boundaries based on ignorance. We have yet to test the limits of our own capacities to understand others, and even to appreciate the difficulties involved. On these issues, see the philosophers Harvey Sarles (1977), Richard Routley (1981), and Mary Midgley (1983); the Dutch human-animal writer Noske (1989, 1992); the philosopher Deborah Moore and the sociologist James Hannon (1993). Tom Tyler (2003) has recently argued for the rejection of the notion of anthropomorphism as it limits our ability to understand human-animal relationships. Also consider the difficulties successfully surmounted (by incorporating the pragmatic dimensions of language into the research paradigm) by the chimpanzee and Bonobo language researcher E. Sue Savage-Rumbaugh (1986) and other animal researchers. Imaginative possibilities are pioneered by the animal trainer and writer Vicki Hearne (1986), the ethologist Robert Mitchell (1987a), and the writer Elizabeth Marshall Thomas (1993). No mental predicates should be dismissed without contemplating such compendia of research on animal sensation, perception, cognition, and emotion as those by the Harvard cognitive ethologist Donald Griffin (1992), the writers Jeffrey Masson and Susan

McCarthy (1995), and the papers collected by Marc Bekoff, Collin Allen and Gordon Burkhardt (2002) and by Robert Mitchell, Nicholas Thompson, and Lyn Miles (1997). Such authors call for shifting the burden of proof to those who deny animal subjectivity in the face of the evidence available. Finally, much work remains to be done to understand species-specific semiotics (see the comment by the sociobiologist Robert Trivers, 1991).

4. The French animal behaviorists Jean-Louis Millot and Jean-Claude Filiatre (1986) noted that children avoid getting close to a dog's muzzle.

5. But the roles are not necessarily evenly shared. In a study of children and their dogs, Millot and Filiatre (1986) found that although 70 percent of the dogs' actions were followed by a modification in the child's behavior, only 40 percent of the child's actions produced a response in the dog.

6. The Dutch educator Margadant-van Arcken (1984, 1989) noted touching (and the passion for knowing animals' names, to be discussed shortly) in her early observations of children and live animals. Millot and Filiatre (1986) observed that young children touched their pet dogs in 68 percent of interactions.

7. In focusing on the individuality of an animal, the children may not be at all wrong. Researchers studying hyenas, chickadees and other animals are detecting stable individual psychological differences akin to human personality traits like boldness versus shyness (Zimmer, 2005).

8. Valerie Sims and her collaborators (2005) tracked and measured how long adults focused their eyes on the parts of human, dog, and cat faces. The images of the faces showed four different emotions. Across species the greatest amount of time was spent looking at the eyes, and the least time was spent on the ears, although ears are important in dogs' and cats' emotional displays.

9. The perception of animal vitality affect and its effects on the person may be unconscious. It might explain a number of findings, e.g., why dogs, aquaria of fish, or other animals can lower adults' and children's blood pressure readings, even in stressful situations; see, e.g., the work of the researchers Aaron Katcher, Erika Friedmann, Alan Beck, and James Lynch (1983); also see Beck and Katcher (1996).

10. One predication of Stern's theory is that infants would begin to register animals differently around 3 months of age, at the same time the core self is gelling. Since writing the first edition of this book, I have had the pleasure of watching our two daughters (and several of their friends) move through this period of life. Of course, I was there with notepad and video camera (I'm sure Piaget would have videotaped at least as much and as representatively as I do, had he had the technology). My records do document that beginning at

age 3 months, our girls started noticing our two cats differently than before: focusing their eyes on the cat, gazing for extended bouts, holding the head erect to see the cats and moving the head to continue seeing them, cooing occasionally, and appearing to reach toward them. By age 5 months, they showed considerable interest in the cats, petting and watching them move. I noted our first child didn't smile at the cats as often as she did at us, but seemed to smile about them sometimes. All these are signs of the infant engaging the cat as a core animate social other. Equally interesting was the difficult adjustment of the cats to our colicky first child, who loudly displaced them from our bed. In addition, the two cats were of quite different temperaments: one quiet and passive, the other (who died not long after our second child was born) was bold but fearful and prone to hiss and swipe. Our first child particularly developed very distinct relationships with these two animals; there is no doubt she registered the interactive differences well within her first year. On a newly discovered neurobiological substrate of cross-modal matching with implications for how infants connect with other species, see chapter 6, note 10.

11. Note that we are considering near-human-scale non-wild animals. But those who sensitively watch even very small creatures under the microscope may also respond to evident agency, coherence, etc.—see an example provided by the Norwegian philosopher Arne Naess (1986/1988). Wild animals show all animate properties, but with much less opportunity for relationships to develop; on children's attitudes to wildlife, see the work of the Yale researchers Stephen Kellert and Miriam Westervelt (1983). In a recent research project with graduate student Ann Russell, I explored the possibility that people with intimate knowledge of wild black bears may develop an articulate sense of self-in-relation to them (Myers and Russell, 2003).

12. This book is unusual in dealing with human-animal interactions across a range of phyla, orders, and species, as well as across stereotypical pet and non-pet species, but others have called for such study also, including the psychologists Timothy Eddy (1995); Aline Kidd, Hellen Kelley, and Robert Kidd (1983); and Julia Nielsen and Lloyd Delude (1989). On the individuality of animals, see note 7, above.

13. The psychologists James Hillman (1991) and Stephen Kellert (1993) have listed several factors behind the radical "otherness" of insects: They have differing spatial-temporal ecological survival strategies; they have a "multiplicity" that affronts selfhood; they have "monstrous" forms; they are associated with mindlessness and absence of feeling; and they demonstrate radical "autonomy" from human will and control. In short they do not evince the four key aspects of a core animate other developed here. On the other hand, the

great popularity of keeping insects among Japanese children gives a different impression. According to Laurent (2000), insects or "mushi" may be referred to as pets, are anthropomorphized in media, but when kept are rarely given names and their deaths are not grieved. So perhaps they provide an exception that proves the dominant pattern developed in this book.

14. The recent commercial availability of sophisticated robotic "dogs" such as Sony AIBO has created a new frontier at which to try to tease apart the properties that make living animate others special. One group of researchers studied young children's interactions with a robot versus with a dog and observed very little spontaneous speech to either dog or AIBO, and few differences in touch, which was the main way of interacting. They concluded that "children at this age appear to treat artificial animals in much the same way as live animals" (Goff et al., 2005). If this is so, then it counts against my contention that animals (at least many near-to-human scale vertebrates) constitute a significant and differentiated category of others for young children. Another research group seems headed toward a more qualified characterization. Kahn and colleagues (2004) compared preschoolers' reasoning about and interactions with a robotic dog and a stuffed toy dog and speculated that the AIBO may not be experienced as either alive or not alive, nor as simply a combination of qualities of both, but rather as a novel type of entity (Kahn et al., 2004). This interpretation was bolstered by parallel research with AIBO and a real dog (Melson et al., 2005). Children across ages 7 and 15 attributed more bodily functions, mental states, sociality, and moral standing to the real dog, and touched it more—all at statistically significant levels (generally $p < .01$). On the other hand, the majority of these children did treat the AIBO in dog-like fashion, supporting Goff et al.'s (2005) idea that the children assimilated the AIBO to the category of living being. This tendency was less, however, among older children. This might be consistent with the emergence of a distinct ontological category that borrows some features from computational artifacts and some from living social others (Kahn et al., 2004). From my interactional perspective the degree of familiarity with the AIBO may also be a critical overlooked variable, with the experimental children having five minutes with the AIBO before questions started, and having altogether about an hour. A more comparable duration of familiarity would be preferable. I would also have questions about the task demands of the verbal questioning for the younger children; and a more subtle coding of behaviors might pick up some of the subtleties of connection and differentiation that the children in my naturalistic study revealed.

15. How the child's cognitive categories (of animals, and in the child's

theory of mind) relate to interactional variation is a topic ripe for future research based on findings presented here.

16. Similarly, Millot and Filiatre (1986) observed that interactions with dogs necessarily differ from those with other children, because the rates of response differ.

17. See, e.g., the psychologists Bruno Bettelheim (1976); Marcel Heiman (1956, 1965); Kerstin Kupferman (1977); Ivan Sherick (1981); and Robert Van de Castle (1983).

18. The implications of attachment for the study of child-pet relations have been described by the psychologist Gail Melson (1990), who discusses four dimensions: time with pet, affect, knowledge, and responsiveness to the pet.

19. Our discussion here omits interpretation of the animal's side of the bond, though it is surely real and important—companion animals are attached to their owners.

Of interest to future researchers, David Anderson (2007) has prepared a collection of instruments for assessing people's bonds with their pets: *Assessing the human-animal bond: A compendium of actual measures* (West Lafayette, IN: Purdue University Press).

20. An important early report on unresponsive psychiatric patients' successes with dogs is by the psychiatrists Samuel Corson, Elizabeth Corson, Peter Gwynne, and Eugene Arnold (1977). The psychologists Laurel Redefer and Joan Goodman (1989) found autistic children's social exchanges were dramatically increased during and immediately after animal intervention; other studies have since confirmed this effect. The child therapist Gerald Mallon (1992) reviews animals in child therapy, as does Melson (2001, ch. 5). Recently Nimer and Lundahl (2005) conducted a meta-analysis of 14 studies that used animals to enhance medical, psychological, and autistic spectrum symptom interventions. They found moderate to strong effect sizes for the use of animals with each kind of the three types of problems, with younger children tending to benefit more from animal-assisted therapy.

21. For more on how pets contribute to social development, see Bryant (1986); A. H. Kidd and R. M. Kidd (1990a, 1990b); Melson (1990, 1991); Melson and Fogel (1988); Myers (1994); Poresky and Hendrix (1990); the German psychologists Detlef Rost and Anette Hartmann (1994); and several authors in the volume edited by the family researcher Marvin Sussman (1985), among others. Several essays in Podberscek et al. (2000) discuss different aspects of pets in family settings; see also Morrow, 1998).

22. Particularly thorough on children and animal abuse is Ascione's book (2005). Ascione suggests a variety of motivations for children's mistreatment of

animals, including curiosity and exploration; peer reinforcement; attempts to modify one's own mood; sexual gratification; coerced or forced animal abuse; abusing an animal as a way to emotionally abuse another person; identification with an aggressor; imitation of adults; posttraumatic play; monetary gain; and others. Any of these may be at work, rather than the often-assumed motivation of rehearsal for interpersonal violence. He discusses and qualifies at length the extent to which this "link" may be valid. Similarly Arluke's (2006) book goes far to paint a more complex picture of animal abuse than presented by the mainstream media—which itself is a focus of his acute sociological analysis of cruelty. Based on interviews with undergraduates who recalled abusing animals, Arluke distinguishes between abuse as displaced aggression and abuse as "dirty play," in which a child consciously casts abuse as similar to power and control exercised by adults. In another interesting section, Arluke details the students' grappling retrospectively with their guilt and self-image. See also Henry (2004a and 2004b) for a discussion of social group factors mediating participation in animal abuse, as recalled later in college.

23. See the work of the historian Gerald Carson (1972); Jared Diamond (1993); the psychologist Harold Herzog and the animal behaviorist Gordon Burghardt (1987); the anthropologist of human-animal relations Elizabeth Lawrence (1982); Menninger (1951); Tuan (1984). Coleman (2004) attempts unflinchingly to answer why killing wolves was not enough, in the collective history of their vicious torture over three centuries during the settlement of America.

24. The perspective I am developing here is in line with theorists who stressed the social self. New concepts about how we understand others are required. For instance, the social psychologist James Youniss (1983) criticizes the concept that "taking the role of the other" equals "understanding" the other, because it assumes there is not the communication requisite to knowing the other in the first place. Similarly, the philosopher Lawrence Blum (1987) argues that the idea that "projection" entails imagining how one would feel and attributing that feeling to the other assumes too sharp a self-other boundary, one too cognitively demanding for very young children, who, counterfactually, *do* understand others. Instead, he claims, "Our ability to grasp another's condition is a more fundamental cognitive process that more specialized uses of inference can only build upon but not replace." One attempt to describe such a process is the philosopher Nel Noddings's (1984) suggestion that it is not by projection but by receptivity or "taking in" the other that the child opens himself or herself to the differences and feelings of the other. Blum (1987) characterizes such responsiveness to others as an "immediate and non-inferential

grasp of another's feelings" (p. 315). This is very akin to the idea of attunement developed by Stern (1985), and emphasized here. New work stemming from the psychologist James Gibson's (1979) ecological theory of perception and from the previously mentioned area of infants' perceptual abilities strengthens such assertions (see Read, 1996; Dent-Read and Zukow-Goldring, 1997). The present study of children with different animals contributes to this direction in contemporary psychology.

25. Examples are provided in Arluke's (2006) discussion of undergraduate students' recollections of violence to animals when they were adolescents. Some of these subjects described as "exciting" the unpredictable reactions animals gave when harmed. These reactions were not of a sort that could be substituted by an inanimate object (see Arluke, 2006, pp. 62–63). Corson et al. (1977, p. 72) discuss "security by rank," perhaps a kindred phenomenon.

26. Here I am suggesting a psychological dynamic akin to the work of self-in-relationship theorists such as Jean Baker Miller (1986) and Judith Jordan (Jordan et al., 1991), who point out how growth in relationships brings new clarity. In a related way, Gendlin's (1978, 1987) work suggests how psychological growth consists of steps of awareness and clarification about the self.

Chapter V

1. See chapter 4, notes 3 and 24.

2. We might be more certain that it *only* arises within human relationships had the few authentic cases of "feral children" raised by nonhuman animals been studied for the possibility that the child's interaffective abilities can work within other species' repertoires of mood and signal. On feral children, see Lucien Malson's assessment and reprinting of Jean Itard's (1799/1964/1972) *The wild boy of Aveyron;* the work of the psychologists Mary McNeil, Edward Polloway and David Smith (1984); and the work of the Indian Reverend J. A. L. Singh and author R. M. Zingg (1939), who cared for the "wolf children" Amala and Kamala. Noske (1989) proposed studying such cases to better understand animals.

3. Selective attunement specifies a nonpsychoanalytic account of feelings similar to those discussed in Freud's (1913/1950) statement that opened chapter 2.

4. At the time the observation was made, I did not know that a child putting his hands in pigeon droppings would run a risk, however slight, of exposure to viral pneumonia, as well as other diseases. The topic of *zoonotic infections* is treated in Gorczyca, Fine and Spain, 2000; also consult *Clinical Infectious Diseases Journal* for current research.

5. Sure examples are in Savage-Rumbaugh's chimpanzee and bonobo language studies (1986; Savage-Rumbaugh et al., 1993). Not only in chimpanzees, bonobos, and gorillas, but in studies of cetaceans and parrots in their own groups or interacting with humans, systems with interintentional and linguistic properties are increasingly well documented (Kako, 1999; Rendell and Whitehead, 2001). Still, the jury shall have to be left out for a long time on the full extent of animals' human language capacities, and much longer on communication using other species' (possible) linguistic systems.

6. The psychologist Ken Shapiro (1989) has described precisely this process in "keep-away" with a dog.

7. Ricard and Allard's (1993) research documents an early step in this development.

8. Research to date on the child's theory of mind has not dealt extensively with attribution of mental properties to nonhuman animals. Other work on children's biological reasoning shows their strong tendency to think of animal properties according to innate potentials and maintenance-of-identity components of an essentialist view (Gelman et al., 1994). An interesting inquiry at the intersection of these domains would be whether and when young children think different species have different trait-like mental qualities. Their tendency to see immanent causes behind animate action, together with their ability to register differences in interactive qualities reported here, suggests they might.

9. For other analyses of adult speech to and for dogs, see Arluke and Sanders (1996) chapter 3, and Mitchell and Edmonson (1999).

10. It could be argued that children are in a favorable position to discover whatever shared communication *is* possible with animals, because they regard animal action as communicative. Even if one lowers the threshold of what is considered conventional and reversible, however, animals in the naturalistic setting of this study did not qualify. This is not to say that under no circumstances *could* they. See Sanders and Arluke (1993); and Arluke and Sanders (1996) for a consideration of the possibilities for enhancing communication with animals. Irvine (2004) argues for intersubjectivity with pet dogs. Also consider great ape language studies, particularly by Sue Savage-Rumbaugh (1986; Savage-Rumbaugh et al., 1993). See Dennett (1995) for a more qualified appraisal of our potential for understanding animal consciousness. I discuss the issue at greater length in Myers (2003).

11. This expectation was also shown by the children in Millot and Filiatre's (1986) study, who gestured more to their dogs when in front of the dogs and used physical contact more when positioned behind them.

12. In my work, I did not examine attribution of second-order intention-

ality (such as communicative intent) according to species. But the psychologists Timothy Eddy and Gordon Gallup and the anthropologist Daniel Povinelli (1993) found that adults attribute more higher-order intentionality the more they perceive the animal as similar to humans.

13. Indeed, classical ethology was able to proceed in cataloguing animal behavior partly because its methodology assumed behavior is transparent. The functions of behavior may not be apparent at first, but the behaviors themselves are relied on as unproblematic data. Only recently has a challenge been raised (Griffin, 1976, 1992).

14. Mallon (1994) found that seven- to sixteen-year-olds in a treatment center spoke to farm animals because they were sure their words would not be repeated.

15. For example, Sanders (1990, 1993a; 1993b) brilliantly describes owner-dog behavior in public, following the sociologist Erving Goffman's (1959) perspective of frame analysis and social impression management.

Chapter VI

1. This and the following are indebted to Hanson (1986, especially chap. 3). Similarly to the spirit of my argument in this section, sociologists Arluke and Sanders (1996), and Alger and Alger (1997) have called for others in their discipline to think beyond Mead regarding the problems of our relationships to animals; see Brandt (2004) for an interactionist approach to human-horse interaction; and Alger and Alger (1997) on humans and cats.

2. Ethologist-psychologist Mitchell's (1990) comparative-developmental analysis of pretend play showed that the design process in pretend play must be *intentional* simulation. Counting against the old idea, suggested by Mead's phrase "ready for expression," that pretend could be a confusion of reality and fantasy, is Harris's (1998) demonstration that pretend instead demonstrates a transfer of knowledge from reality to fiction. Indeed, Lewis and Ramsey (1999) argued that the emergence of consciousness is related to the emergence of pretend because the latter "requires conscious intention and self-awareness in that children know that their actions on objects are not real" (1999, p. 85). See Mitchell (2001) for an interesting set of essays on pretend in humans and animals.

3. That both imitation and pretend play examples are included follows from Mitchell's analyses: Fourth-level imitation includes pretense (1987b), and pretend play can include imitation (1990). The key link is intentionality. Pretend play demonstrates intentional simulation, and fourth-level imitation requires control over the relationship between model and copy. In this chapter,

the imitation examples used were deliberate acts, as evidenced by being directed to a particular other, or otherwise marked. In other words, we will look at imitation that serves communicative goals, albeit sometimes literal rather than make-believe ones.

4. The probability of the relationship I found occurring by chance alone is given by the Fisher exact probability test as 0.048, or less than one in twenty.

5. One commonality between Chen, Billy, Yasmin, and Rosa is that they are younger than average. Drew, a few months to a year older than these four, liked to pretend to be "baby animals, after his bath . . . [a] different one each time." But "Drew hasn't been playing this game in the last few months." One might be tempted to suppose that age is a factor here, but older children accounted for more of the animal-pretend episodes in school. And some of these kids were not reported to pretend at home, i.e., Ivy, Dawn, and Benson (of these, only Ivy had no pets at home). Thus, the context—home or school—may interact with age and exposure to pets, but the question awaits more focused study.

6. The human ecologist Paul Shepard (1978) was among the first to draw attention to animals in children's pretend play and in cognitive development. I hope that this book will substantiate cognate insights for a broader community of psychologists.

7. Analogous pairs of terms are the sociologist Anthony Giddens's (1979) discursive versus practical consciousness, Grice's (1957) non-natural meanings versus natural meanings, and Bruner's (1986) paradigmatic versus narrative thought.

8. See, e.g., works by the psychologist Eugene Gendlin (1962, 1987, 1992).

9. Some argue this is "intersubjectivity," but I have followed Stern's (1985) stricter criteria.

10. Recent functional MRI studies (Chaminade et al., 2005) have substantiated that different areas of the brain are involved in visual-spatial representation of perceived action, than those in the production of the body schema. Different forms of apraxia in which a patient cannot imitate an action involve deficits in one or the other of these different areas. But these separate areas may be integrated via recently revealed "mirror neurons." These specialized cells, distributed in several areas of the brain, fire both when a person does an action, and when the person sees or hears that action done by another. Recent research suggests this matches perfectly with the description preceding this note by Buytendijk of the "original identity of perceptibility and

intelligibility" of behavior. Such neurons were first observed in primates, but reach great complexity and sophistication in humans. The existence of mirror neurons that respond to visual and auditory consequences of actions suggest a basis for the modality-independence underlying core animate relatedness and empathy (see, e.g., Decety & Jackson, 2006; Kaplan & Iacoboni, 2005; Carr et al., 2003; Iacoboni & Lenzi, 2002). To test the theory of human-animal relations advanced here, new research should compare the patterns of activation of mirror neurons during children's observation of animal versus human versus robotic actions to test the idea that children use the same mechanisms in understanding all groups, but that theses mechanisms also differentiate between them (see chapter 4, note 14). Additional research would capitalize on the different movement patterns of different species, perhaps including elicited imitation performances by children, testing the flexibility of the mirror neuron system in the "translation of the body" I discuss in this book. Finally, we should compare the patterns of mirror neuron firings in response to an animal's actions of adults with low versus high levels of psychological defense mechanisms about animal pain. This could help determine whether the latter groups' evident lack of responsiveness to animals' experiences occurs at the basic level of mirroring, or is mediated by other levels of cognitive processing, as predicted by Bandura, 1990 and 1999, and Agnew, 1998.

11. Thus, de Gramont argues that confusion about language (not egocentrism) leads to the phenomena Piaget (1929/1960) termed realism and animism.

12. For a thorough discussion, see de Gramont (1990, chaps. 1 and 6).

13. See, e.g., the historian Sabine Baring-Gould (1865/1995), and the psychiatrists Aaron Kulick, Harrison Pope, and Paul Keck (1990).

14. Arluke and Sax's important 1992 study has been followed up by a book-length treatment by Sax (2000a). This careful historical analysis examines the multiple blurrings of the meaning of human and animal, and how they cohered in a vague but absolute ideology which served Nazi ends. See also Sax, 2000b.

15. If hunting were all that brought about these human abilities, then they would be much more widespread across species. See Mitchell (2001) for scholarly discussions of pretend across species.

Chapter VII

1. See historian Katherine Grier's discussion, summarized above in chapter 2, of the emergence of humane children's literature.

2. Hank Davis, an animal experimentalist, and Dianne Balfour (1992)

proposed that a bond develops between even animal experimentalists and their subjects, requiring some kind of psychic defense. Author Jim Mason (1993) has argued that Western culture is built on a myth of human supremacy, buttressed by such psychodynamics. Other writers have linked the use of animals to systems of human oppression including slavery and the Holocaust—systems maintained by beliefs and mechanisms creating psychological distance (Spiegel, 1996; Patterson, 2002).

3. An attentive student of the related literature will note a divergence between my perspective and that of Kahn (1999) in at least two respects. First, we suggest different developmental patterns in biocentric or animal-related concern; and our underlying theories (and resultant methods) differ. Kahn finds that biocentric reasoning (when it occurs at all) is shown by older children, whereas I suggest a moral sensitivity to harm to animals even at very young ages—and I speculate that that concern is at risk in later ages. Most recently, however, Kahn and Severson (2006) report results supporting the early emergence of biocentrism. Second, Kahn's focus is cognitive moral reasoning or judgment, at the center of the Western deontological tradition of moral philosophy and as studied by the lineage of developmental psychologists including Piaget (1932/1965), Kohlberg (1984), and Turiel (1983; 1998; 2002), and as expressed in in-depth interviews. The youngest age of children with whom such interviews can be conducted is about 6 years, the age of the oldest children at the end of the year in my study. My focus, on the other hand, is better characterized as moral functioning. Its predecessors include most particularly Norma Haan (Haan et al., 1985), who shares with Kohlberg's school the conclusion that the definition of morality must be addressed philosophically before morality can be studied psychologically. While granting an important role to cognition or judgment, Haan's perspective emphasizes emotion, social context, and non-moral psychological factors (such as sense of self, and defense mechanisms) in moral development. The spirit of this approach is in agreement with Schopenhauer (1841/1965), who thought compassion underlies the capacity for moral motivation, and with Hume (1777/1975) who declared "sympathy" to be a key and universal *moral* sentiment and determiner of other-oriented action (see also Kagan, 1984). Beehler points out that even Kant, whose moral system placed reason at its center, admitted that antecedent "feelings" such as love (in the sense of charity) lie "at the basis of morality" (Beehler, 1978, p. 128, quoting Kant, 1797/1964, p. 59). (On care, see also Noddings, 1984.) If indeed emotions and other psychological factors are fundamental in morality, their study should be paramount—but perhaps

more difficult. I do not assume that young children can reliably report their emotions, save in the most favorable circumstances such as to a parent or other trusted adult. In light of the "task demands" researchers can realistically ask of young subjects, my study is based more on orchestrated or naturalistically observed events, and on children's dialog in and about these events. Such evidence allows some inferences about the early moral emotion and experience. Notably, a moral functioning perspective anticipates discontinuities as well as continuities. Philosopher Angus Ross suggests that altruism is more than a mere possibility for our species. When response to perception of another's distress is absent, we may assume it is blocked by some other process. These processes include particularly the distinctions we make between the deserving and the undeserving or between objects of concern and of indifference (Ross, 1983), as illustrated in Bandura's (1990, 1998) work referred to earlier, and in Susan Opotow's work on moral exclusion (2000; Opotow & Brook, 2003). Another kind of blockage is revealed by Betty Bardige's (1988) discussion of the fading of a sense of "moral urgency" in early adolescents. Thus, in as much as Kahn's data show only modest trends toward biocentric reasoning in older ages it is reasonable to ask whether there are obstacles in the socio-moral-emotional part of the equation, as well as a presumed complexification of moral judgment. With these characterizations of these studies noted (however briefly), several fundamental agreements with Kahn's work should be highlighted: a belief that human development matters because it entails the person's integration of genetic and environmental forces, and that it reveals universals (probably cognitive *and* affective!); a stress on interaction with the world as a driver of a psychological constructivist concept of development; a patience with matters philosophical and theoretical as well as with detecting empirical patterns; and an interest in the urgent but under-studied intersection of human development and human ecology.

4. Non-economic values include the idea of "existence value," the benefit people derive from simply knowing that an entity (such as a species) exists, even if they will never see it. Not that economic values are not also at stake. Pets are a $20 billion industry in the U.S. alone; American zoo attendance is higher than at all major sports events combined; bird watching is being reported as the number-one outdoor activity, and animal-oriented outdoor recreation and eco-tourism are major recent trends.

5. This question was not asked about the dog.

6. Each of these three girls was in a separate small group, so they probably did not influence each other's immediate responses.

Chapter VIII

1. See the work of psychologist Wes Schultz and colleagues (2004) for fascinating results from a measure of the extent to which a person implicitly identifies the self with nature.

2. See recent works by me and my colleagues: Myers & Russell, 2004; Myers & Saunders, 2002; Myers, Saunders & Garrett, 2003 & 2004. Other empirical works relating concern for animals to concern for natural environments include Kalof (2000; 2003), and Jerolmack (2003).

References

Agnew, R. (1998). The causes of animal abuse: A social-psychological analysis. *Theoretical Criminology 2*(2), 177–209.

Alger, J. M. & Alger, S. F. (1997). Beyond Mead: Symbolic interaction between humans and felines. *Society and Animals 5*(1), 65–81.

Alibali, M.W., & Goldin-Meadow, S. (1993). Gesture-speech mismatch and mechanisms of learning: What the hands reveal about a child's state of mind. *Cognitive Psychology 24*(4), 468–523.

Anderson, D. (2007). *Assessing the human-animal bond: A compendium of actual measures*. West Lafayette, IN: Purdue University Press.

Aristotle (1984). "Rhetoric." In J. Barnes (Ed.), *The Complete Works of Aristotle*, vol. 2 (Revised Oxford Translation). Princeton, NJ: Princeton Univ. Press.

Arluke, A. (2006). *Just a dog: Understanding animal cruelty and ourselves*. Philadelphia: Temple University Press.

Arluke, A. (2003). Childhood origins of supernurturance: The social context of early human behavior. *Anthrozoös 16* (1), 3–27.

Arluke, A. & Sanders, C. R. (1996). *Regarding animals*. Philadelphia: Temple University Press.

Arluke, A., & Sax, B. (1992). Understanding Nazi animal protection and the Holocaust. *Anthrozoös 5*(1), 6–31.

Ascione, F. R. (1993). Children who are cruel to animals: A review of research and implications for developmental psychopathology. *Anthrozoös 6*(4), 226–247.

Ascione, F. R. (2005). *Children and animals: Exploring the roots of kindness and cruelty*. West Lafayette, IN: Purdue University Press.

Ascione, F. R., Kaufmann, M. E., & Brooks, S. M. (2000). Animal abuse and developmental psychopathology: Recent research, programmatic and therapeutic issues and challenges for the future. In A. H. Fine (Ed.), *Handbook on animal-assisted therapy: Theoretical foundations and guidelines for practice* (pp. 325–354). San Diego, CA: Academic Press.

Ashcraft, R. (1972). Leviathan triumphant: Thomas Hobbes and the politics of wild men. In E. Dudley & M. E. Novak (Eds.), *The wild man within: An image in Western thought from the Renaissance to Romanticism* (pp. 141–181). Pittsburgh, PA: University of Pittsburgh.

Ashley-Montagu, M. F. (1937). *Coming into being among the Australian Aborigines: A study of procreative beliefs of the native tribes of Australia.* London: George Routledge.

Astington, J. W. (1993). *The child's discovery of the mind.* Cambridge, MA: Harvard University Press.

Avis, J., & Harris, P. L. (1991). Belief-desire reasoning among Baka children: Evidence for a universal conception of mind. *Child Development 62,* 460–467.

Bailey, C. (1987). Exposure of preschool children to companion animals: Impact on role-taking skills. *Dissertation Abstracts International 48*(08), 1976A.

Bandura, A. (1990). Selective activation and disengagement of moral control. *Journal of Social Issues 46*(1), 27–46.

Bandura, A. (1999). Moral disengagement in the perpetration of inhumanities. *Personality and Social Psychology Review 3*(3), 193–209.

Barba, B. E. (1995). A critical review of research on the human/companion animal relationship: 1988 to 1993. *Anthrozoös 8*(1), 9–15.

Bardige, B. (1988). Things so finely human: Moral sensibilities at risk in adolescence. In C. Gilligan, J. V. Ward & J. M. Taylor (Eds.), *Mapping the moral domain* (pp. 87–110). Cambridge, MA: Harvard Graduate School of Education.

Baring-Gould, S. (1995). *The book of werewolves.* London: Senate/Studio. (Original work published 1865)

Bates, E. (1976). *Language and context: The acquisition of pragmatics.* New York: Academic Press.

Bates, E. (1979). Intentions, conventions and symbols. In E. Bates (Ed.), *The emergence of symbols: Cognition and communication in infancy* (pp. 33–68). New York: Academic Press.

Bateson, G. (1972). *Steps to an ecology of mind.* New York: Ballantine.

Bateson, G., Jackson, D., Haley, J., & Weakland, J. (1956). Toward a theory of schizophrenia. *Behavioral Science 1,* 251–264.

Beck, A. M., & Katcher, A. H. (1996). *Between pets and people: The importance of animal companionship* (2nd ed.). West Lafayette, IN: Purdue University Press.

Bekoff, M., Allen, C. & Burghardt, G. M. (2002). *The cognitive animal: Empiri-

cal and theoretical perspectives on animal cognition. Cambridge, MA: MIT Press.

Beehler, R. (1978). *Moral life.* Towota, NJ: Rowman & Littlefield.

Beirne, P. (2004). From animal abuse to interhuman violence? A critical review of the progression thesis. *Animals and Society 12*(1), 39–65.

Berger, J. (1980). Why look at animals? In *About looking.* New York: Pantheon.

Berger, P. L., & Luckmann, T. (1966). *The social construction of reality.* Garden City, NY: Doubleday.

Bertenthal, B. (1993). Infants' perception of biomechanical motions: Intrinsic image and knowledge-based constraints. In C. Granrud (Ed.), *Visual perception and cognition in infancy* (pp. 175–214). Hillsdale, NJ: Lawrence Erlbaum.

Bettelheim, B. (1976). *The uses of enchantment.* New York: Vintage.

Bexell, S. (2005). Children and animals: Exploring empathic feelings with animals in four-year-olds in China and the United States. Presentation at the biennial meeting of the Society for Research in Child Development, April 7–10, Atlanta.

Bexell, S. (2006). Effect of a wildlife conservation camp experience in China on student knowledge of animals, care, propensity for environmental stewardship, and compassionate behavior toward animals. Doctoral dissertation, Georgia State University, Atlanta.

Blakeslee, S. (2002). A boy, a mother and a rare map of autism's world. *New York Times,* Nov. 19, F1, F4.

Blonder, L. X., Smith, C. D, Davis, C. E., Kesler-West, M. L., Garrity, T. F., Avison, M. J., Andersen, A. H. (2004). Regional brain response to faces of humans and dogs. *Cognitive Brain Research 20*(3), 384–394.

Blount, M. (1974). *Animal land: The creatures of children's fiction.* London: Hutchinson.

Blum, L. (1987). Particularity and responsiveness. In J. Kagan & S. Lamb (Eds.), *The emergence of morality in young children* (pp. 306–337). Chicago: University of Chicago Press.

Boccella, K. (1996). Gentle Binti just did what gorillas do. *Seattle Times* Aug. 28, p. 3.

Bodson, L. (2000). Motivations for pet-keeping in Ancient Greece and Rome: A preliminary survey. In A. Podberscek, E. Paul & J. Serpell (Eds.), *Companion animals and us: Exploring the relationships between people and us* (pp. 27–41). Cambridge: Cambridge University Press.

Borges, J. L., & Guerrero, M. (1974). *The book of imaginary beings* (N. T. di

Giovanni, Trans.). Middlesex, UK: Penguin. (Original work published 1967)

Bornstein, B., Sroka, H. & Munitz, H. (1969). Prosopagnosia with animal face agnosia. *Cortex 5*(2), 164–169.

Borstelmann, L. J. (1983). Children before psychology: Ideas about children from late antiquity to the late 1800s. In P. Mussen & W. Kessen (Eds.), *Handbook of child psychology: Vol. 1. History, theory and methods* (4th ed., pp. 1–40). New York: Wiley.

Bowd, A. D. (1983). Children's fears of animals. *Journal of Genetic Psychology 142*, 313–314.

Bowd, A. D. (1984). Fears and understanding of animals in middle childhood. *Journal of Genetic Psychology 145*(1), 143–144.

Bowlby, J. (1969). *Attachment and loss*, vol. 1: *Attachment*. New York: Basic Books.

Brandt, K. (2004). A language of their own: An interactionist approach to human-horse communication. *Society and Animals 12*(4), 299–316.

Brazelton, T. B., Tronick, E., & Main, M. (1974). The origins of reciprocity. In M. Lewis & L. Rosenblum (Eds.), *The effect of the infant on its caregiver* (pp. 49–76). New York: Wiley.

Bregman, E. (1934). An attempt to modify emotional attitude of infants by the conditioned response technique. *Journal of Genetic Psychology 45*, 169–198.

Brucklacher, B. (1992). The effects of live- and stuffed-animal displays on the behaviors and attitudes of kindergarten students. *Dissertation Abstracts International 53*(05), 1392A.

Bruner, J. (1969). Modalities of memory. In G. Talland & N. Waugh (Eds.), *The pathology of memory*. New York: Academic Press.

Bruner, J. (1986). *Actual minds, possible worlds*. Cambridge, MA: Harvard University Press.

Bryant, B. K. (1986, August). The relevance of family and neighborhood animals to social-emotional development in middle childhood. Abstract of paper presented at meeting of the Delta Society, Boston.

Bucke, W. F. (1903). Children's thoughts, reactions and feelings toward pet dogs. *Pedagogical Seminary (Journal of Genetic Psychology) 10*, 459–513.

Burghardt, G. (1992). Human-bear bonding in research on black bear behavior. In H. Davis and D. Balfour (Eds.) *The inevitable bond* (pp. 365–82). Cambridge: Cambridge University Press.

Butcher, C. & Goldin-Meadow, S. (2000). Gesture and the transition from one- to two-word speech: When hand and mouth come together. In D.

McNeill, (Ed.), *Language and gesture* (pp. 235–257). Cambridge: Cambridge University Press.

Campbell, D. T. (1975). "Degrees of freedom" and the case study. *Comparative Political Studies 8*(2), 178–193.

Carey, S. (1985). *Conceptual change in childhood.* Cambridge: MIT Press.

Carr, L., Iacoboni, M., Dubeau, M., Mazziotta, J. C., & Lenzi, G. L. (2003). Neural mechanisms of empathy in humans: A relay from neural systems for imitation to limbic areas. *Proceedings of the National Academy of Sciences, 100*(9), 5497.

Carroll, L. (1946). *Through the looking glass.* New York: Random House. (Original work published 1871)

Carson, G. (1972). *Men, beasts and gods: A history of cruelty and kindness to animals.* New York: Scribner.

Carson, H. (1917). The trial of animals and insects: A little known chapter of medieval jurisprudence. *American Philosophy 56*, 410–415.

Chaminade, T., Meltzoff, A. N. & Decety, J. (2005). An fMRI study of imitation: Action representation and body schema. *Neuropsychologia 43*(1), 115–127.

Cirillo, L., & Wapner, S. (Eds.). (1986). *Value presuppositions in theories of human development.* Hillsdale, NJ: Lawrence Erlbaum.

Cohen, E. (1994). Animals in medieval perceptions: The image of the ubiquitous other. In A. Manning & J. Serpell (Eds.), *Animals and society: Changing perspectives* (pp. 59–80). New York: Routledge.

Clark, E. (1979). Building a vocabulary: Words for objects, actions, and relations. In P. Fletcher & M. Garmon (Eds.), *Language acquisition: Studies in first language development* (pp. 149–160). Cambridge, UK: Cambridge University Press.

Coleman, J. (2004). *Vicious: Wolves and men in America.* New Haven CT: Yale Univ. Press.

Coley, J. D. (1995). Emerging differentiation of folkbiology and folkpsychology: Attributions of biological and psychological properties to living things. *Child Development 66*(6), 1856–1874.

Coley, J. D., Solomon, G. E. A., & Shafto, P. (2002). The development of folkbiology: A cognitive science perspective on children's understanding of the biological world. In P. H. Kahn, Jr. & S. R. Kellert (Eds.), *Children and nature: Psychological, sociocultural and evolutionary investigations* (pp. 65–91). Cambridge, MA: MIT Press.

Cormier, L. A. (2003). *Kinship with monkeys: The Guajá foragers of eastern Amazonia.* New York: Columbia Univ. Press.

Corsaro, W. A. (1981). Entering the child's world: Research strategies for field entry and data collection in a preschool setting. In J. L. Green & C. Wallat (Eds.), *Ethnography and language in educational settings* (pp. 117–146). Norwood, NJ: Ablex.

Corsaro, W. A. (1985). Friendship and peer culture in the early years. Norwood, NJ: Ablex.

Corsaro, W. A. & Streeck, J. (1986). Studying children's worlds: Methodological issues. In J. Cook-Gumperz, W. Corsaro & J. Streeck (Eds.), *Children's worlds and children's language* (pp. 13–36). New York: Mouton de Gruyter.

Corson, S. A., Corson, E. O'L., Gwynne, P. H., & Arnold, L. E. (1977). Pet dogs as nonverbal communication links in hospital psychiatry. *Comprehensive Psychiatry 18*, 61–72.

Creager, A. & Jordan, W. C. (Eds.) (2002). *The animal/human boundary: Historical perspectives*. Rochester, NY: University of Rochester Press.

Crocker, J. C. (1985). My brother the parrot. In G. Urton (Ed.), *Animal myths and metaphors in South America* (pp. 13–47). Salt Lake City, UT: University of Utah Press.

Csikszentmihalyi, M. (1990). *Flow: The psychology of optimal experience*. New York: Harper & Row.

Daly, B. & Morton, L. L. (2003). Children with pets do not show higher empathy: A challenge to current views. *Anthrozoös 16*(4), 298–314.

Damon, W. (Ed.) (1998). *Handbook of child psychology*, fifth edition, vols. 1–4. New York: John Wiley & Sons.

Damon, W., & Hart, D. (1988). *Self-understanding in childhood and adolescence*. Cambridge: Cambridge University Press.

Darwin, C. (1874). *The descent of man and selection in relation to sex* (2nd ed). New York: Appleton. (Original work published 1871)

Darwin, C. (1965). *The expression of emotion in man and animals*. Chicago: University of Chicago Press. (Original work published 1872)

Davidson, D. (1985). *Inquiries into truth and interpretation*. Oxford, UK: Clarendon.

Davis, H., & Balfour, D. (Eds.). (1992). *The inevitable bond: Examining scientist-animal interaction*. Cambridge, UK: Cambridge University Press.

Decety, J., & Jackson, P. L. (2006). A social neuroscience perspective on empathy. *Current Directions in Psychological Science 15*, 54–58.

de Gramont, P. (1990). *Language and the distortion of meaning*. New York: New York University Press.

Dennett, D. C. (1978). Beliefs about beliefs. *Behavioral and Brain Sciences 1*, 568–570.

Dennett, D. C. (1987). *The intentional stance*. Cambridge: MIT Press.

Dennett, D. C. (1995). Animal consciousness: What matters and why. *Social Research* 62(3), 691–710.

Dent-Read, C. & Zukow-Goldring, P. (Eds.). (1997). *Evolving explanations of development: Ecological approaches to organism-environment systems.* Washington, DC: American Psychological Association.

Denzin, N. K. (1982). The significant others of young children: Notes toward a phenomenology of childhood. In K. M. Borman (Ed.), *The social life of children in a changing society* (pp. 29–46). Hillsdale, NJ: Lawrence Erlbaum.

de Saussure, F. (1959). *Course in general linguistics.* New York: Philosophical Library.

Descartes, R. (1971). Discourse on method. In *Descartes philosophical writings* (E. Anscombe & P. T. Geech, Trans. & Ed.). Indianapolis, IN: Bobbs-Merrill. (Original work published 1637)

Descartes, R. (1972). *Treatise of man.* (T. S. Hall, Trans.). Cambridge, MA: Harvard University Press. (Original work published 1632)

Diamond, J. (1992). *The third chimpanzee.* New York: HarperCollins.

Diamond, J. (1993). New Guineans and their natural world. In S. R. Kellert & E. O. Wilson (Eds.), *The biophilia hypothesis* (pp. 251–271). San Francisco: Island Press.

Dobrin, S. I. & Kidd, K. B. (Eds.). (2004). *Wild things: Children's culture and ecocriticism.* Detroit: Wayne State University Press.

Dombrowski, D. A. (2002). Bears, zoos and wilderness: The poverty of social constructionism. *Society and Animals* 10(2), 195–202.

Douglas, M. (1975). *Implicit meanings: Essays in anthropology.* Boston: Routledge & Kegan Paul.

Durkheim, E., & Mauss, M. (1963). *Primitive classification.* Chicago: University of Chicago Press. (Original work published 1903)

Eaton, W. M. (1980). *The sociology of mental disorders.* New York: Praeger.

Eddy, T. J. (1995). Human cardiac responses to familiar young chimpanzees. *Anthrozoös* 8(4), 235–243.

Eddy, T. J., Gallup, G., & Povinelli, D. (1993). Attribution of cognitive states to animals: Anthropomorphism in comparative perspective. *Journal of Social Issues* 49(1), 87–101.

Erikson, E. H. (1958). *Young man Luther: A study in psychoanalysis and history.* New York: Norton.

Erikson, P. (2000). The social significance of pet-keeping among Amazonian Indians. In A. Podberscek, E. Paul & J. Serpell (Eds.), *Companion animals and us: Exploring the relationships between people and us.* (pp. 7–26). Cambridge: Cambridge University Press.

Evans, J. L., Alibali, M. W. & McNeil, N. M. (2001). Divergence of verbal expression and embodied knowledge: Evidence from speech and gesture in children with specific language impairment. *Language and Cognitive Processes 16*(2–3), 309–331.

Evans-Pritchard, E. E. (1940). *The Nuer.* Oxford, UK: Oxford University Press.

Evernden, N. (1993). *The natural alien: Humankind and environment* (2nd ed.). Toronto: University of Toronto Press.

Felthous, A. R., & Kellert, S. R. (1987). Childhood cruelty to animals and later aggression against people: A review. *American Journal of Psychiatry 144*(7), 10–17.

Ferenczi, S. (1916). *Contributions to psychoanalysis* (E. Jones, Trans.). Boston: R. G. Badger.

Fernandez, J. W. (1986). *Persuasions and performances: The play of tropes in culture.* Bloomington, IN: Indiana University Press.

Fine, A. H. (Ed.). (2000). *Handbook on animal-assisted therapy: Theoretical foundations and guidelines for practice.* San Diego, CA: Academic Press.

Fine, G. A. & Sandstrom K. L. (1988). *Knowing children: Participant observations with minors.* Thousand Oaks, CA: Sage Publications.

Fisher, A. (2002). *Radical ecopsychology: Psychology in the service of life.* Albany: SUNY Press.

Fisher, J. A. (1987). Taking sympathy seriously: A defense of our moral psychology toward animals. *Environmental Ethics 9*, 197–215.

Flavell, J. H., Green, F. L., & Flavell, E. R. (1986). Development of knowledge about the appearance-reality distinction. *Monographs of the Society for Research in Child Development 51*(1, Serial No. 212).

Freud, S. (1950). *Totem and taboo: Some points of agreement between the mental lives of savages and neurotics* (J. Strachey, Trans.). New York: Norton. (Original work published 1913)

Freud, S. (1955). Analysis of a phobia in a five-year-old boy "Little Hans." In J. Strachey (Ed. & Trans.), *Case histories* (vol. 1, pp. 165–312). Middlesex, UK: Pelican. (Original work published 1909)

Freud, S. (1965). *The interpretation of dreams* (J. Strachey, Trans.). New York: Avon/Basic. (Original work published 1900)

Frith, U. (1989). *Autism: Explaining the enigma.* Oxford: Basil Blackwell.

Fuentes, A. & Wolfe, L. D. (Eds.). (2002). *Primates face to face: Conservation implications of human-nonhuman primate interconnections.* Cambridge: Cambridge University Press.

Gallegos, E. S. (1991). *Animals of the four windows.* Santa Fe: Moon Bear.

Garcia, J. (1981). Tilting at the paper mills of academe. *American Psychologist 36*(2), 149–158.

Gardner, H. (1983). *Frames of mind.* New York: Basic Books.

Gardner, H. (1999). *Intelligence reframed: Multiple intelligences for the 21st century.* New York: Basic Books.

Gelman, S. A., Coley, J. D., & Gottfried, G. M. (1994). Essentialist beliefs in children: The acquisition of concepts and theories. In L. A. Hirschfeld & S. A. Gelman (Eds.), *Mapping the mind: Domain specificity in cognition and culture* (pp. 341–365). Cambridge, UK: Cambridge University Press.

Gendlin, E. T. (1962). *Experiencing and the creation of meaning: A philosophical and psychological approach to the subjective.* New York: Macmillan.

Gendlin, E. T. (1978). *Focusing.* New York: Bantam.

Gendlin, E. T. (1987). A philosophical critique of the concept of narcissism: The significance of the awareness movement. In D. Levin (Ed.), *Pathologies of the modern self: Postmodern studies on narcissism, schizophrenia and depression* (pp. 251–304). New York: New York University Press.

Gendlin, E. T. (1992). The primacy of the body, not the primacy of perception. *Man and World 25*(3–4), 341–353.

Gibson, J. J. (1979). *The ecological approach to visual perception.* Boston: Houghton Mifflin.

Giddens, A. (1979). *Central problems in social theory.* London: Macmillan.

Gillberg, C., & Rasmussen, P. (1994). Brief report: Four case histories and a literature review of Williams syndrome and autistic behavior. *Journal of Autism and Developmental Disorders 24* (3), 381–393.

Gilligan, C., & Wiggins, G. (1987). The origins of morality in early childhood relationships. In J. Kagan & S. Lamb (Eds.), *The emergence of morality in young children* (pp. 277–305). Chicago: University of Chicago Press.

Glaser, B. G. & Strauss, A. L. (1967). *The discovery of grounded theory: Strategies for qualitative research.* New York: Aldine de Gruyter.

Goff, L. G., Sims, K. & Chin, M. G. (2005). Preschoolers' interactions with live and robotic dogs. Abstract of paper presented at the International Association for Anthrozoology 14th Annual Conference, July 11–12, Niagara Falls.

Goffman, E. (1959). *The presentation of self in everyday life.* Garden City, NY: Doubleday.

Golinkoff, R. M., & Halperin, M. S. (1983). The concept of animal: One infant's view. *Infant Behavior and Development 6,* 229–233.

Goodall, J. 1990. *Through a window: My thirty years with the chimpanzees of Gombe.* Boston: Houghton Mifflin.

Gopnik, A. (1982). Words and plans: Early language and the development of intelligent action. *Journal of Child Language 9,* 303–318.

Gopnik, A., & Astington, J. W. (1988). Children's understanding of representational change and its relation to their understanding of false belief and the appearance-reality distinction. *Child Development 58*, 26–37.

Gorczyca, K., Fine, A. H., Spain, C. V. (2000). History, theory and development of human-animal support services for people with AIDS and other chronic/terminal illnesses. In A. H. Fine (Ed.), *Handbook on animal-assisted therapy: Theoretical foundations and guidelines for practice* (pp. 253–302). San Diego, CA: Academic Press.

Gould, S. J. (1977). *Ontogeny and phylogeny.* Cambridge, MA: Harvard University Press.

Grene, M. (1968). *Approaches to a philosophical biology.* New York: Basic Books.

Grice, H. P. (1957). Meaning. *Philosophical Review 66*, 377–388.

Grice, H. P. (1975). Logic and conversation. In P. Cole & J. L. Morgan (Eds.), *Syntax and semantics: 3. Speech acts* (pp. 43–58). New York: Academic Press.

Grier, K. C. (1999). Childhood socialization and companion animals: United States, 1820–1870. *Society and Animals 7*(2), 95–120.

Griffin, D. R. (1976). *The question of animal awareness: Evolutionary continuity of mental experience.* New York: Rockefeller University Press.

Griffin, D. R. (1992). *Animal minds.* Chicago: University of Chicago Press.

Haan, N, Aerts, E. & Cooper, B. (1985). *On moral grounds: The search for a practical morality.* New York: New York University Press.

Hall, G. S. (1897). A study of fears. *American Journal of Psychology 8*, 147–249.

Hall, G. S., & Browne, C. E. (1904). The cat and the child. *Pedagogical Seminary (Journal of Genetic Psychology) 11*, 3–29.

Hallowell, A. I. (1975). Ojibwa ontology, behavior, and world view. In D. Tedlock & B. Tedlock (Eds.), *Teachings from the American earth* (pp. 141–178). New York: Liveright. (Original work published 1960)

Hanson, K. (1986). *The self imagined: Philosophical reflections on the social character of the psyche.* New York: Routledge & Kegan Paul.

Haraway, D. (1989). *Primate visions: Gender, race and nature in the world of modern science.* New York: Routledge.

Harris, P. L. (1998). Fictional absorption: Emotional responses to make-believe. In S. Bråten (Ed.), *Intersubjective communication and emotion in early ontogeny* (pp. 336–353). Cambridge: Cambridge Univ. Press.

Harris, S. H. (1993). The everyday life experiences of three to six-year-old children with comforting possessions. (Doctoral dissertation, University of San Diego, San Diego). *Dissertation Abstracts 51* (6): 2805.

Hart, L. (1994). The Asian elephant-driver partnership: The drivers' perspective. *Applied Animal Behaviour Science 40*, 297–312.

Hart, L. & Sundar (2000). Family traditions for mahouts of Asian elephants. *Anthrozoös 13* (1), 34–42.

Hearne, V. (1986). *Adam's task: Calling animals by name*. New York: Vintage.

Heerwagen, J. H. & Orians, G. H. (2002). The ecological world of children. In P. H. Kahn, Jr. & S. R. Kellert (Eds.), *Children and nature: Psychological, sociocultural and evolutionary investigations* (pp. 29–63). Cambridge, MA: MIT Press.

Heidegger, M. (1962). *Being and time*. New York: Harper & Row.

Heiman, M. (1956). The relationship between man and dog. *Psychoanalytic Quarterly 25*, 568–585.

Heiman, M. (1965). Psychoanalytic observations on the relationship of pet and man. *Veterinary Medicine/Small Animal Clinician 60*, 713–18.

Hendrickson, K. , McCarthy, T. & Goodwin, J. (1990). Animal alters: Case reports. *Dissociation 8*, 18–221.

Henry, B. C. (2004a). Exposure to animal abuse and group context: Two factors affecting participation in animal abuse. *Anthrozoös 17*(4), 290–305.

Henry, B. C. (2004b). The relationship between animal cruelty, delinquency, and attitudes toward the treatment of nonhuman animals. *Society and Animals 12*(3), 185–207.

Herzog, H. A., & Burghardt, G. M. (1987). Attitudes toward animals: Origins and diversity. *Anthrozoös 1*(4), 214–222.

Hillman, J. (1991). *Going bugs*. Gracie Sta., NY: Spring Audio.

Hinde, R. A. (1976). On describing relationships. *Journal of Child Psychology and Psychiatry 17*, 1–19.

Hirschfeld, L., & Gelman, S. (Eds.). (1994). *Mapping the mind: Domain specificity in cognition and culture*. Cambridge, UK: Cambridge University Press.

Hirsh-Pasek, K., & Treiman, R. (1982). Doggerel: Motherese in a new context. *Journal of Child Language 9*, 229–237.

Hobbes, T. (1965). *Leviathan* (W. G. Pogson Smith, Ed.). Oxford, UK: Oxford University Press. (Original work published 1651)

Hodge, C. F. (1902). *Nature study and life*. Boston: Ginn.

Hoelscher, K. & Garfat, T. (1993). Talking to the animal. *Journal of Child and Youth Care 9*(3): 87–93.

Hoffman, M. (1987). The contribution of empathy to justice and moral judgment. In N. Eisenberg & J. Strayer (Eds.), *Empathy and its development* (pp. 47–80). Cambridge, UK: Cambridge University Press.

Houston, J. (1982). *The possible human: A course in enhancing your physical, mental and creative abilities.* Los Angeles: Tarcher-Houghton.

Howells, J. G. (Ed.) (1975). *World history of psychiatry.* New York: Brunner/Mazel Pub.

Hume, D. (1975). *Enquiries concerning human understanding and concerning the principles of morals.* (L. A. Selby-Bigge, Ed.) Oxford: Clarendon Press. (Original work published 1777)

Humphrey, N. K. (1984). *Consciousness regained: Chapters in the development of mind.* Oxford: Oxford University Press.

Iacoboni, M., & Lenzi, G. L. (2002). Mirror neurons, the insula and empathy. *Behavioral and Brain Sciences 25*(1), 39.

Ingold, T. (1988a). Introduction. In T. Ingold (Ed.), *What is an animal?* (pp. 1–16). London: Unwin Hyman.

Ingold, T. (1988b). The animal in the study of humanity. In T. Ingold (Ed.), *What is an animal?* (pp. 84–99). London: Unwin Hyman.

Inhelder, B. & Piaget, J. (1958). The growth of logical thinking from childhood to adolescence: An essay on the construction of formal operational structures (A. Parsons & S. Milgram, Trans.). New York: Basic Books.

Irvine, L. (2004). *If you tame me: Understanding our connection with animals.* Philadelphia: Temple University Press.

Isaacs, S. (1930). *Intellectual growth in young children.* New York: Harcourt, Brace.

Isbell, B. J. (1985). The metaphoric process: "From culture to nature and back again." In G. Urton (Ed.), *Animal myths and metaphors in South America* (pp. 285–313). Salt Lake City: University of Utah.

Jackson, M. (1988). Knowledge of the body. *Man (N.S.) 18*, 327–345.

James, W. (1890). *The principles of psychology.* New York: Dover.

James, W. (1961). *Psychology: The briefer course.* New York: Harper. (Original work published 1892)

Jerolmack, C. (2003). Tracing the profile of animal rights supporters: A preliminary investigation. *Society and Animals 11* (3), 245–266.

Jersild, A., & Holmes, F. B. (1935). Children's fears. *Child Development Monographs 20.* New York: Teachers College Press.

Johnson, A. (1995). Constructing the child in psychology: The child-as-primitive in Hall and Piaget. *Journal of Phenomenological Psychology 26*(2), 35–57.

Jordan, J. V., Surrey, J. L., Kaplan, A. G., Miller, J. B. & Stiver, I. P. (1991). *Women's growth in connection: Writings from the Stone Center.* New York: Guilford Press.

Jung, C. G. (1971). *The portable Jung*. (B. F. C. Hall, Trans., & J. Campbell, Ed.). New York: Viking.

Kagan, J. (1984). *The nature of the child*. New York: Basic Books.

Kagan, J. (1990). The concepts of self: A dialogue. In D. Cicchetti & M. Beeghly (Eds.), *The self in transition: Infancy to childhood* (pp. 363–383). Chicago: University of Chicago Press.

Kahn, P. H., Jr. (1999). *The human relationship with nature: Development and culture*. Cambridge, MA: MIT Press.

Kahn, P. H., Jr., Friedman, B., Perez-Granados, D. R., Freier, N. G. (2004). Robotic pets in the lives of preschool children. *Extended Abstracts of the CHI 2004 Conference on Human Factors in Computing Systems*. (pp. 1449–1452). New York: Association for Computing Machinery.

Kahn, P. H., Jr., & Severson, R. L. (2006, October). Biocentrism in a technological world. Abstract of paper presented at the 14th meeting of the Society for Human Ecology, Bar Harbor, ME.

Kako, E. (1999). Elements of syntax in the systems of three language-trained animals. *Animal Learning and Behavior 27* (1), 1–14.

Kalof, L. (2000). The multi-layered discourses of animal concern. In H. Addams & J. Proops (Eds.), *Social discourse and environmental policy: An application of Q methodology* (pp. 174–195). Northampton, MA: Edward Elgar.

Kalof, L. (2003). The human self and the animal other: Exploring borderland identities. In S. Clayton & S. Opotow (Eds.), *Identity and the natural environment* (pp. 161–178). Cambridge, MA: MIT Press.

Kant, I. (1964). *The doctrine of virtue*. (H. J. Paton, Trans.) New York: Harper & Row. (Original work published 1797)

Kaplan, J. T., & Iacoboni, M. (2005). Listen to my actions! *Behavioral and Brain Sciences 28*(2), 135.

Katcher, A., Friedmann, E., Beck, A., & Lynch, J. (1983). Looking, talking and blood pressure: The physiological consequences of interaction with the living environment. In A. Katcher & A. Beck (Eds.), *New perspectives on our lives with companion animals* (pp. 351–359). Philadelphia: University of Pennsylvania Press.

Kaylor, M. A. (1909). Feelings, thought and conduct of children toward animal pets. *Journal of Genetic Psychology 16*, 205–239.

Keil, F. C. (1990). Concepts, kinds and cognitive development. Cambridge: MIT Press.

Kellert, S. R. (1993). The biological basis for human values of nature. In S. R. Kellert & E. O. Wilson (Eds.), *The biophilia hypothesis* (pp. 42–69). Washington DC: Island Press.

Kellert, S. R., & Westervelt, M. O. (1983). *Children's attitudes, knowledge and behaviors toward animals (Phase 5)*. Washington DC: U.S. Fish and Wildlife Service.

Kessen,W (1965). *The child.* New York: Wiley.

Kidd, A. H., Kelly, H., & Kidd, R. (1983). Personality characteristics of horse, turtle, snake and bird owners. *Psychological Reports 52,* 719–729.

Kidd, A. H., & Kidd, R. M. (1987a). Reactions of infants and toddlers to live and toy animals. *Psychological Reports 61,* 455–464.

Kidd, A. H., & Kidd, R. M. (1987b). Seeking a theory of the human/companion animal bond. *Anthrozoös 1*(3), 140–157.

Kidd, A. H., & Kidd, R. M. (1990a). Factors in children's attitudes toward pets. *Psychological Reports 66,* 775–786.

Kidd, A. H., & Kidd, R. M. (1990b). Social and environmental influences on children's attitudes toward pets. *Psychological Reports 67,* 807–818.

Kidd, R. M. (1986, August). *Children and animals: Symbol and reality.* Abstract of paper presented at meeting of the Delta Society, Boston.

Kohlberg, L. (1984*). Essays on moral development.* San Francisco: Harper & Row.

Kulick, A. R., Pope, H. G., Jr., & Keck, P. E., Jr. (1990). Lycanthropy and self-identification. *Journal of Nervous and Mental Disease 178*(2), 134–137.

Kupferman, K. (1977). A latency boy's identity as a cat. *Psychoanalytic Study of the Child 32,* 363–385.

Lakoff, G. (1987). *Women, fire and dangerous things.* Chicago: University of Chicago Press.

Langdon, T. (1975). Food restrictions in the medical system of the Barasana and Taiwano Indians of the Colombian Northwest Amazon. Doctoral dissertation, Tulane University, New Orleans, LA.

Lasher, M. (1998). A relational approach to the human-animal bond. *Anthrozoös 11*(3), 130–133.

Laurent, E. L. (2000). Children, "insects" and play in Japan. In A. Podberscek, E. Paul & J. Serpell (Eds.), *Companion animals and us: Exploring the relationships between people and pets* (pp. 61–89). Cambridge: Cambridge University Press.

Lawrence, E. A. (1982). *Rodeo: An anthropologist looks at the wild and the tame.* Chicago: University of Chicago Press.

Lawrence, E. A. (1989). Neoteny in American perceptions of animals. In R. J. Hoage (Ed.), *Perceptions of animals in American culture* (pp. 57–76). Washington DC: Smithsonian Institution.

Le Guin, U. K. (1990). *Buffalo gals.* New York: Penguin.

Leslie, A. M. (1991). The theory of mind impairment in autism: Evidence for a modular mechanism of development? In A. Whiten (Ed.), *Natural theories of mind: Evolution, development and simulation of everyday mind reading* (pp. 63–78). Oxford, UK: Basil Blackwell.

Lévi-Strauss, C. (1966). *The savage mind.* Chicago: University of Chicago Press.

Levin, D. M. (1997). *Language beyond postmodernism: Saying and thinking in Gendlin's philosophy.* Evanston, IL: Northwestern University Press.

Levinson, B. M. (1969). *Pet-oriented child psychotherapy.* Springfield, IL: Charles C. Thomas.

Levinson, B. M. (1972). *Pets and human development.* Springfield, IL: Thomas.

Levinson, R. A. & Sanders, J. (1986). *An educational curriculum and the psychological needs of the student: A case study of interactions.* Unpublished ms., Sonia Shankman Orthogenic School, Chicago.

Levy-Bruhl, L. (1966). *How natives think.* New York: Washington Square Press.

Lewis, M. & Ramsay, D. (1999). Intentions, consciousness and pretend play. In P. Zelazo, J. Astington & D. R. Olson (Eds.), *Developing theories of intention: Social understanding and self-control* (pp. 77–94). Mahwah, NJ: Lawrence Erlbaum Assoc.

Linzey, A. (1990). For God so loved the world. *Between the Species* 6(1), 12–16.

Loren, B. K. (2001). Dancing the animal body: The heart of gong fu. *Orion* (Autumn), 12–14.

Lorenz, K. Z. (1962). *King Solomon's ring.* New York: Time. (Original work published 1952)

Lovejoy, A. (1961). *The great chain of being.* Cambridge, MA: Harvard University Press. (Original work published 1936)

Maccoby, E. (1980). *Social development: Psychological growth and the parent-child relationship.* New York: Harcourt, Brace, Jovanovich.

Malamud, R. (1998). Poetic animals and animal souls. *Society and Animals* 6(3), 263–277.

Malcarne, V. (1983). North American Association for Humane Education special report: Empathy and humane education. East Haddam, CT: North American Association for Humane Education.

Mallon, G. P. (1992). Utilization of animals as therapeutic adjuncts with children and youths: A review of the literature. *Child and Youth Care Forum* 21(1), 53–67.

Mallon, G. P. (1994). Cow as co-therapist: Utilization of farm animals as therapeutic aides with children in residential treatment. *Child and Adolescent Social Work Journal 11*(6), 455–474.

Malson, L., & Itard, J. M. G. (1972). *Wolf children and the problem of human nature* and *The wild boy of Aveyron* (E. Fawcett, P. Ayrton, & J. White, Trans.). New York: Monthly Review Press. (Malson's original work published in French 1964; Itard's original work published 1799)

Mandell, N. (1988). The least-adult role in studying children. *Journal of Contemporary Tthnography 16*(4), 433–467.

Margadant-van Arcken, M. (1984). "There's a real dog in the classroom?": The relationship between young children and animals. *Children's Environment Quarterly 1*(3), 13–16.

Margadant-van Arcken, M. (1989). Environmental education, children and animals. *Anthrozoös 3*(1), 14–19.

Marsh, M. A. (1902). Children and animals. In E. Barnes (Ed.), *Studies in Education 2* (pp. 83–99). New York: Stechert.

Mason, J. (1993). *An unnatural order: Uncovering the roots of our domination of nature and each other*. New York: Simon and Schuster.

Masson, J. M., & McCarthy, S. (1995). *When elephants weep: The emotional lives of animals*. New York: Delacorte.

Matthews, G. B. (1978). Animals and the unity of psychology. *Philosophy 53*, 437–454.

McLinton, B. S. & Meir, B. G. (1978). *Beginnings: Psychology of early childhood*. St. Louis: Mosby.

McNeil, M. C., Polloway, E. A., & Smith, J. D. (1984). Feral and isolated children: Historical review and analysis. *Education and Training of the Mentally Retarded 19*(1), 70–79.

McNeill, D. (1992). *Hand and mind: What gestures reveal about thought*. Chicago: University of Chicago Press.

McNeill, D. (Ed.) (2000). *Language and gesture*. Cambridge: Cambridge University Press.

Mead, G. H. (1913). The social self. *Journal of Philosophy, Psychology, and Scientific Methods 10*, 374–380.

Mead, G. H. (1962). *Mind, self and society from the standpoint of a social behaviorist*. Chicago: University of Chicago Press. (Original work published 1934)

Melson, G. (1990). Studying children's attachment to their pets: A conceptual and methodological review. *Anthrozoös 4*(2), 91–99.

Melson, G. (1991, April). The relationship between children's attachment to pets and socioemotional development. Paper presented at the biennial meeting of the Society for Research in Child Development, Seattle.

Melson, G. (2001). *Why the wild things are: Animals in the lives of children.* Cambridge, MA: Harvard Univ. Press.

Melson, G. F., & Fogel, A. (1988). Children's ideas about animal young and their care: A reassessment of gender differences in the development of nurturance. *Anthrozoös 2*(4), 265–273.

Melson, G. F., Kahn, Jr., P. H., Beck, A. M., Friedman, B., Roberts, T., & Garrett, E. (2005). Robots as dogs?: Children's interactions with the robotic dog AIBO and a live Australian Shepherd. *Extended Abstracts of the CHI 2005 Conference on Human Factors in Computing Systems.* (pp. 1649–1652). New York: Association for Computing Machinery.

Meltzoff, A. N., & Gopnik, A. (1993). The role of imitation in understanding persons and developing a theory of mind. In S. Baron-Cohen, H. Tager-Flusberg, & D. Cohen (Eds.), *Understanding other minds: Perspectives from autism* (pp. 335–366). New York: Oxford University Press.

Meltzoff, A. N. & Moore, K. M. (1995). A theory of the role of imitation in the emergence of the self. In P. Rochat (Ed.), *The self in infancy: Theory and research. Advances in psychology 112* (pp. 73–93). Amsterdam: North-Holland/Elsevier Science Publishers.

Menninger, K. A. (1951). Totemic aspects of contemporary attitudes toward animals. In G. B. Wilber & W. Muensterberger (Eds.), *Psychoanalysis and culture: Essays in honor of Geza Roheim* (pp. 42–74). New York: International Universities Press.

Merleau-Ponty, M. (1962). *Phenomenology of perception* (C. Smith, Trans.). London: Routledge. (Original work published 1945)

Midgley, M. (1983). *Animals and why they matter.* Athens, GA: University of Georgia Press.

Midgley, M. (1988). Beasts, brutes and monsters. In T. Ingold (Ed.), *What is an animal?* (pp. 35–46). London: Unwin Hyman.

Miller, J. B. (1986). *Toward a new psychology of women. Second edition.* Boston: Beacon Press.

Miller, P. J., & Hoogstra, L. (1989, November). How to represent the native child's point of view: Methodological problems in language socialization. Paper presented at the meeting of the American Anthropological Association, Washington, DC.

Millot, J.-L., & Filiatre, J.-C. (1986). The behavior sequences in the communication system between the child and his pet dog. *Applied Animal Behaviour Science 16*, 383–390.

Mitchell, R. W. (1987a). Projects, routines, and enticements in interspecies play between familiar and unfamiliar dogs and people. *Dissertation Abstracts International 8*(07), 2136B.

Mitchell, R. W. (1987b). A comparative-developmental approach to understanding imitation. In P. P. G. Bateson & P. H. Klopfer (Eds.), *Perspectives in ethology*, vol. 7: *Alternatives* (pp. 183–215). New York: Plenum Press.

Mitchell, R. W. (1990). A theory of play. In M. Bekoff & D. Jamieson (Eds). *Interpretation and explanation in the study of animal behavior*, vol. 1: *Interpretation, intentionality and communication* (pp. 197–227). Boulder, CO: Westview Press.

Mitchell, R. W. (1994). Review of *The biophilia hypothesis. Anthrozoös* 7(3), 212–214.

Mitchell, R. W. (1997). A comparison of the self-awareness and kinesthetic-visual matching theories of self-recognition: Autistic children and others. *Annals of the New York Academy of Sciences 818*, 39–62.

Mitchell, R. W. (Ed.). (2001). *Pretending in animals and humans*. Cambridge: Cambridge Univ. Press.

Mitchell, R. W. & Edmonson, E. (1999). Functions of repetitive talk to dogs during play: Control, conversation or planning? *Society and Animals* 7(1):55–82.

Mitchell, R. W., Thompson, N. S., & Miles, H. L. (1997). *Anthropomorphism, anecdotes and animals*. Albany, NY: SUNY Press.

Moore, D. E., & Hannon, J. T. (1993). Animal behavior science as a social science: The success of the empathic approach in research on apes. *Anthrozoös* 4(3), 173–189.

Morrow, V. (1998). My animals and other family: Children's perspectives on their relationships with companion animals. *Anthrozoös 11*(4), 218–226.

Myers, O. E., Jr. (1994). Young children's sense of connection to animals: The developmental basis of an ecological self. Doctoral dissertation, University of Chicago, Chicago.

Myers, O. E., Jr. (1996). Child-animal interaction: Nonverbal dimensions. *Society and Animals 4* (1), 19–35.

Myers, O. E., Jr. (1998). *Children and animals: Social development and our connections to other species*. Boulder, CO: Westview Press.

Myers, O. E., Jr. (1999). Human development as transcendence of the animal body and the child-animal association in psychological thought. *Society and Animals* 7(1), 121–140.

Myers, O. E., Jr. (2001). Young children's animal-role pretend play. In R. Mitchell (Ed.), *Pretending in animals and humans* (pp. 154–166). Cambridge: Cambridge Univ. Press.

Myers, O. E., Jr. (2002). Symbolic animals and the developing self. *Anthrozoös* 15(1), 19–36.

Myers, O. E., Jr. (2003). No longer the lonely species: A post-Mead perspective on animals and the self. *International Journal of Sociology and Social Policy* 23(3), 46–68.

Myers, O. E., Jr. (2005). Review of *If you tame me: Understanding our connection with animal,* by Leslie Irvine. *American Journal of Sociology 111*(1): 1846–1848.

Myers, O. E., Jr., & Russell, A. (2004). Human identity in relation to wild black bears: A natural-social ecology of subjective creatures. In S. Clayton & S. Opotow (Eds.), *Identity and the natural environment* (pp. 67–90). Cambridge, MA: MIT Press.

Myers, O. E., Jr., & Saunders, C. (2002). Animals as links to developing caring relationships with the natural world. In P. H. Kahn Jr. & S. R. Kellert (Eds.), *Children and nature: Theoretical and scientific foundations* (pp. 153–178). Cambridge, MA: MIT Press.

Myers, O. E., Jr., Saunders, C. & Birjulin, A. (2004). Emotional dimensions of watching zoo animals: An experience sampling study building on insights from psychology. *Curator 47*(3), 299–321.

Myers, O. E., Jr., Saunders, C. D. & Garrett, E. (2003). What do children think animals need? Aesthetic and psycho-social conceptions. *Environmental Education Research 9*(3), 305–325.

Myers, O. E., Jr., Saunders, C. D. & Garrett, E. (2004). What do children think animals need? Developmental trends. *Environmental Education Research 10*(4), 545–562.

Naess, A. (1988). Self realization: An ecological approach to being in the world. In J. Seed, J. Macy, P. Fleming, & N. Naess, *Thinking like a mountain* (pp. 19–30). Philadelphia: New Society Publishers. (Originally delivered as the Fourth Keith Roby Memorial Lecture, Murdoch University, Murdoch, Australia, March 12, 1986)

Nelson, K. A. (Ed.). (1989). *Narratives from the crib.* Cambridge, MA: Harvard University Press.

Nelson, R. K. (1983). *Make prayers to the raven: A Koyukan view of the northern forest.* Chicago: University of Chicago Press.

Nevers, P., Gebhard, U. & Billmann-Maheca, E. (1997). Patterns of reasoning exhibited by children and adolescents in response to moral dilemmas involving plants, animals and ecosystems. *Journal of Moral Education* 26(2):169–186.

Nielsen, J. A., & Delude, L. A. (1989). Behavior of young children in the presence of different kinds of animals. *Anthrozoös 3*(2), 119–129.

Nimer, J. & Lundahl, B. W. (2005). Animal assisted therapy with children and adolescents: A meta-analysis. Abstract of paper presented at the International Association for Anthrozoology 14th Annual Conference, July 11–12, Niagara Falls.

Noddings, N. (1984). *Caring: A feminine approach to ethics and moral education.* Berkeley: University of California Press.

Noske, B. (1989). *Humans and other animals: Beyond the boundaries of anthropology.* London: Pluto.

Noske, B. (1992). Deconstructing the animal image: Toward an anthropology of animals. *Anthrozoös 5*(4), 226–230.

Öhman, A. (1986). Face the beast and fear the face: Animal and social fears as prototypes for evolutionary analyses of emotion. *Psychophysiology 23* (2), 123–145.

Opotow, S., & Brook, A. (2003). Identity and exclusion in rangeland conflict. In S. Clayton & S. Opotow (Eds.), *Identity and the natural environment: The psychological significance of nature* (pp. 249–272). Cambridge, MA: MIT Press.

Opotow, S., & Weiss, L. (2000). Denial and the process of exclusion in environmental conflict. *Journal of Social Issues 56*(3), 475–490.

Patterson, C. (2002). *Eternal Treblinka: Our treatment of animals and the Holocaust.* New York: Lantern Books.

Paul, E. S. (2000). Empathy with animals and humans: Are they linked? *Anthrozoös 13*(4), 194–202.

Perner, J., Leekam, S., & Wimmer, H. (1987). Three-year-olds' difficulty with false belief: The case of a conceptual deficit. *British Journal of Developmental Psychology 5*, 125–137.

Piaget, J. (1963). *The origins of intelligence in the child.* New York: Norton. (Original work published 1936)

Piaget, J. (1975). *The child's conception of the world.* (J. Tomlinson & A. Tomlinson, Trans.). Totowa, NJ: Littlefield, Adams. (Original work published 1929)

Piaget J. (1965). *The moral judgment of the child* (M. Gabain, Trans.). New York: Free Press. (Original work published 1932)

Plous, S. (1993). Psychological mechanisms in the human use of animals. *Journal of Social Issues 49*(1), 11–52.

Plumwood, V. (2002). *Environmental culture: The ecological crisis of reason.* New York: Routledge.

Podberscek, A. L., Paul, E. S., & Serpell, J. A. (Eds.). (2000). *Companion animals and us: Exploring the relationships between people and pets.* Cambridge: Cambridge University Press.

Poresky, R. H., & Hendrix, C. (1990). Differential effects of pet presences and pet-bonding on young children. *Psychological Reports 67*, 51–54.

Poresky, R. H. (1996). Companion animals and other factors affecting young children's development. *Anthrozoös* 9(4), 159–168.

Ramachandran, V. S. (Ed.). (1994). *Encyclopedia of human behavior.* San Diego: Academic Press.

Redefer, L., & Goodman, J. (1989). Pet-facilitated therapy with autistic children. *Journal of Autism and Developmental Disorders* 19(3), 461–467.

Reed, E. S. (1996). *Encountering the world: Toward an ecological psychology.* New York: Oxford University Press.

Rendell, L. & Whitehead, H. (2001). Culture in whales and dolphins. *Behavioral and Brain Sciences 24,* 309–382.

Ricard, M., & Allard, L. (1993). The reaction of 9- to 10-month-old infants to an unfamiliar animal. *Journal of Genetic Psychology 154*(1), 5–16.

Richards, D. D., & Siegler, R. (1986). Children's understanding of the attributes of life. *Journal of Experimental Child Psychology 42,* 1–22.

Ritvo, H. (1995). Border trouble: Shifting the line between people and other animals. *Social Research 62*(3), 481–500.

Rizzo, T. A., Corsaro, W A., & Bates, J. E. (1992). Ethnographic methods and interpretive analysis: Expanding the methodological options for psychologists. *Developmental Review 12,* 101–123.

Roberts, K., & Cuff, M. D. (1989). Categorization studies of 9- to 15-month-old infants: Evidence for superordinate categorization? *Infant Behavior and Development 12,* 265–288.

Rochberg-Halton, E. (1985). Life in the Treehouse: Pet therapy as family metaphor and self-dialogue. In Sussman, M. (Ed.), *Pets and the family* (pp. 175–189). New York: Haworth Press.

Rosen, G. (1968). *Madness in society: Chapters in the historical sociology of mental illness.* London: Routledge & Kegan Paul.

Rosengren, K. S., Gelman, S. A., Kalish, C. W, & McCormick, M. (1991). As time goes by: Children's early understanding of growth in animals. *Child Development 62,* 1302–1320.

Ross, A. (1983). The status of altruism. *Mind (N.S.) 92* (366), 204–218.

Ross, G. (1980). Categorization in 1- to 2-year-olds. *Developmental Psychology 16,* 391–396.

Ross, N., Medin, D., Coley, J. D. & Atran, S. (2003). Cultural and experimental differences in the development of folkbiological induction. *Cognitive Development 81*(1), 25–47.

Rost, D. H., & Hartmann, A. (1994). Children and their pets. *Anthrozoös* 7(4), 242–254.

Rothenberg, D. (1991). The greenhouse from down deep: What can philosophy do for ecology? In M. S. Sontag, S. D. Wright, & G. L. Young (Eds.), *Human ecology: Strategies for the future. Selected papers from the Fourth Conference of the Society for Human Ecology* (pp. 243–247). Fort Collins, CO: Society for Human Ecology.

Rothfels, N. (Ed.) (2002). *Representing animals.* Bloomington, IN: Indiana University Press.

Rousseau, J.-J. (1979). *Emile* (A. Bloom, Trans.). New York: Basic Books. (Original work published 1762)

Rousseau, J.-J. (1986). Discourse on the origins of inequality. In *The first and second discourses* and *Essay on the origins of languages* (V. Gourevitch, Trans. & Ed.). New York: Harper & Row. (Original work published 1755)

Routley, R. (1981). Alleged problems in attributing beliefs, and intentionality, to animals. *Inquiry 24,* 385–417.

Röver, M. (1996). Die Entwicklung kinderlicher Einstellungen gegenüber Tieren. Ergebnisse von Gruppendiskussionen in der 3. und 9. Klassenstufe. Master's thesis, University of Hamburg, Hamburg, Germany.

Rusca, G., & Tonucci, F. (1992). Development of the concepts of living and animal in the child. *European Journal of Psychology of Education 7*(2), 151–176.

Sanders, C. R. (1990). The animal "Other": Self-definition, social identity and companion animals. *Advances in Consumer Research 17,* 662–668.

Sanders, C. R. (1993a). Understanding dogs: Caretakers' attributes of mindedness in canine-human relationships. *Journal of Contemporary Ethnography 22,* 205–226.

Sanders, C. R. (1993b). Excusing tactics: Social responses to the public misbehavior of companion animals. *Anthrozoös 6*(2), 82–90.

Sanders, C. R. (1999). *Understanding dogs: Living and working with canine companions.* Philadelphia: Temple University Press.

Sanders, C. R., & Arluke, A. (1993). If lions could speak: Investigating the animal-human relationship and the perspectives of nonhuman others. *Sociological Quarterly 34*(3), 377–390.

Sarles, H. (1977). *After metaphysics: Toward a grammar of interaction and discourse.* (*Studies in Semiotics 13*). Lisse, The Netherlands: Peter De Ridder.

Savage-Rumbaugh, E. S. (1986). *Ape language: From conditioned response to symbol.* New York: Columbia University Press.

Savage-Rumbaugh, E. S., Murphy, J., Sevcik, R. A., Brakke, K., Williams, S. L., & Rumbaugh, D. M. (1993). Language comprehension in ape and child. *Monographs of the Society for Research in Child Development 58*(3–4, Serial No. 233).

Sax, B. (2000a). *Animals in the Third Reich: Pets, scapegoats and the Holocaust.* New York: Continuum.

Sax, B. (2000b). The Holocaust and blood sacrifice. *Anthrozoös 13*(1), 22–33.

Schopenhauer, A. (1965). *On the basis of morality.* (E. F. J. Payne, Trans.) Indianapolis: Bobbs-Merrill. (Original work published 1841)

Schowalter, J. E. (1979). When dinosaurs return: Children's fascination with dinosaurs. *Children Today 8,* 2–5.

Schultz, P. W., Shriver, C., Tabanico, J., & Khazian, A. (2004). Implicit connections with nature. *Journal of Environmental Psychology 24,* 31–42.

Schutz, A. (1951). Making music together: A study in social relationship. *Social Research 18*(1), 76–97.

Searle, J. R. (1983). *Intentionality: An essay in the philosophy of mind.* Cambridge, UK: Cambridge University Press.

Searles, H. F. (1960). The nonhuman environment in normal development and in schizophrenia. *Monograph Series on Schizophrenia 5.* New York: International Universities Press.

Serpell, J. A. (1986). *In the company of animals: A study of human-animal relationships.* New York: Basil Blackwell.

Serpell, J. A. (2000). Creatures of the unconscious: Companion animals as mediators. In A. Podberscek, E. Paul & J. Serpell (Eds.), *Companion animals and us: Exploring the relationships between people and pets.* (pp. 108–121). Cambridge: Cambridge University Press.

Shapiro, K. (1985). *Bodily reflective modes: A phenomenological method for psychology.* Durham, NC: Duke University Press.

Shapiro, K. (1989). Understanding dogs through kinesthetic empathy, social construction, and history. *Anthrozoös 3*(3), 184–195.

Shepard, P. (1973). *The tender carnivore and the sacred game.* New York: Charles Scribner's Sons.

Shepard, P. (1978). *Thinking animals: Animals and the development of human intelligence.* New York: Viking.

Shepard, P. (1996). *The others: How animals made us human.* Washington DC: Island Press.

Sherick, I. (1981). The significance of pets for children: Illustrated by a latency age girl's use of pets in her analysis. *Psychoanalytic Study of the Child 36,* 193–215.

Sherrod, L. R. (1981). Issues in cognitive-perceptual development: The special case of social stimuli. In M. E. Lamb & L. R. Sherrod (Eds.), *Infant social cognition: Empirical and theoretical considerations* (pp. 11–36). Hillsdale, NJ: Lawrence Erlbaum.

Shweder, R. A. (1984). Anthropology's romantic rebellion against the enlightenment, or there's more to thinking than reason and evidence. In R. A.

Shweder & R. A. LeVine (Eds.), *Culture theory* (pp. 27–66). Cambridge, UK: Cambridge University Press.

Shweder, R. A., Mahapatra, M., & Miller, J. G. (1987). Culture and moral development. In J.Kagan & S. Lamb (Eds.), *The emergence of morality in young children* (pp. 1–83). Chicago: University of Chicago Press.

Sims, V. K., Chin, M. G., Sushil, D. J., Ellis, L. U. & Jones, R. (2005). Eye movements when judging affect in cats and dogs. Abstract of paper presented at the International Association for Anthrozoology 14th Annual Conference, July 11–12, Niagara Falls.

Singer, P. (1975). *Animal liberation.* New York: Avon.

Singh, J. A. L., & Zingg, R. M. (1939). *Wolf children and feral man.* New York: Harper & Brothers.

Soares, C. J. (1985). The companion animal in the context of the family system. *Marriage and the Family Review 8,* 49–62.

Spelke, E. (1979). Perceiving bimodally specified events in infancy. *Developmental Psychology 15,* 626–636.

Spelke, E., Phillips, A., & Woodward, A. (1995). Infants' knowledge of object motion and human action. In D. Sperber, D. Premack, & A. Premack (Eds.), *Causal cognition: A multidisciplinary debate* (pp. 44–78). Oxford, UK: Clarendon.

Spiegel, M. (1996). *The dreaded comparison: Human and animal slavery.* New York: Mirror Books.

Stallones, L. (1994). Pet loss and mental health. *Anthrozoös 7*(1), 43–54.

Staub, E. (1986). A conception of the determinants and development of altruism and aggression: Motives, the self, and the environment." In C. Zahn-Waxler, E. M. Cummings, & R. Iannotti (Eds.), *Altruism and aggression: Biological and social origins* (pp. 135–164). Cambridge, UK: Cambridge University Press.

Stern, D. (1985). *The interpersonal world of the infant.* New York: Basic Books.

Stewart, M. F. (1999). *Companion animal death.* Oxford: Butterwood Heinemann.

Strayer, J. (1987). Affective and cognitive perspectives on empathy. In N. Eisenberg & J. Strayer (Eds.), *Empathy and its development* (pp. 218–244). Cambridge, UK: Cambridge University Press.

Strum, S. C. (1987). *Almost human: A journey into the world of baboons.* New York: Random House.

Sullivan, H. 5. (1953). *The interpersonal theory of psychiatry.* New York: Norton.

Sully, J. (1896). *Studies of childhood.* New York: D. Appleton.

Sussman, M. (Ed.). (1985). Pets and the family [Special issue]. *Marriage and Family Review* 8(3/4).

Symcox, G. (1972). The wild man's return: The enclosed vision of Rousseau's *Discourses*. In E. Dudley & M. E. Novak (Eds.), *The wild man within: An image in Western thought from the Renaissance to Romanticism* (pp. 223–247). Pittsburgh, PA: University of Pittsburgh Press.

Tambiah, S. J. (1969). Animals are good to think and good to prohibit. *Ethnology 8*, 423–459.

Tammivaara, J. & Enright, D. S. (1986). On eliciting information: Dialogues with child informants. *Anthropology and Education Quarterly 17*, 218–238.

Tester, K. (1991). *Animals and society: The humanity of animal rights*. New York: Routledge.

Thomas, E. M. (1993). *The hidden life of dogs*. Boston: Houghton Mifflin.

Thomas, K. (1983). *Man and the natural world: A history of the modern sensibility*. New York: Pantheon.

Thorslev, P. L. (1972). The wild man's revenge. In E. Dudley & M. E. Novak (Eds.), *The wild man within: An image in Western thought from the Renaissance to Romanticism* (pp. 281–307). Pittsburgh, PA: University of Pittsburgh Press.

Triebenbacher, S. (1998). Pets as transitional objects: Their role in children's emotional development *Psychological Reports 82*, 191–200.

Tiedemann, D. (1927). Observations on the mental development of a child. (C. Murchisan & S. Langer, Trans.). *Journal of Genetic Psychology 35*, 205–230. (Original work published in 1787)

Trivers, R. (1991). Deceit and self-deception: The relation between communication and consciousness. In M. H. Robinson & L. Tiger (Eds.), *Man and beast revisited* (pp. 175–191). Washington DC: Smithsonian Institution.

Tuan, Y. F. (1984). *Dominance and affection: The making of pets*. New Haven, CT: Yale University Press.

Turiel, E. (1983). *The development of social knowledge*. Cambridge: Cambridge University Press.

Turiel, E. (1998). Moral development. In N. Eisenberg (Ed.), *Handbook of child psychology*, vol. 3: *Social, emotional and personality development* (5th ed., pp. 863–932). New York: Wiley.

Turiel, E. (2002). *The culture of morality: Social development and social opposition*. New York: Cambridge University Press.

Turner, D. C. & Rieger, G. (2001). Singly living people and their cat: A study of human mood and subsequent behavior. *Anthrozoös 14*(1), 38–46.

Tyler, T. (2003). If horses had hands… *Society and Animals 11*(3), 267–281.

Ulrich, R. S. (1993). Biophilia, biophobia, and natural landscapes. In R. Kellert

& E. O. Wilson (Eds.), *The biophilia hypothesis* (pp. 73–137). Washington, DC: Island Press.

Unti, B. O. (2002). The quality of mercy: Organized animal protection in the United States 1866–1930. Doctoral dissertation, American University, Washington, DC.

Urton, G. (Ed.). (1985). *Animal myths and metaphors in South America.* Salt Lake City: University of Utah Press.

von Uexküll, J. (1982). The theory of meaning (B. Stone & H. Weiner, Trans.). *Semiotics 42*(1), 25–82. (Original work published 1940)

Van de Castle, R. (1983). Animal figures in fantasy and dreams. In A. H. Katcher & A. M. Beck (Eds.), *New perspectives on our lives with companion animals* (pp. 148–173). Philadelphia: University of Pennsylvania Press.

Varela, F. J. , Thompson, E., & Rosch, E. (1991). *The embodied mind: Cognitive science and human experience.* Cambridge: MIT Press.

Vizek-Vidović, V. Vlahović-Stetić, V. V. & Bratko, D. (1999). Pet ownership, type of pet, and socioemotional development of school children. *Anthrozoös 12* (4), 211–217.

Vollum, S., Buffington-Vollum, J. & Longmire, D. R. (2004). Moral disengagement and attitudes about violence toward animals. *Society and Animals12*(3), 209–235.

Waksler, F. (1986). Studying children: Phenomenological insights. *Human Studies 9*, 71–82.

Watson, J. B., & Rayner, K. (1920). Conditioned emotional reactions. *Journal of Experimental Psychology 3*, 1–14.

Watzlawick, P., Beavin, J. H., & Jackson, D. D. (1967). *Pragmatics of human communication: A study of interactional patterns, pathologies and paradoxes.* New York: Norton.

Wellman, H. M. (1990). *The child's theory of mind.* Cambridge: MIT Press.

White, S. H. (1983). The idea of development in developmental psychology. In R. M. Lerner (Ed.), *Developmental psychology: Historical and philosophical perspectives* (pp. 55–77). Hillsdale, NJ: Lawrence Erlbaum.

Wilson. E. O. (1994). *Naturalist.* San Francisco: Island Press.

Winnicott, D. W. (1989). *Playing and reality.* New York: Tavistock/Routledge. (Original work published 1971)

Wolfe, J. (1977). The use of pets as transitional objects in adolescent interpersonal functioning. *Dissertation Abstracts International 38*, 2391B.

Woods, S. M. (1965). Psychotherapy and the patient's pet. *Current Psychiatric Therapies 5*, 119–21.

Yin, R. K. (1989). *Case study research: Design and methods.* Revised edition. Thousand Oaks: Sage Publications.

Youniss, J. (1983). Understanding differences within friendship. In R. L. Leahy (Ed.), *The child's construction of social inequality* (pp. 161–178). New York: Academic Press.

Zahn-Waxler, C., Radke-Yarrow, M., Wagner, E. & Chapman, M. (1992). The development of concern for others. *Developmental Psychology 28*(1), 126–136.

Zahn-Waxler, C. & Smith, K. D. (1992). The development of prosocial behavior. In M. Hersen (Ed). (1992). *Handbook of social development: A lifespan perspective* (pp. 229–256). New York: Plenum Press.

Zimmer, C. (2005). Looking for personality in animals, of all people. *New York Times*, March 1, pp. D1, D6.

Zimmer, H. (1960). *The king and the corpse.* New York: Meridian.

Index